NICHOLA FLETCHER'S

ULTIMATE *Venison* COOKERY

To the ship's captain

Illustrations by Nichola Fletcher

NICHOLA FLETCHER'S

ULTIMATE

Venison

COOKERY

Quiller

First published in the UK in 2007 by Quiller,
an imprint of Quiller Publishing Ltd
Reprinted 2008

British Library Cataloguing-in-Publication Data
A catalogue record for this book
is available from the British Library

ISBN 978 1 904057 60 4

Book design by Sharyn Troughton
Printed in China

Quiller

An imprint of Quiller Publishing Ltd
Wykey House, Wykey, Shrewsbury, SY4 1JA
Tel: 01939 261616 Fax: 01939 261606
E-mail: info@quillerbooks.com
Website: www.countrybooksdirect.com

Contents

Acknowledgements

A book that is the distillation of thirty years' work is clearly the spirit of many peoples' generosity. There are so many, and some sadly no longer with us, that it is impossible to list them individually. It was Sue Varvill of the British Deer Society who urged me to produce this book, and finally, in impatience at my inertia, put me in touch with Andrew Johnston and his team at Quiller Publishing, so to The British Deer Society and to Sue in particular I remain grateful. There are many other societies which have helped with information and enthusiasm: The Veterinary Deer Society, who in return for some convivial venison banquets have always provided balanced scientific advice; the Game Conservancy in Scotland, for whom I have demonstrated venison and game cooking at the Scottish Fair for more years than I care to remember. And, of course, the British Deer Farmers Association, with whom we have discovered and worked out many fascinating things about deer and venison.

Our international network of friends can always be relied upon to provide specialist knowledge. They come from Britain and Europe, from New Zealand and Canada, from Australia and America, from Persia and China. Ecologists, researchers, veterinarians, deer farmers, park managers, stalkers, game dealers, wildlife rangers, chefs, writers, historians, factors and academics, not to mention the eager team of voluntary recipe testers – you know who you are, and I thank you all. Food writers relish discussions about the delicious world of food production, ingredients, cooking, and eating, and I am no exception. So to my learned international friends at Eat Words, and to colleagues at The Guild of Food Writers, I raise my glass in companionship. I should also like to acknowledge the many newspaper, radio and television journalists who greeted our stories with such enthusiasm. Without them, the task of spreading the word about venison would have been more difficult.

Probably the largest group I should acknowledge here is our loyal army of customers who over the years have been so positive in their feedback. Through them, I have learnt what people like, don't like, wish for, feel uncertain about, and want to know more about, when it comes to venison. I have relived memorable meals with them, had fun planning new ones, celebrated successes in cookery competitions, helped their pets back to health, shared stories and discussed a myriad of interesting topics. I realise how lucky I am to have such appreciative and communicative customers.

Finally, I should like to give three cheers for our excellent team here: for Graeme Braid, our master butcher who stood, knife poised, as I made diagrams; for David Stewart who looks after our deer so conscientiously; and for Pauline who helps in the butchery, farmers' markets and in the office. Our daughters Stella and Martha remain in touch with the farm, to our delight. But it is John, 'The Ship's Captain' who deserves my gratitude most of all, for without him there would have been no voyage of venison, and no book.

Introduction

The sheer pleasure of venison

> *'There are very few things in life that you can enjoy doing and are also good for you. I can only think of two, and one of those is eating venison.'*
>
> John Fletcher

When it comes to choosing what meat (or indeed food) to cook, there are many positive aspects to venison. Apart from the fact that it is delicious and offers significant health benefits, there is much to offer the conscience as well as the body – an increasingly important aspect for people who want to feel reassured about what they eat as well as enjoy its taste.

I wrote my first venison cookery book in 1983. A novice at food writing, I produced it in response to questions from customers eager to know how to cook it. John and I had been producing venison for ten years by then, selling it directly to people in Britain instead of exporting it, as most game dealers did at the time. When we started working with our deer in 1973, restaurants that featured venison on their menu were rarities, and of those that did, too many dished up overcooked roasts or stewed it to a stringy death. Consumers had barely heard of venison, far less eaten or cooked it. English market stalls and a few specialist shops were the only places to buy it if you didn't shoot your own. Those that had heard of venison were full of anxieties, many of them perfectly understandable given some of the misconceptions current at the time. And a tragic number of people came to us with horror stories of uneatable venison that even their dogs wouldn't touch. Actually they still do, but thankfully not very many. We had a lifetime's task ahead of us to change all that, but thirty years of exploration and discovery have been a privilege. They took us all over the world, into generous peoples' homes, to parks, estates, ranches and farms, to research institutes, deer societies, game larders, hunting communities, and sometimes into politicians' lairs. We found that the world of venison is populated with larger-than-life characters. Sometimes we revised our original opinions, sometimes we had them reinforced, invariably we learned something entirely new. Always the deer were there with us, teaching us, and they still are.

Much has changed since those early days. More venison is now sold within Britain than exported. Indeed, the demand is topped up with farmed imports from New Zealand. Throughout America and Europe, wild deer are hunted less and numbers are increasing so fast that in some areas they are causing environmental damage and need heavier culling. Fortunately, consumption is increasing all over the world. Venison is commonly seen on restaurant and bistro menus, with a new generation of chefs keen to try out innovative recipes. Venison lends itself well to a wide variety of dishes, and the imagination of these chefs has inspired their customers to try cooking it at home. Farmers' markets have brought venison regularly into many town centres, along with people able to give advice. Even the much-maligned supermarkets have played their part, though I do wish they would not instruct people to overcook it – more of that later.

But, but ... we haven't quite got there yet. The journey is not finished. There is still incorrect advice churned out. Writers still come out with astonishing pronouncements that are either quite wrong or miss the point completely. Are these statements based on a single experience or simply prejudice? Whichever it is, those mantras of misinformation are copied from one erroneous publication to the next. As a result, too many people still labour under hoary old myths which ruin their dishes, missing the infinitely more interesting and delicious truth. There is still a deep lack of knowledge in some parts of the catering trade. There are still some game dealers, processors and butchers who throw their normal high standards out of the window when confronted with a deer carcase. And there are still thousands of people who have not yet experienced this exceptional meat, for which the only essential ingredient is an open, enquiring mind.

One of the biggest differences between venison and conventional domestic meat is that it comes from deer of very different sizes, ages, sources and species so it helps to understand the effects these could have on the cooking. And being so lean, it sometimes needs different cooking methods from the fattier meats most people are used to dealing with. No one can successfully recreate dishes from a foreign country without information about the cooking methods, the culture and how the ingredients react to cooking. And for many people, the world of venison is a foreign land. So I make no apology for including the necessary technical information. On the contrary, the more you know about what you are cooking and eating, the more you enjoy it. It makes good dinner conversation, too.

To produce a venison book containing only recipes would be of limited use, however wonderful the recipes might be. Because with venison, far more than other meat, it is necessary to have some background information in order to understand what you are buying, what you are cooking with and how that cooking will work. Only then do you understand the effect that certain techniques will have on the meat, and only then do you finally understand that it is actually all wonderfully simple. The recipes are, if you like, the cream on the cake.

I hope this book will help venison in its long and honourable journey back into many more peoples' lives, for that is where it belongs.

Nichola Fletcher,
Auchtermuchty, 2007

My wish-list for venison

- Don't overcook it. Cook it LESS not MORE
- Remember it is versatile: Eat it MORE not LESS
- Feed your children on it
- Assess and grade your venison and discard poor quality
- Provide more information about species, if not age
- Shoot younger deer – you can't eat trophies.
- Eat a deer and save a tree (or a songbird's nest)

1. *First catch your deer*

Sources of venison, species and their sizes

The English word 'venison' originally covered meat from a large variety of species. In former times, it was used to describe the meat of other hunted animals as well as deer, in the same way that the German word *wild* is used for 'game meat' today. The Spanish word *venados* is the same and, like 'venison', comes from the Latin word *venare* meaning 'to hunt'. So some old recipe books call for 'hare, or boar, or other venison'. Today, although venison now means only the meat of deer, not all deer are necessarily hunted. The majority are wild and shot by hunters, but significant numbers are reared in parks and farms throughout the world.

The two most important variables from the cook's point of view are the differences in ages and sizes of deer. Any young deer, wild or enclosed, cleanly killed, well hung and carefully prepared, produces magnificent venison. Conversely, many really old deer, wild or enclosed, will not. There are forty different species[1] of deer with a huge range of sizes and this can sometimes lead to confusion – e.g. many eighteenth and nineteenth century cookery books assume their readers are cooking fallow deer from the parks so their recipes don't always work with roe and red venison.

In Europe there are three main sizes of deer. The large species are roughly twice the size of the medium, which in turn are twice the size of the small ones. So a whole red deer haunch would be about twice the size of a fallow deer haunch but four times the size of a roe deer haunch. The same goes for fillets, chops, and so on.

---

[1]This is forty different species of deer, not different breeds. So even though a red deer and a reindeer may both have antlers and look slightly similar, they are no more closely related than a cow and a sheep, which both have horns though they look rather more different. Normally only subspecies of deer can interbreed.

SOURCES OF VENISON

WILD DEER

Wild deer inspire deep-seated emotions. As well as being fascinating and beautiful animals to study, they clearly symbolise 'the wild' in a way that other animals do not. As such they appeal to the basic human challenge to hunt, though they also provoke strong emotions, especially among urban dwellers who believe that all deer should live in the wilderness, without perhaps realising that when left uncontrolled with no natural predators, deer are apt to eat their own wild paradise and then die from lack of food and shelter.

Any wild deer that is not too old, which is cleanly and swiftly killed, and then well prepared, makes magnificent eating. Wild venison for sale is culled by large estates or hunters. In the EU it must be handled by licensed game dealers, but current legislation allows up to three hundred to be sold locally by each hunter with no health checks other than voluntary codes of practice by stalkers and hunters, though this may change. Deer in the USA are culled in great numbers by individuals under licence. Some years ago, the *New York Times* calculated that if you combined the manpower of the world's ten largest armies, this would still amount to fewer than the number of Americans who go off every

Wild red deer in the Scottish Highlands

year in pursuit of white-tailed deer. Even so, in many parts of the world the numbers of hunters are declining and the numbers of wild deer increasing.

The primary reasons for shooting wild deer are recreation (i.e. hunting mature males for trophy antlers) and to control populations. In these circumstances, the venison is a by-product. However skilled the hunter or stalker, it is difficult to attain a perfect kill every time. Consequently, wild venison has the widest variation in condition as well as age, ranging from the delicious to the inedible. It needs careful grading and, sometimes, substantial trimming. Enormous improvements in handling wild venison have taken place in the last ten years by far-sighted processors like Highland Game who do a superb job at trimming and presenting wild venison, though of course they are not alone. The Deer Commission now run training courses for estates, stalkers and game dealers which, hopefully, will provide examples of how to present venison in the way it deserves.

In Britain there are currently about 500,000 roe deer and 360,000 red. The roe are evenly distributed but there are only 12,500 red deer in England – most live in the Scottish Highlands. Because red deer are bigger they contribute the most venison. Fallow deer number about 100,000 and are found mainly in England; there are around 40,000 muntjac. Between the 1970s and 1990s, all species doubled except muntjac, whose numbers increased eightfold. Throughout Europe red and roe prevail and in North America, whitetail, mule deer and wapiti. In the north of both continents, elk and reindeer dominate.

PARK DEER

Park Deer are also classed as wild game in the EU and are therefore subject to the same health regulations and close seasons as wild deer. For centuries, the deer park was an integral part of the stately home, gradually changing from being a convenient on-site hunting larder to being part of the landscape gardener's vision – many National Trust properties still have active deer parks. Fallow and red deer are the main species in European parks, though some have a number of exotics. Woburn Abbey, for example, keeps nine species. Park deer are likely to be culled younger than wild venison and shot at closer range in the head or neck, like many farm deer. Nowadays most parks provide winter feed, consequently their deer are kept in good condition. Throughout Europe there are deer parks ranging from the huge French royal hunting park at Chambord to the thousands of two-hectare parks in Germany which provide for the owners' families and friends, and which collectively account for considerable amounts of venison.

Fallow buck

FARMED DEER

Farmed Deer come under the same EU meat inspection legislation as cattle, sheep, pigs and goats. They have no close season so farm venison is available all year round. The greatest difference between farmed deer and other domestic animals in the EU is that farmed deer are allowed to be field shot – they are not required to be killed in an abattoir – a privilege not allowed to other farm animals. Such farms are little different from parks, the only legal distinction being that of intent, a subject that taxes bureaucrats in Brussels.

Red deer are the most commonly farmed species in Britain. Fallow are farmed too, but are more common in the rest of Europe. Red, wapiti and a few fallow are farmed in New Zealand, and red, fallow and rusa in Australia. In North America, only some states allow the sale of farmed venison. Where allowed, North American deer farmers keep fallow and red deer (originally imported from Europe) or the larger wapiti (native).

If there is no on-farm processing facility, farmed deer are transported to specially adapted abattoirs. Provided they are used to being handled like other livestock, they behave similarly. In New Zealand, where deer farming is a huge industry, and also in Australia, all farmed deer are processed through highly efficient dedicated deer abattoirs, which allow chilled transport into markets all over the world.

The privilege of being able to shoot farmed deer in the field is considerable. The deer are entirely unstressed before slaughter since they are not transported, or handled in unfamiliar pens, or wounded. From the point of view of animal welfare it has to be the perfect system. From the consumer's point of view, the quality of the meat is excellent, because farm deer can be shot in the head so that death is always instantaneous and completely stress-free; there is no bruising, and no adrenalin surge to damage the meat. Everything is in place for producing a fine carcase that can be hung to perfection.

IMPORTED VENISON

Britain is still a net exporter of venison so imports of wild venison are insignificant. The main source of imported venison is New Zealand farmed. It is sold widely to the catering trade, and is also used by some processors of venison products. At the time of writing, most venison in British supermarkets is from New Zealand. From the chef's point of view, it is reliable and very well presented.

THE SIZE OF DIFFERENT SPECIES OF DEER

The largest deer in the world is the elk (known as moose in North America) with its huge pendulous nose and vast, heavy flat antlers. They stand up to 2 m (6½ ft) high at the shoulder and weigh up to 800 kg (1800 lb). Smallest is the tiny South American pudu, though Muntjac deer, increasingly common in Britain, are not much bigger, standing 50 cm (20 ins) and weighing only 10–15 kg (22–33 lb). And there are all sizes in between. Venison from large deer is coarser grained than that from small deer, though not necessarily tougher – that depends on age. The list below covers only the species most likely to be encountered by readers of this book. The first in each category are the most common British ones.

Information sources list different weights for deer: 'live' weight, 'larder' weight or 'dressed carcase' weight. Larder weight includes the skin and feet, but not the head or the stomach, i.e. the way most wild deer are brought back to a game larder after gralloching, ready for collection by the game dealer. A 'dressed' carcase, contrary to its name, is actually *un*dressed, i.e. it's skinned and gutted, with head, feet, heart and liver removed and is all ready to butcher. I use the dressed carcase weight, since this is the part butchers, cooks and chefs are interested in. It is roughly 55% of the live weight. Females weigh about 20% less than males, and farmed deer are near the middle of the weight range as, even though better grown than their wild counterparts, they are relatively young.

Tinted deer from left to right: muntjac, reindeer/caribou, roe, elk/moose
White deer from left to right: red deer, fallow, white-tailed deer
The relative sizes of different species of deer.
Clearly, cuts from these deer will vary greatly in size

LARGE DEER

Large deer include the red deer (*Cervus elaphus*), the elk or moose (*Alces alces*) and the wapiti or American elk (*Cervus canadensis*) – arguably a subspecies of red deer as they can interbreed even though wapiti are nearly twice as big.

There are large wild populations of red deer in Europe, and stags (harts) have been the subject of mythology and legend for thousands of years. A grass grazer, red deer is the species most commonly farmed in Britain and some other European countries, and also, with the wapiti, in New Zealand and North America. Landseer's famous painting *The Monarch of the Glen* is of a red deer stag.

The elk, (moose) in North America, is vast, though being a selective browser of leaves and shrubs, they share many features with the tiny roe deer. People in Sweden used to ride elk, but the practice was banned in the seventeenth century because robbers kept escaping from the police whose horses couldn't catch these long-legged giants.

The wapiti looks like an outsized red deer; the two are related and can interbreed. As you travel east from Europe through Russia to Canada, the European red deer becomes larger, changes colour and starts to whistle instead of roaring, until in Canada it has become the huge wapiti. Wapiti is their native name, but they are often called elk in America. This confuses Europeans for whom elk means the deer the Americans call moose. The reason Americans call wapiti elk is that when the first settlers arrived and saw wapiti they were so amazed at their huge size that they thought they must be a kind of elk.

LARGE DEER: DRESSED CARCASE WEIGHT OF MALES

red deer 35–100 kg (78–225 lbs)
wapiti 120–225 kg (270–500 lbs)
elk/moose: 200–400 kg (450–900 lbs)

Red deer in parks are larger than those in the Scottish Highlands.

MEDIUM DEER

Medium Deer include fallow deer (*Dama dama*), reindeer or caribou (*Rangifer tarandus*), white-tailed deer (*Odocoileus virginianus*), mule deer (*Odocoileus hemionus*), sika (*Cervus nippon*) and rusa (*Cervus timorensis*).

Fallow deer originated in the Middle East and are one of the most common species in European deer parks; there are also wild populations dotted throughout Europe. They are farmed in Europe (particularly in Germany) as well as in Australia and USA. They have flattened (palmated) antlers like the moose and can become remarkably tame. Despite their size, they can jump higher than red deer.

Over a million reindeer are still managed in huge herds by nomadic Saamis and other peoples in the far north of Europe and Russia. These reindeer are thoroughly domesticated, being ridden like mules and used for pulling sledges as well as being milked and used for meat. In addition, there are similar numbers of completely wild reindeer in Russia, and also in North America where they are called by the native name of caribou. There is a huge culture of history and myth surrounding this romantic species. It is far more interesting than just being Santa's assistant – for example, they are the only deer where females grow antlers.

White-tail buck. Native of N. America, these are said to be the oldest of all deer species

Mule and white-tailed deer are exclusively American species with feeding habits similar to roe deer and, like roe, are experiencing an impressive population explosion; Bambi is a white-tailed deer. They are now ranched in North America for trophies and big bucks fetch big bucks.

The Asian rusa is widespread throughout Indonesia and is also farmed, both in Asia and in Australia. Like the sika below, it is closely related to red deer.

Sika (the Japanese word for 'deer') were introduced into the West Highlands of Scotland from Japan in the nineteenth century. Closely related to red deer, they can and do hybridise in some areas, reducing the body size and antlers of wild 'red' deer hybrids. The way the fur grows on their foreheads makes sika stags look as though they are frowning. Perhaps they have a problem understanding Gaelic.

Sika Stag

MEDIUM SIZED DEER: DRESSED CARCASE WEIGHT RANGE OF MALES

fallow deer 25–47 kg (56–105 lbs)
sika 25–35 kg (56–78 lbs)
reindeer 50–130 kg (115–290 lbs)
rusa deer 100–125 kg (225–280 lbs)
white-tailed deer 40–60 kg (90–140 lbs)
mule deer 40–60 kg (90–140 lbs)

SMALL DEER

Small deer include roe (*Capreolus capreolus*), Chinese water deer (*Hydropotes inermis*) and muntjac (*Muntiacus reevesi*).

Roe deer are widespread throughout Europe and Asia. Because they live in small family groups and are territorial, they are not suited to being enclosed, so they are always wild. Of all the wild British species, they produce the most reliable, fine- grained meat since they are small and don't live too long. Roe are adept at nibbling their way into new habitats and their numbers are increasing rapidly everywhere, where they are welcomed (except by foresters and gardeners) as they look very dainty. Roe venison (*chevreuil*) is favoured above all by French chefs, possibly because so much of their red deer venison comes from *chasse à courre* (hunting with hounds), which increases adrenalin in the venison. However, Sir

Roe buck

Walter Scott, a noted gourmet, disagreed: 'The learned in cookery . . . hold the roe venison dry and indifferent food, unless when dressed in soup and Scotch collops.'

Muntjac and Chinese water deer in Britain escaped from parks where they were introduced from Asia in the nineteenth century. Like roe deer, they have adapted themselves well to our landscape. But although they may look cute, in many areas of Britain muntjac wreak environmental havoc with native species of plants, trees and birds, not to mention becoming, like their American white-tail counterparts, an irritation to suburban and country gardeners. So while half of the population takes road traffic victims along to wildlife treatment centres and illegally releases the patched up survivors into new locations, the other half does its best to eliminate an invasive pest. Chinese water deer can become quite fat, not unlike lamb.

Muntjac

SMALL DEER: DRESSED CARCASE WEIGHT RANGE OF MALES

roe 8–13 kg (18–30 lbs)
Chinese water deer 6–9 kg (12–20 lbs)
muntjac 5–9 kg (11–20 lbs)

WHY ARE ANTELOPE AND GAZELLE NOT DEER, AND DOES IT MATTER ANYWAY?

The simplest distinction is that deer have antlers whereas antelope have horns. Antlers are shed annually and re-grow every year, which is a remarkable thing. Horns, however, are permanently attached to the animal throughout its life and simply get bigger each year. Animals that have horns are called bovids and include cattle, sheep, goats, gazelles, antelope (springbok, eland etc.), and many other species. Deer, with their antlers, are called cervids. This is an important distinction when it comes to the type of diseases certain species are prone to getting – BSE (bovine spongiform encephalopathy or mad cow disease) for example. However, the meat of many of the little wild bovids that scamper about the world is so similar to deer meat that in the culinary sense of the word (and in the old-fashioned sense of the word) it is to all intents and purposes venison.

CLOSE SEASONS FOR WILD DEER

At the time of writing, it is illegal to 'take' (i.e. capture as well as kill) wild deer in the close season unless they are marauding crops or unless it is done under license. Fresh venison may be legally sold during the open season and for a short period after the close season starts. That is the law. But so much 'marauding' goes on in forestry plots that some game dealers now handle more venison out of season than in it, so fresh wild venison is available all the time. There are no close seasons for farmed deer in Britain, and wild muntjac and Chinese water deer have no close seasons either. Park deer follow the same close seasons as wild deer. The law on selling frozen wild venison out of season is hazy and not enforced. There are different seasons in England, Scotland and every other country in the world. In other words, the whole system is confusing and is being reviewed with a view to change; gone are the days when Escoffier was sent to prison for selling out-of-season venison at the Savoy.

VENISON FOR THE GOURMET TRAVELLER

European countries generally list the species of deer (and sometimes the sex as well) on their menus, which is helpful and interesting for the consumer. In North America, Britain, Australia and New Zealand, venison is usually just called venison or deer meat, though occasionally a restaurant will qualify the species. New Zealand has spent many years marketing its prime red deer venison in North America under the trade name of Cervena which sometimes appears on menus. Below are the European names of the most common species. The names are similar in closely related languages.

ENGLISH	FRENCH	GERMAN	ITALIAN	SPANISH	DANISH
roe deer	chevreuil	Reh	capriolo	el corzo	rådyr
fallow deer	daim	Damhirsche	daino	el gamo	dådyr
reindeer	renne	Rentier	renna	el reno	rensdyr
red deer	cerf, daguet, or biche (f),	Rotwild	cervo	el ciervo or el venado	krondyr
venison	venaison	wild	carne di cervo	carne de venado	viltkød

2. The eating quality of venison

Tenderness, flavour, smell, succulence, juiciness and diet

Good eating quality comes from the perfect balance of tenderness, taste, smell, succulence and juiciness. Sometimes it is difficult to define exactly what it is that is so appealing: I have often heard people comment, 'it tastes delicious – so tender', yet tenderness is quite different from taste. Everyone's priorities are different.

Carefully handled venison is a superb product, and now that wild game is being handled so much better, this is becoming the norm. Unfortunately, though, some less good meat still finds its way onto the market. Venison has far greater variability than other red meats due it its wide variety of sources, size, age and killing methods, and there is little point in thinking you can achieve the impossible with a really low-grade carcase. Few people would imagine that a cattle beast that had been pounding up and down the hills for fourteen years (or was wounded, or chased for a few hours, or stressed by poor handling and transportation) before being despatched, would make good beef. Why should it be any different with venison? You can certainly improve it, but never transform it into the best. These notes will help people to understand what makes their venison the way it is, and offers some suggestions for remedying any shortcomings, should there be any.

TENDERNESS

Tenderness is more important nowadays than it used to be; it is arguably the most important attribute of meat for some people. It varies according to the age of the animal and also the way it was killed. Any deer under three years old should be tender enough to cook without any further preparation and, in the normal course of events, correctly prepared venison will be more tender and finer-grained than premium beef, much to many peoples' surprise and delight. If it isn't tender at this young age, the most likely

Stressed deer produce adrenalin which can toughen meat

cause is stress at slaughter – if death is not instant, adrenalin can toughen meat. Or it could be that the carcase was chilled too quickly (this is called 'cold shortening' but is unlikely with wild venison). It is difficult to do much about either of these things other than long, slow cooking or processing.

After the age of three, although the actual red meat may remain tender, the sinews that run through and around it start to thicken up. Sinews shrink with fierce cooking and cause a joint or steak to curl and twist – they also harden into a rubbery layer, which someone aptly described as like eating knicker elastic. New Zealand trials show that venison from hinds remains tender up to the age of six so long as all the skin and sinew is completely removed. Stags start the toughening process after eighteen months. So careful butchery and trimming becomes increasingly important with older animals.

Ways of tenderising venison include hanging the whole carcase, ideally in a dry atmosphere of -2°–0°C (28–32°F), with a fan to circulate the air. Under these conditions, a red deer carcase can mature for three weeks or more, whereas a roe carcase could achieve the same result in a week because it is so much smaller. Warmer temperatures accelerate maturation too; every 10°C (20°F) increase halves the time required. Marinating meat for a long time is a traditional way of tenderising meat; the spiced wines and oil exclude the air and prevent spoilage. However, acids in wine or vinegar can adversely affect the texture of meat (see p.49) and tenderising on its own can be achieved just as successfully

Deer despatched peacefully yield more tender venison

either by using the correct cooking techniques or else by leaving the meat completely covered in oil for anything up to two weeks. Meat can also be matured in a vacuum pack or shrink-wrap. The wholesale market matures most of its meat like this. It is essentially the same process as marinating as it excludes all the air, but vacuum packing meat doesn't produce the same kind of flavour change as either open hanging or marinating. Up to three weeks is usual, and some systems allow it to be kept fresh for as long as twelve weeks. This is how fresh meat arrives from New Zealand. A Chinese method of tenderising cheap tough cuts of meat commonly used in restaurants is bicarbonate of soda or baking powder mixed with sugar, wine and potato flour or cornflour paste. The natural enzyme found in fruits like raw pineapple and papaya can also be used to break down tough muscle tissue; it is either pulped and spread over raw meat, or cooked with it. Some people have even been known to use Coca Cola as a tenderiser. It does work. Naturally, some cuts are more tender than others, so making the correct choice of cut (see chapter 3) and even more importantly the correct method of cooking for that cut will determine the degree of tenderness of the finished dish.

FLAVOUR AND SMELL

Flavour and smell (closely related) can be affected for good or for bad by hanging, marinating, bruising, stress at slaughter, vacuum packing and the other ingredients used in the cooking process. Hanging enhances the flavour of a good carcase though damaged and bruised meat is not improved by it. Venison matured in cold dry conditions matures slowly, giving the carcase an attractive rich but bright smell and the venison a deep, rich mahogany colour – a sign that all is going well. If meat is matured in warm or moist conditions, moulds and yeasts can form. Some of these taste delicious but others impart a musty or acrid flavour with curious overtones of petrol. This is more likely (though not inevitable, of course) in carcases hung with the fur on because fur retains moisture. If hung with other damp game, venison can acquire musty, sometimes bitter overtones. Many people think this flavour, which is sometimes quite strong, is the natural taste of gamy venison. It isn't, it's the product of the environment it has been hanging in. (A good analogy would be the difference between a cheese that is kept in a musty fridge and comes out imbued with a mouldy flavour, and a cheese carefully ripened in optimal conditions by a skilled *affineur*. I know which I'd rather have!) However, so long as all the surface is carefully trimmed off without contaminating the inside meat, such venison can still make good eating. Marinating or spicing any meat introduces the flavours and perfumes of the ingredients used; see chapter 4 for more details. Bruising caused by bullet damage or poor handling gives a rich, livery, sometimes bitter taste to the meat, which always remains dark and rather bloody. Stress at slaughter affects flavour drastically by producing adrenalins which convert glycogen into lactic acid, reducing the pH of the meat. It also switches the blood flow into the muscle of limbs. This makes the meat dark with a bitter liver flavour and sour smell. Vacuum packing only affects the flavour if it has been kept in the pack too long, in which case it not only smells but also tastes sour (see p.272–273). Probably the most dramatic way of altering flavour is with the other ingredients used to cook the dish.

SUCCULENCE

Succulence comes from fat, or anything else that gives a slippery texture to meat. This could come in the form of a sauce surrounding small pieces of venison. It could come from minced fat or vegetables like mushrooms, aubergines, slow-cooked carrots etc. incorporated into made dishes – sausages and pies, for example. It could come from the gelatinous texture of slowly cooked shin, which lends fabulous succulence to a dish. Or it could be introduced by inserting fat (larding) into larger pieces like joints. There is more on larding on p.133 and 140.

JUICINESS

Juiciness (moisture) can only be retained by cooking venison rare or medium rare. Venison has a high moisture content, so as long as there is still pinkness (blood) in the cooked meat, it is physically impossible for it to be dry – so simple when you think about it. Venison immersed in a liquid and cooked very slowly stays moist as long as it remains in the liquid, but the minute it is removed or cooled, it dries out. Meat cooked long and slowly will always have a slightly more fibrous texture.

VENISON FAT

It is often claimed that venison is very lean. When speaking of the red meat (muscle), this is generally true because venison is not marbled like beef, and young deer lay down little fat. But deer can become very fat indeed when fully mature and after a good summer's grazing in preparation for the winter. The fat on deer is largely on the outside of the muscle, so is easily trimmed off if not wanted. Historically, people used to wax lyrical about fat venison, and many stalkers still relish it. But for those not keen on fat, it has to be admitted that venison fat is one of the least attractive, being hard and having a high melting point which means it congeals in the mouth. This is why many old books recommended serving venison on very hot plates, and why it used to be served up on special hollow dishes filled with hot water. However, when lean venison is served rare, the plates need only to be warm; scalding hot plates could risk overcooking it.

THE DEER'S DIET

People wax lyrical about 'the flavour of the hills': it conjures up a lovely image. But the disappointing fact is that a deer's diet makes virtually no difference to the taste of its meat, unless it is very fatty (which mostly it isn't). Ruminants, with their multiple stomachs, don't seem to pass on the flavour of their food into the muscle tissue, but rather into the fats present. (Animals like pigs and poultry with only one stomach are quite different; diet affects their flavour considerably.) Cattle and sheep have plenty of fat distributed throughout the muscle meat, and of course milk contains fat. So flavours such as turnips, seaweed, heather or fish meal can be passed into both marbled meat and milk. But deer are so lean and unmarbled that diet doesn't have a noticeable effect. I won't say 'no effect', but it is so small as to be indiscernible. (Someone once turned their deer onto a field of surplus onions which did affect the flavour, but that was an extreme case). The other factors described above make so much more difference that they drown out the minute differences of diet. This sounds incredible, and is bound to disappoint some people, but several trials using professional tasters have shown it to be the case, and I have done dozens of tastings for people myself to demonstrate it. For example, if diet affects flavour, you would imagine that roe deer with their varied diet would yield a more complex flavour than red deer that had been eating just grass. But we found that roe deer, hung for only three days tasted insipid compared to the red deer that had been hung for three weeks. In other words, it was the hanging that made the red deer venison taste more interesting.

3. Basics: The venison tool kit

Venison cuts, portion sizes, ingredients and information sources

In thirty years of working with venison, I have come across heartbreaking instances of consumers, writers, chefs and wholesalers talking at cross-purposes. For this reason I have broken down a venison carcase into its component parts with the correct names (including some international terms), highlighting the commonly mis-used ones. Chapter 16 contains more detailed information, of interest to the chef who needs to cost his purchases, and to those wishing to butcher venison.

WHAT TO BUY: THE CUTS OF VENISON

See chapter 1 for the different species and sizes of deer
See chapter 2 for factors affecting the flavour and eating quality of venison.

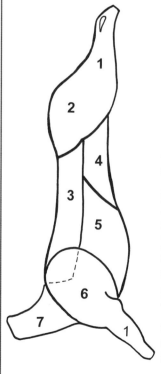

SUITABLE CUTS FOR COOKING METHODS

Grill/fry/stir-fry/fondue: loin, fillet, haunch
Roast: saddle, loin, haunch (plus shoulder if young)
Stew, casserole: haunch, shoulder, neck, shank
Braise: haunch, shoulder

1. Shank/Shin
Shank joint, Ossobuco, diced shin, mince

2. Haunch
Bone-in haunch joint, boned and rolled haunch joint, rump (steak, joint), topside (steak, joint), silverside (steak, joint), thick flank (steak, joint), diced haunch

3. Saddle
Wholesale saddle, saddle joint, rack/French rack, chops, cutlets, striploin/sirloin, loin, loin eye, fillet/filet mignon

4. Flank
Rolled stuffed joint, processing mince

5. Rib/Breast/Brisket
Processing mince, rolled stewing joint

6. Shoulder
Bone-in joint, boned and rolled joint, diced shoulder, shoulder steak, mince

7. Neck
Diced neck, mince

SADDLE (BACK, SADDLE-BACK)

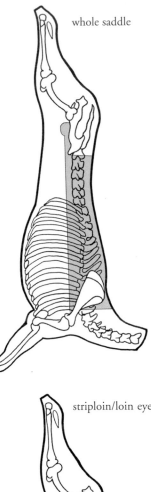

whole saddle

> WARNING! SOMETIMES RECIPES ASK FOR SADDLE
> WHEN THEY MEAN LOIN (BELOW).

The saddle is the part of the back where you'd put a saddle. It is made up of the loin, the fillet (filet mignon), the skin and the bones all joined together into the best roasting cut of all. But as soon as you bone it out it stops being saddle.

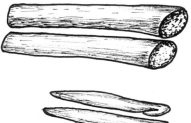

saddle roast

2 loins (striploin, sirloin, loin eye, loin fillet, back fillet, backstrap)

2 fillets (filet mignon, undercut, tenderloin)

LOIN (STRIPLOIN, SIRLOIN, LOIN EYE, LOIN FILLET, BACK FILLET, BACKSTRAP) The muscles that run along the top of the saddle from rump to shoulder are called the loin. It is beloved of restaurant chefs because it can be cooked in the time it takes for customers to eat their first course. Sliced loin may be called sirloin steaks, loin steaks, medallions, collops or noisettes. When sliced almost through and opened out, they are called butterfly or Valentine steaks. Loin and fillet (below) are the two best cuts and remain most tender when cooked past the pink stage. The front end of the loin parts into two muscles.

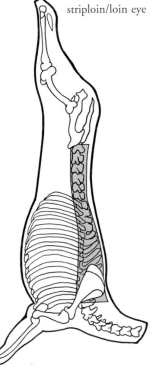

striploin/loin eye

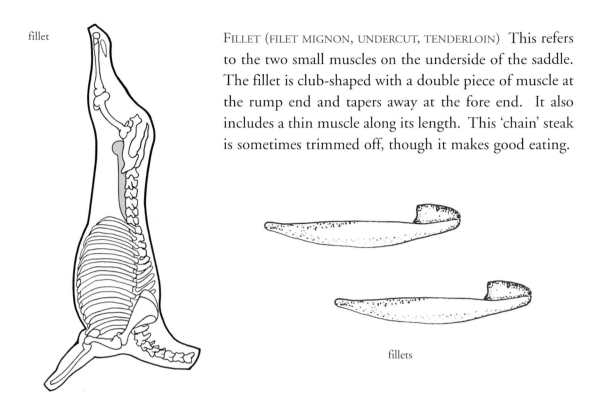

fillet

FILLET (FILET MIGNON, UNDERCUT, TENDERLOIN) This refers to the two small muscles on the underside of the saddle. The fillet is club-shaped with a double piece of muscle at the rump end and tapers away at the fore end. It also includes a thin muscle along its length. This 'chain' steak is sometimes trimmed off, though it makes good eating.

fillets

WARNING! Some suppliers, writers and chefs incorrectly refer to the loin as fillet, perhaps because venison loin looks like a small beef fillet. And the true fillets from small deer are so very small that their loins are often wrongly called fillets. If the word fillet is used to describe loin, it should always be qualified by calling it a loin fillet or back fillet. It is well worth checking this with a supplier, because the real fillet is dramatically different from loin and cooks differently too. The true fillet is only half the diameter of loin and one third of the length, so a 500 g (18 oz) whole fillet is a completely different shape and thickness from a 500 g (18 oz) slice of loin. Equally, loins and fillets from different species are completely different sizes.

RIB (RIB ROAST, RACK, CROWN ROAST) The rib is the front part of a saddle after the best end containing the fillet has been cut off. On small species it usually includes both sides of the back; in large species it is split into two halves. When the halved rib has the backbone and all outer skin removed, and all the meat removed between the ribs it is called a French rack. This is time-consuming to prepare so is an expensive cut to purchase. Two racks sewn back-to-back become a crown roast ready to stuff the centre. When sliced, the rack turns into chops (cutlets). Nearer to the rump are double loin chops which include the fillet, and Barnsley chops which are sliced across the saddle. Chops from roe and other small species are nicest cut with two or three rib bones per portion to give a good thick chunk of meat.

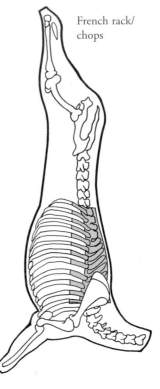

French rack/ chops

French rack

chops

HAUNCH (LEG, HIND LEG, HINDQUARTER)

The haunch includes the whole back leg with the rump. A haunch from a large red deer or elk can weigh 12–15 kg (26–33 lbs) and is usually cut into smaller joints or boned out, whereas a whole haunch from a roe deer may only weigh 2–3 kg (4–7 lbs) and makes a delightful roasting joint. A haunch roasted on the bone makes a splendid festive joint, especially if the butcher has removed the awkward-to-carve pelvic bone. When referring to old cookery books, bear in mind that, until

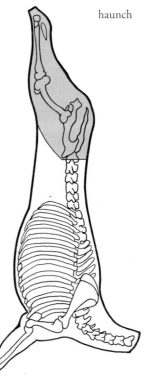

haunch

haunch
(original
definition)
sometimes
called
'pistol'

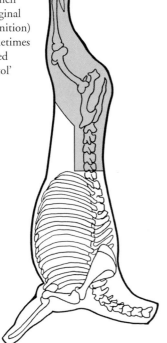

haunch roast: bone-in

boned and rolled haunch

well into the twentieth century the term 'haunch' meant the leg and the loin together, as in the illustration here. This is still the dictionary definition. Once a leg is boned, it can be divided into four main muscles plus the shank. All four muscles can be further split into two smaller ones. Good quality offcuts of haunch make excellent stir-fries, brochettes, kebabs, fondue, stroganoff and tagine.

rump

RUMP (POPE'S EYE, PAVÉ) The rump is the least easy part to cut neat steaks from, and also the muscle that has the greatest covering of fat on a mature animal. What meat there is, however, is good quality, being next to the saddle.

Rump: whole muscle, parted into two
muscles, and sliced into steak

TOPSIDE (TOP ROUND, PAVÉ) This is roughly triangular-shaped muscle, one of the best for steaks and roasting. Steaks off the topside are the largest of all.

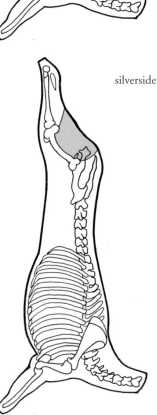
topside

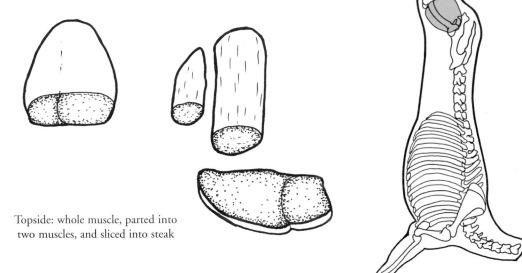

Topside: whole muscle, parted into two muscles, and sliced into steak

SILVERSIDE (OUTSIDE, BOTTOM ROUND, PAVÉ) This oblong muscle is also good for steaks and roasts. When divided, the small chunky muscle is called the salmon cut (haunch fillet, side) and makes a good substitute for fillet. Silverside is sometimes a paler colour than topside, no one seems to know why.

silverside

 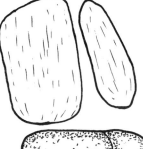

Silverside: whole muscle, parted into two muscles, and sliced into steak

thick flank

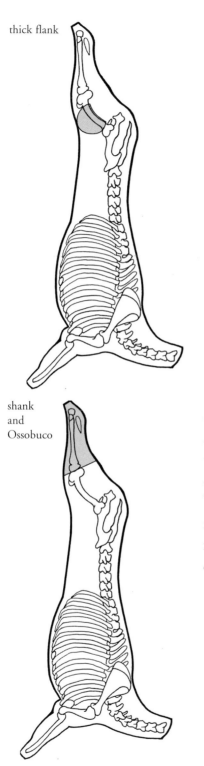

THICK FLANK (KNUCKLE END, FLESHY END, CUSHION) Nearest to the shank, this muscle is made up of five small muscles with sinew between, so is not suitable for steaks or roasts if from an old animal – it is better stewed. However, from a young/small deer, it makes good rolled roasts, frying steaks and stir-fries.

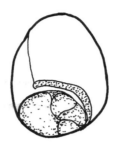

Thick flank: whole muscle, parted into two muscles, and sliced into steak

shank and Ossobuco

SHIN (SHANK, OSSOBUCO) One of the toughest parts of the haunch, but when very slowly cooked, the thick sinews turn into a fabulous gelatinous texture which complements venison beautifully. Can be cooked on the bone or diced into chunks. Thick slices of shin that include the marrowbone are called ossobuco. Watch out for the tiny pin-like bone near the marrow-bone – if you can, pull it out before serving.

shank

Ossobuco

FOREQUARTER (FORE)

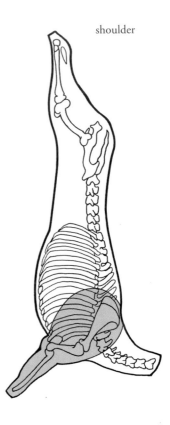

shoulder

NECK Makes excellent stock, soup and hotpots. Boned out and trimmed, it produces good diced meat for a stew if from young animals; if not it makes good quality mince for making into sausages, pies etc.

SHOULDER Can be roasted on or off the bone if from a young/small deer which won't have thick sinews, otherwise it is best slowly braised, diced for stews and pies, or minced.

boned and rolled shoulder   section of shoulder roast

LOIN EYE (NECK FILLET) This is the front part of the loin that divides into two muscles with a sinew between them. It is not such good quality as the loin further back on the saddle but nevertheless makes good steaks or roast if from young/small deer.

BRISKET This can be rolled and/or stuffed for a stewing joint, or diced, or minced. At the end of the summer, some older animals' brisket can be very fatty.

FLANK Generally minced for processing and can contain much hard fat on old animals, but on young/small animals it can be rolled into a slow-cooking cheap joint which benefits from stuffing.

SHANK See previous page.

OTHER CUTS

LIVER AND KIDNEY It is crucial that both these cuts are very fresh. Equally important, neither liver nor kidneys should ever be used from mature and rutting males. However, from females and immature deer these are gourmet delicacies, rightly sought-after by discerning gastronomes. Although dark in colour because it is so rich in iron, venison liver at its best is wonderfully sweet, tender and mild, and has fewer tubes in it than other livers.

HEART Like liver, heart is best thinly sliced and very quickly cooked, or else very slowly braised for a very rich stew. It's full of flavour.

TONGUE Deer tongues are very small and tender. Prepared and used in the same way as lamb tongues, they are a treat see p.209. Save up several in the freezer to cook at once.

SWEETBREADS (THYMUS AND PANCREAS) The thymus is difficult to obtain because it is only available from immature animals. The pancreas, though marginally less choice, is present throughout the animal's life. Most cognoscenti never tell anybody else about them but greedily keep them secret, for they are delicious.

OBSCURE PARTS For the sake of interest, and also because I believe that once an animal has been killed then every part should be used, some people may be glad to know that, somewhere in the world, the following parts are eaten, drunk or turned into buttons, medicines, drums, clothing, tools, footwear, whistles, fishing flies, trophies, macrobiotic fertilizers, purses, hair shirts, leather burnishers and glue: hard antler, velvet antler, heads, skins, hair, tendons, intestines, stomach, pizzles, tails, scrota, lungs, cheeks, blood, spleens, feet and bones.

PORTION SIZES

It is difficult to give firm advice, because people's ideas of 'enough' varies so much. It depends on the number of courses in the meal, the style of meal, the age of the diners and whether or not you want second helpings or leftovers. Venison is leaner, denser and more filling than beef, so most people are satisfied with about three-quarters the amount of venison, i.e. 225 g (8 oz) beef for a main course = 180 g (6 oz) venison. Most of the recipes in this book use 180 g (6 oz) of boneless venison (e.g. steaks, stew, small joints) for a main course portion. Light dishes and starters use about 100 g ($3^1/_2$ oz) per person. Cured and smoked venison is so intensely flavoured that 25 g (1 oz) is usually enough for a starter.

For venison joints on the bone, allow 350 – 450 g (12 oz – 16 oz) per person, to allow for second helpings, since a roasting joint is one of those things that lends itself to generosity and can be eaten cold at a second meal. For medium-sized boneless joints, allow 225–350 g (8–12 oz) to provide second helpings. Oddly, boneless roasts for large numbers (weddings, banquets, large dinners) can be reduced to 150 g (5 oz).

REDUCING THE USE OF FAT AND OIL

Being so lean, venison is perfect for people who wish to reduce the use of fat and oil in their diet. It is at its most succulent when served pink. However, many people following a low-fat diet use oil rather than butter to brown meat. But, especially when using very small amounts of oil, it often does not get hot enough to really brown the meat (especially small pieces like steaks or casserole chunks) before it overcooks. If you rub a very little salt over the meat, it draws out a small amount of blood, and this helps it to brown more quickly so the interior of the meat is left pink. Other suggestions for reducing fats can be found in chapters 6, 7, 8 and 13.

USING THE RECIPES

When cooking steaks and joints, the most important part is the general guidelines at the beginning of these chapters. Make sure that you read through them first, as the recipes assume you have done so. Some of the starters and light dishes are also easier if you have already read the guidelines for cooking steaks. Sauces and vegetables that go with steaks will work with roast venison too, and vice versa. The slow cooking section also has accompaniments that can be used with other dishes if wished, they are all there to be used as you wish. The suggested number of servings are a guide only, since appetites vary so much (see above).

Some dishes seem more likely to be cooked for two people whilst others are likely to be cooked for larger numbers, so that is how I have written them. But if you want to cook for larger or smaller numbers, it is very easy to increase or decrease the recipes. Unless otherwise stated, pepper in the recipes is freshly milled black pepper. Salt can be ordinary table salt, or fine ground sea salt unless otherwise stated. For browning meat, I use a half-and-half mixture of light olive oil and rapeseed or grape seed oil, though they can all be used on their own.

METRIC CONVERSIONS

Use either the metric or the imperial weights. In order to avoid cumbersome conversions like, for example, 500 g = 1 lb 2 oz, I have often translated it as 500 g = 1 lb+, i.e. a generous pound. Where I have done this, it really doesn't matter whether the extra 2 oz is there or not. Equally, although $^1/_2$ pint is 284 ml, I have rounded it up to 300 ml. If exact amounts are needed they are written exactly. I have used fluid ounces where exactitude is necessary but fractions of pints for more approximate measurements.

EQUIPMENT

Apart from the usual cook's demand for sharp knives, the only piece of equipment I would recommend above all is a meat thermometer. It amazes me that people are prepared to spend substantial amounts of money buying superb meat and expensive kitchen equipment and then baulk at paying £5 or £6 for a simple piece of equipment that makes it so easy to cook meat successfully. See p.132.

STORE CUPBOARD INGREDIENTS FOR VENISON

OIL For browning food, use virgin olive oil, rape seed, grape seed or groundnut oil. Grape seed and groundnut have the highest smoking points and little flavour. Virgin olive oil is great for cooking as long as it is not too highly flavoured. Some oils cancel out the beneficial qualities of Omega-3 fats, but neither olive nor rape seed oil do this. Walnut oil doesn't affect Omega-3 either, though it should not be used for high temperature cooking. It is wonderful for low-temperature cooking and superb for salads, as are most nut oils.

JUNIPER BERRIES (The classic seasoning) Despite their name they are treated like a spice (like whole cloves) rather than a fruit. Their strong flavour comes from the oil in the berries which should be moist enough to be squashed by your fingers or with the back of a spoon. They should immediately release a pungent aroma and remain slightly sticky. If they crunch up into a dry powder, throw them away - you might as well add dried sawdust to your dish. It is juniper berries that give gin its characteristic flavour, so it is quite logical to use gin in cooking venison. And sloe gin, as long as it is nice and tangy, is superb. Use juniper berries sparingly or they can be overpowering.

GINGER (Both dried or fresh root ginger) A complementary flavour for many venison dishes especially used with garlic as well. It's particularly good in stir-fries, and also in superior home-made burgers, sausages, terrines and other 'made' dishes. In the old days powdered ginger was used to preserve venison haunches in transit. It acted as a fly-repellent and flavoured the joint pleasantly as well.

NUTMEG Good for rich stews and all 'made' dishes. If you can be bothered to grate your own whole nutmeg, you will be rewarded with an invigorating burst of aroma.

CLOVES Best used sparingly especially when ground, as it is a strong flavour. Cloves add a dusky almost-bitter richness to slow-cooked winey dishes. Cloves are dried flower buds of *Syzygium aromaticum* that grows in Indonesia, Madagascar and Zanzibar. When fresh, the tight little buds are bright scarlet. Only the round tip has real flavour; the 'stalk' is useful to spike it into onions.

MUSTARD Wholegrain mustard is great in sauces or added to the cooking liquid of a slowly cooked joint. If you cook with mustard, you can usually manage without using salt, which is a health bonus. Crushed mustard seeds used to be put into country peoples' socks to keep their feet warm.

PAPRIKA For those wonderful fiery-red Hungarian venison dishes. There are different grades of paprika, all of which add their orangey-red colour to the dish. They range from very mild – essentially dried sweet peppers – to extremely hot chilli powder.

COCOA POWDER Not to be confused with drinking chocolate under any circumstances. Cocoa powder is pure ground cocoa beans and is unsweetened. It is a powerful, rich savoury flavour which adds a luscious velvetiness to rich stews and sauces. But it should be used sparingly, especially if there are sweet ingredients.

NUTS Pine nuts are a traditional accompaniment to venison dishes in Germany and France. I think almonds are brilliant almost anywhere, and both almonds and walnuts are wonderful fried, either plain or spiced, and scattered over a venison salad. All nuts lose vitality once shelled, so if you don't use them quickly, the freezer is the best place to keep them, tightly wrapped. Chestnuts are also good added to a venison stew. You can buy peeled, vacuum-packed chestnuts now, which removes a lot of the work.

THYME AND ROSEMARY   Both strong, oily flavoured herbs, and good in many venison dishes. Lovely in an oily marinade for a summer barbecue, but also punchy enough for winter stews and strewn on roasted potatoes. Their flowers are nice in a summer salad with smoked or cured venison.

LOVAGE   (Lover's parsley) With its strong celery-aniseed flavour, lovage needs using in moderation. It's good in marinades. Not commonly sold, but easy to grow in the garden. It grows up to two metres (six feet), looking a bit like celery that has gone berserk.

SPICY SALAD HERBS AND LEAVES   The deep rich flavour of venison needs more than just a plain lettuce salad. My salads for venison use barely 25% lettuce. The rest is a mixture of as many of the following as I can lay my hands on: marjoram, basil, chervil, chive flowers, parsley, garland chrysanthemum (shungiku), marigold petals, rocket, mizuna, wild garlic, nasturtium leaves. Salads made of perfumed herbs are almost a staple part of Persian (Iranian) cooking.

ORANGES   As with many gamey dishes, the sweet-sourness of oranges makes them a good marinade ingredient, being only slightly acid.

PEARS
These are a classic German accompaniment to venison. They are cored and halved and either baked or poached, then often served with redcurrant jelly.

BERRIES   Nearly all berries (except strawberries which are too bland) are good for making sauces for venison: raspberries, redcurrants, black currants, blackberries and their wild form, brambles. Blueberries and elderberries can be insipid and may

need a squeeze of lemon juice added to enhance the flavour and acidity. Redcurrant jelly is used in many classic game sauces.

ROWAN BERRIES (The fruit of the mountain ash tree, *Sorbus aucuparia*) Many people think they are poisonous as the raw berries are bitter and not at all juicy, but the birds know better. Rowan berries make wonderful full-strength tart jelly for enriching sauces or as an accompaniment to joints and steaks (see below). The American equivalent, mayhaw jelly, is paler and sweeter by comparison. Many old Scottish houses have rowan trees nearby as they are supposed to ward off evil.

CRANBERRIES AND POMEGRANATES Both make excellent tart sauces and jellies for sauces. Many bought sauces are too sweet as you need astringency to make the sauce interesting.

STONE FRUITS: In both plums and apricots the dried form (prunes and dried apricots) brings out the slight acidity of the fruit, though grilled fresh plums are delicious with venison.

CELERY, CELERIAC, BULB (FLORENCE) FENNEL, FENNEL SEED These are all especially good flavours for venison. If you particularly like their lightly aniseed taste, then add some fennel, caraway or aniseed to them as they cook.

CARROTS The sweetness of carrots, and their texture when well cooked, is perfect in many guises, whether puréed, cooked in large chunks and glazed to a slow buttery softness, mashed with other vegetables, or as a crisp, raw grated addition to a selection of salads. For the best flavour, don't peel them, says my carrot-grower.

4. Enrichments

Jelly, stock, marinades and rubs

4. Enrichments

Jelly, stock, marinades and rubs

Rowan jelly

Makes about 10–11 x 450 g (1 lb) pots

A staple venison ingredient as far as I am concerned, as rowan jelly is far more interesting than redcurrant. Use it as an accompaniment to roasts or steaks, add it to the pan while steaks are resting to make a quick sauce, or put a dollop into a casserole. The smell of rowan berries being boiled is the very essence of autumn. Yellow and orange berries, in my limited experience of them, tend to make the jelly bitter rather than tart. The best berries are bright red ones, preferably growing in thick, heavy clusters. Pick the whole bunch, leaving the bud tip behind to provide next year's crop. There will be one leaf attached to the cluster. Remove it, leaving all the other stalks on. To make one batch, I pick a full carrier bag, which weighs about 3 kg (7 lbs). If you make smaller quantities, the formula for the strained juice is 750 g of sugar to every 1 litre of juice (1 lb sugar to 1 pint juice).

3 kg (7 lbs) rowanberries in bunches

6 litres (10 pts) water

3.2 kg (7 lbs) sugar (optional)

150 ml (¼ pt) liquid pectin

Tip the berries into a huge pan and add the water. Bring slowly to the boil, and then reduce the heat to a simmer. With a sturdy potato masher, pound the berries from time to time to pulp them into a thin porridge. This process takes about an hour. The berries need a long simmering to release the sweetness from the starchy interior. Short simmering leaves it too bitter.

Strain the pulp through a jelly bag. There should be about 4.2 litres (7 pints) of rosy red , slightly cloudy liquid. If there is significantly less, pour a little extra hot water carefully into the jelly bag and allow it to filter through the pulp.

Wash the jelly pan and return the strained juice. Add the sugar and dissolve it slowly. Bring to a rolling boil, then turn the heat down to stop it boiling over. Allow it to boil and reduce. Keep testing to see if it has set (it could take 45 minutes or more). Put a few drips of jelly onto a cold dry plate and after a few minutes, push your finger across it. If it wrinkles and you are able to lift up a slightly jellied blob, it is ready. Skim off any scum diligently and then pour the crystal clear jelly into warm pots.

Rowan jelly takes longer than other jellies to set, as it doesn't have much pectin. A lightly set jelly is better for making sauces, but if you want it stiffer add about 150 ml (1/4pt) of bottled pectin right at the end, bring it to the boil, skim the jelly, and remove from the heat. Allow it to sit for five minutes, then stir it once more and pour it into pots.

VENISON STOCK

It surprises me that more people don't make their own stock. It is a pleasant job, you know exactly what's in it, and you can make enough to last for months. Having said that, it is much easier to buy reasonable additive-free stock nowadays. Avoid any that contain flavour enhancers, stabilisers or other ingredients that you would not have in your own kitchen. In particular, avoid stocks that contain monosodium glutamate.

EMERGENCY STOCK-IN-A-HURRY

If you don't have time, patience or bones, and can't buy any stock, here is a tip given to me by chef Anne Nicol. Trim your meat to the perfect shape and reserve the trimmings. If it is already a perfect shape, just cut a thin slice off each end and dice them really small. Dice a small shallot, a tiny piece of carrot and any other suitable vegetables to hand too. Brown the trimmings and vegetables, making sure they are caramelised to a deep brown (but not burnt). Add 150 ml ($^1/_4$ pint) water, and, scraping up all the pan juices, allow it to simmer while you prepare the rest of the dish. After the meat in your recipe has been browned, pour the simmering stock and trimmings into that pan to scrape up all those brownings too. You now have a little stock to add flavour to your dish.

SERIOUSLY STUCK

If you have neither home-made nor bought stock, then as a last resort try some of the following, but with caution so as not to drown the flavours of the recipe: soy sauce, teriyaki sauce, oyster sauce, tart fruit jelly, tomato purée, port, sweet stout, stock cubes, cocoa powder, Worcestershire sauce.

PROPER STOCK

Use good quality scraps but discard anything that is bruised or very high as it will give a bitter and/or mouldy flavour. However, trimmings that are only a little too well hung for normal cooking should not be spurned – they are going to be boiled for a very long time. To make lovely silky sauces, you need to include bones with cartilage. Neck bones are good, but best of all are the ends of the shin and shank bones. If they are also sawn in two, they will release the marrow too.

The more meat and vegetables in the initial stock, the less reducing it needs later. Vegetables like carrots and onions add sweetness; celery is also good. The meat, bones and vegetables should be thoroughly browned first for flavour and colour. Roast them in the oven or under the grill after brushing with oil, and turn them around so that they get browned all over.

Then get a large pan and completely cover the meat, bones and vegetables with water. Don't add seasoning. Bring to the boil and lower the heat to a gentle simmer for 4–5 hours, on the stove top or in a low oven. After 3 or 4 hours, give everything a good stir as some of the meat will detach from the bones and give out more flavour. Then strain the stock into a large bowl and allow it to cool. When completely cold, you can remove the layer of fat on top. The top layer of stock is the purest; on the bottom will be some sludge which is fine for soups, so don't throw it away. I usually make a secondary stock once the 'first pressing' has been strained off. It needs more reducing but is useful nevertheless.

The strained stock may be used as it is for soup, stews or diluting gravy, or it may be reduced to make strong stock for sauces, or even further to make a 'jus' which is ready to add to a frying pan after steaks are cooked. Or it can be boiled right down to a jelly. Freeze it in small cartons and ice cube containers and it is fantastically useful for making really good quick sauces, adding to soup or filling terrines and pies. This elixir (meat glaze or demi-glace) will also keep, covered, in the fridge for about a week.

MARINATING

Yes or no? I recently read the draft of a cookery book that urged the reader to use marinades only 'with desecration, and with a purpose'. The vision conjured up by this lovely misprint describes what some marinades achieve, often because so many people assume that you have to marinate venison, even though they wouldn't consider marinating other kinds of meat.

Marinades in some cookery books are harsh, virtually pickles, using hefty quantities of acids. Alexis Soyer writes in 1846 in *The Gastronomic Regenerator*: 'The flesh of the doe or roebuck is a kind of black meat, and possesses a wild gamey taste; it is seldom used without being pickled in a marinade and is sent to table with a sharp and savoury sauce.' He soaks his venison for up to a week in two parts vinegar to one of broth. Meg Dods, in her *Cook and Housewife's Manual* of 1826, wrote 'Some cooks marinate the meat in wine and other seasonings for a night, or for some hours prior to baking. This, no doubt, imbues the venison with the flavour of the seasonings, but at the same time drains off the juices, and hurts the natural flavour of the meat, so that we discountenance the practice.' I am inclined towards Meg Dods' view.

It is interesting though, that countless European recipes survive for transforming inferior meats into 'venison' by soaking and cooking them in wine, vinegar, lemon juice and the types of spices that they would use for venison. In the seventeenth century, Samuel Pepys noticed with disapproval a venison pasty 'that was palpable beef and not handsome' and another one which 'proved a pasty of salted pork'. Lengthy marinating of venison seems to have taken off in the mid nineteenth century. Perhaps it was caused by increased amounts of stalked venison in contrast to the mild young park venison that people had been used to eating; perhaps it was the Germanic influence of Prince Albert (Germany, Austria and Switzerland still tend to heavily marinate their venison).

Properly matured venison has a fabulous flavour of its own. Like any well-prepared meat, its flavour is deep, rich, but bright, and needs no marinade to make it tender, succulent or delicious. However, there is no doubt that for some people, the whole idea of marinating venison is part of its romance, and far be it from me to spoil anyone's fun. But there is an important difference between cooking meat in rich wines and spices, and leaving it to soak for days in acidic liquids. Contrary to what many people imagine, acids like wine, vinegar, lemon juice and so on, actually make the surface of the meat tougher and drier rather than more tender. This is because, as Meg Dods pointed out, the astringency draws moisture from the meat, and if left for long in such a marinade, the outside of the meat eventually becomes pale, fuzzy and slightly 'cooked' in texture.

So leave lengthy marinades for really large joints with proportionately less outside surface and more inside. And don't marinate small pieces of meat in acid mixtures for long, as they have such a lot of surface to be dried out. Instead, ask the question: what is the purpose of the marinade? Is it to tenderise the meat? Is it to mask 'off' tastes of badly killed and processed venison, or is it to impart delicious new flavours? There may be other ways of achieving the goal.

If you buy venison, it shouldn't be tough. But if it is, gentle and lengthy cooking in a liquid will eventually tenderise the toughest cut without any marinade. If you want to serve it pink, put it in a deep bowl and completely submerge it in a light-flavoured oil, excluding all the air and keep it in a cold place for up to ten days. If you want, add spices and herbs and other flavourings to the oil, but not acids. Eventually, meat kept like this will become so tender it is quite mushy, so don't overdo it unless you are dentally challenged.

'Off' flavours caused by poor handling sometimes only affect the surface of the meat. In this case, simple trimming or even washing of the outside helps a lot. For 'off' flavours caused by stress, even lengthy marinating can't penetrate more than the outside layers anyway so it is best just to dice it up and cook the venison in a well-spiced liquid to make a sauce that will improve the overall flavour.

I have given tutored venison tastings to hundreds of people, and a surprising number begin by confusing the flavour of marinades with the natural flavour of venison, which it isn't. But marinade flavours have a levelling effect – they brighten up insipid meat and mask over-strong taste. So if you want to impart the lovely perfumes of spices and herbs

to venison steaks, then an hour or two is usually long enough. With slow-cooked dishes there is no need to marinate at all; simply cooking it with the spices or liquids is enough. An advantage of using marinades to cook rather than soak the meat, is that you don't need to pat lots of small pieces dry before browning them.

However, having said all that, if you still think it necessary to souse your venison in marinade for many days, there does need to be enough acid in the mix to prevent the other liquids fermenting.

A final point to note about marinades is that many children are not keen on the taste of food cooked with alcohol, so use it with caution when cooking for them, and start them off with simpler flavours.

SPICE RUBS

A delicious alternative to marinating venison is to simply rub some spices and pungent herbs into its surface, bind it up tightly in cling-film, and leave it for a few hours. Small pieces (stew and steaks) are best with milder spicing whereas joints can cope with stronger spicing since it won't drown the flavour of the venison. Scrape the spices off before cooking for a subtle flavour; leave them on for the full blast. Choose from the following: crushed juniper, crushed whole caraway seed, grated or ground ginger, crushed fennel seed, cracked black, pink or szechuan peppercorns, toasted cumin or coriander seed, chopped chilli, thyme, lovage, rosemary or any other favourite herb or spice.

ENRICHED COOKING LIQUIDS AND MILD MARINADES

If you have an awkwardly shaped joint, or find that the marinade doesn't cover the meat, put them both in a thick plastic bag and tie it tightly round the meat so that all the air is excluded. If you want to speed up the process, leave the meat to marinate at room temperature. If you want to slow it down, keep it in the fridge. It is always best to turn meat around in its marinade if it is there for more than an hour or two because the oil rises to the top. There are many lovely flavoured oils available now which help to impart flavour. If you use a mild marinade as the stewing liquid, allow 300–500 ml per 1 kg (4 – 7 fl oz per 1lb) of meat. The marinade recipes at the end of this section are strongest.

Fletcher's cooking marinade

Makes 900 ml (1½ pts)

Best simply used as a cooking liquid, though the meat can be left in it overnight as there is not too much acid in it.

500 ml (¾ pt) red wine

150 ml (¼ pt) olive oil

5 tablespoons orange juice

5 tablespoons mild wine vinegar

5 tablespoons brandy

1 tablespoon rowan jelly

1 teaspoon crushed juniper berries

½ teaspoon ground ginger

Sweet cider marinade

Makes 1.2 litres (2 pts)

Hazelnut oil is powerfully flavoured, but the marinade is still good without it. Fry the apples briskly in the olive oil till browned, add the vinegar or Calvados, and remove from the heat. Add these to the other ingredients, and when cool, soak the venison in it. Use the honey if the cider is very dry. This is good for making into a stew, but retrieve the cinnamon stick before serving.

2 apples, peeled, cored and sliced

3 tablespoons hazelnut oil

1 tablespoon cider vinegar or Calvados

1 litre (1¾ pts) cider

¼ teaspoon ground black peppe

¼ teaspoon ground cloves

5 cm (2 in) piece cinnamon stick (optional)

2 teaspoons hazelnut oil (optional)

1 teaspoon honey

Ginger and garlic marinade

Makes 100 ml (3¹/₄ fl oz)

This is great for venison steaks, hence the smaller quantities. Use some of the marinade to deglaze the pan, if wished. Gently sauté the ginger and garlic in the sesame oil. Add them to the other ingredients, and once it is cool, turn the meat around in it for an hour or so.

3 cm (1 ¹/₄ in) fresh ginger root, grated

3 cloves garlic, peeled and chopped

2 tablespoons sesame oil

2 tablespoons soy sauce

2 tablespoons rice wine or white wine

1 teaspoon honey

Mustard and Strong Ale Marinade

Makes 1 litre (1³/₄ pts)

Mix together and use this as a cooking liquid to for a stew or to braise a joint. There is no need to soak it beforehand.

1 litre (1³/₄ pts) strong brown ale

2 tablespoons wholegrain mustard

Hindberry marinade

Makes 200 ml (7 fl oz)

Hindberries is an old country name for raspberries. I like to think of hinds nibbling them as they pass through the dappled woods. Crush the raspberries and beat all the ingredients together. I would use this to marinate steaks or a small joint for an hour or so.

2 tablespoons raspberry vinegar

150 ml (¼ pint) light olive oil

1 clove garlic, crushed

1 shallot, peeled and sliced

100 g (4 oz) fresh raspberries

Summer marinade

Makes 350 ml (12 fl oz)

Pare the rind of the lemon and break it into pieces with half the juice. Add all the rest of the ingredients. Because this is mostly oil, the aromas of the lemon, garlic, and herbs will permeate it nicely, and it will do no harm to be left overnight or longer.

200 ml (7 fl oz) light olive, walnut or grapeseed oil

Rind of 1 lemon

125 ml (4 fl oz) medium-sweet sherry

1 dessertspoon fresh thyme

1 dessertspoon fresh rosemary

1 tablespoon fresh parsley

1 clove garlic, peeled and crushed

Brandy and walnut oil marinade

Makes 250 ml (8 fl oz)

This is strong so you only need a little. Keep turning the meat in it as it will not be covered completely. Good for steaks on a cold day.

125 ml (4 fl oz) brandy

125 ml (4 fl oz) walnut oil

$^1/_2$ teaspoon ground black pepper

Yoghurt marinade

Makes 300 ml ($^1/_2$ pt)

Another good soak for steaks or chops. Marinate the venison in it for no more than two hours, and scrape it off before cooking so that the meat browns properly. Add some of the marinade to deglaze the pan to provide a simple sauce but don't let it boil or it will curdle. If the yoghurt and lemon is too acid for you, use cream instead.

300 ml ($^1/_2$ pt) natural yoghurt

Zest of $^1/_2$ small lemon

2 tablespoons fresh parsley, chopped

1 tablespoon fresh mint, chopped

1 dessertspoon garam masala

Freshly ground black pepper

Simple barbecue marinade

Makes 350 ml (12 fl oz)

2 tablespoons red wine

300 ml ($^1/_2$ pt) light olive oil

1 teaspoon crushed juniper berries

1 teaspoon caraway or fennel seed

3 cloves garlic, crushed

Fresh herbs, especially thyme

Classic red wine marinade

Makes 1 litre (1$^3/_4$ pts)

Bring all the ingredients to the boil, boil for two minutes, then allow to cool. Immerse the meat in it as desired; anything from two hours to two days. Wipe dry thoroughly before browning the meat, and use it as the cooking liquid if desired.

750 ml (1 bottle) red wine

100 ml (3 fl oz) red wine vinegar

150 ml ($^1/_4$ pint) olive oil

1 teaspoon crushed juniper berries

$^1/_4$ teaspoon ground black pepper

2 onions, sliced

2 bay leaves

1 teaspoon dried thyme

To recover venison that is tainted

From Gervase Markham's *The English Housewife* of 1615:

'Take strong ale, and put to it of wine vinegar as much as will make it sharp: then set it on the fire, and boil it well, and scum it, and make of it a strong brine with bay salt, or other salt: then take it off, and let it stand till it be cold, then put your venison into it, and let it lie in it full twelve hours: then take it out from that mere sauce, and press it well; then parboil it, and season it with pepper and salt, and bake it.'

Tough old buck venison marinade

Makes 300 ml (¹/₂ pint)

This is Harold Webster's recipe which he guarantees is the one to use for getting rid of the over gamy smell of tainted venison. An avid hunter and cook, he studied the effects that killing and handling have on the venison. He compared deer of similar age and species the only difference being the way they were shot and handled. 'The deer that was rested and harvested [shot] cleanly had a fresh meat smell. The deer that was tired and badly shot smelled wild and gamy.' Harold's suggestion of injecting the marinade deep into the meat is good; if you don't have a syringe, then make some deep slits in the meat to allow the marinade to penetrate. 'If this marinade will not remove the wild smell, nothing will.'

150 ml (¹/₄ pt) red wine

3 tablespoons balsamic vinegar

3 tablespoons olive oil

2 tablespoons sorghum molasses (or treacle)

2 tablespoons fresh thyme, chopped

2 tablespoons fresh rosemary, chopped

1 tablespoon juniper berries, crushed

3 cloves garlic, minced

Zest of 3 unwaxed oranges

Zest of 3 unwaxed lemons

8 whole cloves

8 whole peppercorns

2 bay leaves

³/₄ teaspoon salt

Combine all the ingredients. Inject some of the marinade deep into the venison. Place the marinade and venison in a plastic, glass or stainless steel container, cover and refrigerate overnight.

5. Enough is good for a feast

Light dishes, starters, salads and stir-fry

5. Enough is good for a feast

Light dishes, starters, salads and stir-fry

There are so many different eating styles nowadays that it is difficult to know how best to group recipes. This section consists of dishes that will make good starters and, apart from the first four, are ideal for a quick meal – a lunch, perhaps, a little supper treat for two, or a tasty snack for curling up in front of the telly. Pâté and terrine recipes are in chapter 11. These recipes can be easily halved or doubled if wished to suit different appetites. Guidelines for cooking steaks are on pages 100-108.

Seared venison with asparagus, Parmesan salad and truffle dressing

Serves 4

This makes a great dinner party starter – for a main course, multiply by one and a half. It is a recipe from New Zealand chef Hamish Brown and has a lovely fresh spring feeling that emphasises the lightness of venison, though it would also be good with 100 g (4 oz) Jerusalem artichokes or parsnips in the winter. Filet mignon or loin may also be used here. When using haunch (leg), it should be trimmed into a log shape approx 5 cm (2 ins) in diameter. Some suppliers offer a single leg muscle of this shape.

400 g (14 oz) piece of venison haunch

salt and pepper

oil for browning

12 asparagus spears

80 g (3 oz) whole Parmesan

1 tablespoon salted capers

1 handful rocket leaves

For the truffle dressing

½ teaspoon Dijon mustard

Juice ½ lemon

1½ tablespoons Champagne or white wine vinegar

1½ tablespoons truffle oil

3 tablespoons olive oil

Pinch of chopped chervil

Season the venison with salt and pepper and brown it in a hot pan until evenly coloured on all sides (5 – 6 minutes). Remove from the pan and cool. The meat should be very rare inside.

Make the truffle dressing: whisk the mustard, lemon juice and vinegar together, then slowly whisk in the oils. Add the chopped chervil and adjust seasoning with salt and pepper.

Once the venison is cool enough to handle, lay it onto a sheet of plastic clingfilm and add two tablespoons of the truffle dressing. Seal it in the clingfilm and chill.

Trim and clean the asparagus spears and cook until only just tender then plunge them into iced water to cool immediately. Drain .

To assemble Shave the Parmesan cheese. Thinly slice the venison and lay it out onto the plates evenly. Toss the asparagus in the dressing and arrange neatly on the venison. Garnish with remaining ingredients and serve immediately. Any spare dressing can be passed round separately or kept for future use.

Venison and celeriac consommé

Serves at least 8

It is worth making a fuss about consommé – a simple but elegant starter or between-course offering. It is easy to make: all you need is time, so it is worth making plenty at once and freezing the surplus. Make sure there is plenty of meat and include some bones with cartilage as these simmer down into gelatine, which gives the consommé its smooth unctuous texture. Because it is so pure, consommé can of course be served absolutely plain. However, it does lend itself to finishing touches: these should be small and exquisite without being too overpowering. It is the carnivorous Western version of Japanese bowls of miso soup, each containing some tiny edible treasure. It's nice to make these reflect the season.

2.5 kg (5 lbs) meaty venison bones and trimmings (neck, shin)

1 small celeriac root

500 g (1 lb+) mixture of onions, carrots, celery

Bay leaves, thyme, parsley

Oil, butter or dripping for browning

1 teaspoon black peppercorns

water

2 egg whites

Medium dry sherry and seasoning to taste

Finishing touches, see next page

If you want to cut out shapes from carrot and celeriac (see below), do this now and use the rest for the stock. Cut vegetables into large chunks, and you can leave the skin of the onion on after removing the roots and the dirty outer skin – it helps to colour the stock. Brush the bones, trimmings, mixed vegetables and celeriac with oil or fat and roast or grill until browned all over. Be careful not to cook them till black as this makes the stock bitter – a deep brown is best. Put them into a large stockpot with the peppercorns and herbs, cover with water, and simmer over a very low heat (or put into a low oven) for at least 6 hours – longer is better. Give it a stir from time to time.

Strain the stock as thoroughly as possible using first a sieve and then a cloth. Allow to cool completely, then skim off all the fat. For eight people you will need about 2.2 litres (3^1/$_2$pts). If there is too much, it can either be reduced to intensify the flavour, or the surplus frozen. Bring the stock up to blood temperature. Then beat the egg whites and whisk them into the tepid stock. Gradually allow it to simmer for 20–30 minutes without disturbing it. The egg whites attract all the small particles, leaving crystal clear consommé. Have ready a sieve or colander lined with a double layer of tea towel or linen cloth (not your best ones). Place it over a bowl and, using a ladle, carefully lift out as big a piece as you can of this now rather dirty-looking crust and let it drain through the cloth. Then gently ladle the rest through the hole you have made. Season very carefully with sherry and salt. Garnish as wished: see suggestions below.

The consommé can also be reduced by half and served as a chilled jelly in hot weather.

Garnish suggestions
• Tiny slices or chopped pieces of fresh truffle. Add them at the last minute to retain their perfume.
• Flowers that taste, such as chive, rosemary or peppery-tasting nasturtium flowers.
• Flakes of gold leaf floating on top.
• Tiny wild fungi such as chanterelles or ceps, simmered in salty water till soft. If they are not small enough, cut them into thin slices instead.
• Vegetables, either cut into thin matchsticks or sliced paper-thin and cut into shapes with a knife or miniature pastry cutter. Simmer briefly in salted water till barely soft, then refresh in cold water. Drain and keep till ready to serve, where they will swirl merrily in the clear consommé. I use little stag shapes.
• A tiny poached quenelle of vegetable or venison. See the recipe for frikadellar on p.94. Since the consommé is made in advance, you have time to poach these just before serving.

Spiced venison parcels with fresh tomato sauce

Serves 4

Another good starter or light lunch dish.

300 g (11 oz) venison mince

Heaped tablespoon chopped spinach

1 dessertspoon chopped parsley

1 tablespoon olive oil

$\frac{1}{2}$ teaspoon each of nutmeg, turmeric and cumin

Black pepper, salt

250 g (9 oz) puff pastry

Beaten egg to glaze

For the sauce

4 tablespoons chopped tomatoes

1 tablespoon finely chopped carrot

1 tablespoon finely chopped onion

1 clove garlic, crushed

Zest of $\frac{1}{4}$ lemon, grated

1 dessertspoon olive oil

150 ml ($\frac{1}{4}$ pt) white wine

Tiny pinch ground cloves

50 g (2 oz) butter (optional)

Fresh basil or mint to finish

To make the sauce, put the carrot, onion, garlic, lemon zest, olive oil and wine into a small pan and simmer until reduced by two-thirds, then add the chopped tomato. Season with salt and pepper and just a hint of cloves and warm it through. Keep aside until ready to serve, then just before serving, warm it through and whisk in the butter if used; this gives it a silkier texture.

To make the parcels, mix together all the ingredients except the pastry and beaten egg and form into four balls. Roll out the pastry into four squares. Place a ball of mince in the centre of each square and brush the pastry edges with water, milk or beaten egg. Bring up the four corners of each square into the centre like a square pyramid and crimp the edges firmly together. If you twist the top and then press it gently down, it stops them from bursting. Brush with beaten egg and cook in a fairly hot oven (Gas 6, 200°C, 400°F) for about 25 minutes. If the pastry looks as though it will brown too much, turn the heat down a little. The parcels should be golden brown and the pastry puffed up.

Serve with the tomato sauce with torn basil or mint scattered over it.

Trygves Solheim's extra easy venison recipe
Serves 4

This dish can be used as a starter as well as round a campfire in the woods. You need a cheese slicer. Norwegian flatbread can be substituted with ultra-thin oatcakes if necessary. Flatbread is made with a mixture of flour (rye, wheat, oat or barley) that varies according to region. Whatever is used, the flatbread must be rolled paper-thin.

680 g (1½ lb) tender venison haunch or shoulder

180 g (6 oz) block of pure butter, chilled

Balsamic vinegar

Flaked sea salt

For the Norwegian flatbreads

250 g (8 oz) oatmeal flour

250 g (8 oz) barley flour

250 g (8 oz) rye flour

1 teaspoon salt

700 ml (24 fl oz) milk or water

First make the flatbreads. Mix together the flours and salt. Moisten with the liquid to form a soft dough. Dust a board with oat or barley flour. Divide the dough into pieces and roll each one out as thinly as possible – 3 mm (⅛ in) maximum. Prick them with a fork. Lightly oil a large heavy frying pan and heat until smoking hot. One by one, place the rolled-out circles onto the frying pan and cook until the base begins to brown. Then turn it over gently and cook the other side. Keep turning until it is dry and crisp but not more than medium brown.

Put some butter in a hot frying pan and cook the venison quickly, leaving it nicely browned all over but red and juicy in the middle – about 5 minutes, though this depends on the thickness of the meat.

Let the venison rest for a few minutes, then slice it thinly. Put two or three slices onto each piece of flatbread, then, using a cheese slicer, cut a thick slice of pure butter and lay it on top of the venison. Add a few drops of best Balsamic vinegar and finally a few flakes of salt. Before the butter melts, pass this to your friends. 'Don't swallow your tongue,' says Trygve.

Venison steak tartare

Serves 2

Venison is perfect for steak tartare as it is so lean. Make sure all the sinew is removed before mincing. Ideally, mince your own just before serving, but if that is not possible, then ask to have some de-sinewed steak minced, and tell the butcher it is for steak tartare. There are some good alternatives to sturgeon caviar now, ranging from reformed seaweed, through salty lumpfish roe to one made of reformed herring which I like the best. Not like genuine caviar of course, but good in its own right, and good for this purpose.

150 g (5 oz) lean minced venison

1 small onion

2 eggs

2 teaspoons caviar or alternative

Black pepper, paprika

12 caper berries

Aioli (garlic mayonnaise), mustard, horseradish sauce, chilli jam or others to taste

Slice the onion and reserve two good rings. Finely chop the rest and add these to the minced venison. Form this into two patties. Make a well in the centre and place an onion ring in it. Separate the eggs carefully without breaking the yolks. Place a yolk into each onion ring. Dust with paprika and black pepper, scatter with the caviar, and serve with the caper berries and sauces.

SMOKED, CURED, AND RAW VENISON CARPACCIO

Most of the following recipes can be interchanged and they are best suited to starters and canapés. Suggestions for accompaniments are below, followed by some recipes using them. Since cured venison has an intense flavour, a small amount feeds a lot of people. For a starter, allow 35 g (1½ oz) per person if it is to be laid out on a plate, but if snipped into strips 25 g (1 oz) per person will suffice. As well as smoked venison, you can buy venison dry-cured into a raw ham, like Parma or jambon. Serve it laid out on plates, or snip the slices into thin ribbons like tagliatelli (kitchen scissors are easier than a knife), which makes it easier for people to eat – it's handy for canapés snipped this way and for dividing it up amongst large numbers too. Pile these into a little heap on each plate with the accompaniments. Dry sherry goes well with smoked and cured venison. To cure or smoke your own venison, see Chapter 12.

Serving suggestions for smoked and cured venison
• Hot-smoked venison with horseradish sauce, beetroot and rocket.
• Smoked or dry-cured venison with gratin dauphinoise (p.178).
• Hot-smoked venison with red pepper stew and Parmesan wafers.
• Smoked venison with thinly sliced seared pineapple scattered with fresh chilli.
• Dry-cured venison with oven-dried tomatoes, basil and mozzarella.
• Cold smoked venison with ripe melon and a little freshly grated ginger.
• Dry-cured venison with rémoulade (grated celeriac in a mustard mayonnaise) and truffle oil.

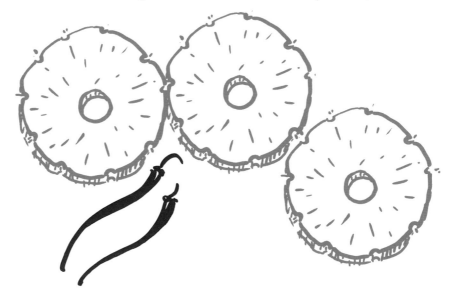

Carpaccio of venison

Serves 4

Carpaccio of beef was the invention of Harry's Bar in Venice. They called it carpaccio because the raw meat was the shade of red used by the sixteenth-century Venetian painter Carpaccio. Nowadays it has come to mean wafer thin slices of anything – tuna, pineapple, salmon, cured meats. Being perfectly lean, venison is lovely served raw and it is also a rich, vibrant red. As with most simple things, the ingredients must be perfect. For information on eating raw venison, see p.102.

225 g (8 oz) venison loin, or haunch muscle trimmed into a log shape

Butter and oil for browning

Olive oil

Whole Parmesan or strong Cheddar cheese

50 g (2 oz) rocket or spicy salad leaves

Black pepper

4 or 5 pickled caper berries each (optional)

Most people prefer to sear the outside of the venison before chilling and slicing it. If so, melt a knob of butter in a frying pan with a tablespoon of olive oil till the butter stops frothing and turns brown. Sear the meat speedily over a high heat till all sides are nicely browned but the inside is still raw. Then remove from the pan and cool quickly. If you don't have a meat slicer, it is easier to cut wafer-thin slices if you freeze the meat for an hour till it starts stiffening up. You need a very sharp knife. As you slice the venison, lay it out on plates so that the surfaces are covered. Drizzle olive oil over the slices and shave some Parmesan over the top. Serve with the spicy rocket leaves, a turn of coarse black pepper and the pickled caper berries.

Smoked venison soufflés with watercress salsa
Serves 6

The contrast of the smoky flavour and the sharp watercress is a good one. You can use this recipe with almost any hot-smoked meat or fish, and indeed I first made this with de-boned kippers. Use hot-smoked venison as it pulverises more easily.

100 g (4 oz) hot-smoked venison

grated zest of 1 unwaxed lemon

30 g (1 oz) butter

1¹/₂ tablespoons flour

300 ml (¹/₂ pt) milk

2 eggs

For the salsa

75 g (3 oz) watercress

juice of ¹/₂ lemon

2 tablespoons balsamic vinegar

200 ml (¹/₃ pt) olive oil

12 cherry tomatoes halved

Oil six metal soufflé moulds of about 100 ml (3¹/₂ fl oz) capacity. Grate the rind off the lemon. Put this zest into a blender with the smoked venison and pulverise till smooth. Make a fairly thick white (béchamel) sauce by melting the butter, stirring in the flour and whisking in the milk. Keep stirring till it has thickened, then remove from the heat. Separate the eggs. Beat the venison and the egg yolks into the white sauce. You don't need salt. Whisk the egg whites till stiff and fold them in. Divide the mixture between the moulds and place them in a large, deep frying pan. Carefully pour in enough boiling water to come half way up the moulds, then cover the pan with a domed lid or make a domed lid out of foil. Allow the soufflés to simmer and steam gently for 15 – 20 minutes.

Meanwhile make the salsa. Wash the watercress and put it in a blender, adding the juice of half the lemon, the balsamic vinegar and olive oil. Blend until it looks slightly creamy but the watercress is not completely pulverised. Dice the cherry tomatoes. When the soufflés are done (they should only rise to the top of the moulds) carefully turn them out onto individual plates. Put a generous puddle of the salsa and a heap of diced sweet tomatoes next to each soufflé. Serve at once.

Ceviche of venison with caramelised shallots

Serves 4-6

Ceviche is a South American way of serving raw fish. The acid in the marinade appears to cook the outside of the fish, or, in this case, the meat, though it actually remains raw. I have used this technique with woodpigeon and rabbit as well as venison and had thought that to cure meat like this was entirely my own invention until I went to Norway and was given something remarkably similar – sweet-cured raw venison – which goes to show there is little new in the culinary world.

This is also good served with deep-fried parsnip chips and caperberries.

Because it is eaten raw, it is important to be scrupulous about your hygiene, and also to cut your slices from an unbroken muscle. See p.102 for information on eating raw venison. It is important to slice the meat very thinly, as thick raw meat is not pleasant to eat. In small quantities, as a little starter or canapé, it is delicious. Its texture is at its best after about an hour; any longer and the outside 'cooked' texture permeates the whole slice, losing its internal succulence.

180 g (6 oz) venison loin or haunch

Juice of 1 lemon or lime

1 tablespoon soy sauce

1 tablespoon port

$^1/_2$ tablespoon balsamic vinegar

$^1/_2$ teaspoon salt

Ground black pepper

For the caramelised shallots

12–18 shallots, peeled

1 tablespoon olive oil

1 wineglass medium sherry or sweet vermouth

2 teaspoons honey

1 teaspoon balsamic or wine vinegar

To serve

Rocket or spicy salad leaves

6 dabs wasabi or English mustard (optional)

Completely trim the meat. Put it into the freezer for 1 hour to firm it. Mix together in a bowl all the remaining ceviche ingredients. Cut the meat into very thin slices, like smoked salmon and stir it into the cure. Leave for 20 minutes – 1 hour, giving it an occasional stir. It will take on a slightly 'cooked' appearance because of the vinegar and lemon juice.

While the venison cures, caramelise the shallots. Roast the shallots with the oil in a hot oven (Gas7, 220ºC, 425ºF) for 20 minutes until till they begin to brown and soften. Add the sherry, honey and wine vinegar, and roll them around to coat them. Cook for a further 20 minutes until they are nicely softened and well coated. Cool.

Strain the ceviche from its cure and serve it draped over the cool spicy salad leaves with the warm caramellised shallots on top and the fiery wasabi paste or mustard to one side.

Hot-smoked venison with parsnip and avocado

Serves 4

One of those marriages made in heaven: the smoky venison being complemented perfectly by the sweet earthiness of parsnip and the luscious oiliness of avocado. Very often independent shops and markets are the best source of ripe avocados. This also works with cold-smoked venison. Jerusalem artichokes make a wonderful alternative to the parsnips.

100 g (4 oz) hot-smoked sliced venison

3–4 large parsnips

2 tablespoons wine vinegar

2 teaspoons wholegrain mustard

6 tablespoons olive oil

Black pepper, pinch of salt

1 large or 2 small ripe avocados

Flat-leaved parsley or chervil

Peel the parsnips and slice into sticks, then boil them till soft. They cook quite quickly. While they cook, make up the dressing by whisking together the vinegar, mustard, oil, salt and pepper. Drain the parsnips and immediately pour the dressing over them so it soaks in while they cool. When ready to serve, remove the stones from the avocado, cut it into chunks and gently mix the chunks with the parsnips. Cut the smoked venison into wide strips and serve with the parsnip/avocado, dredging some roughly cut parsley or chervil over the top.

Swedish tjälknöl

Serves 8

This hot-cured venison is easy to make at home but needs preparing one to seven days in advance. It's a great way to produce a lot of venison for a buffet. Instructions for making it are on p.229 and serve at least thirty for a starter. It's good with the following mustard and dill sauce. Swedish mustard is very mild. If you want salad with the tjälknöl, try raw sliced bulb fennel dressed with black pepper and oil, or some of the wonderful Eastern European or Russian pickled vegetables. Delicious. Cumberland sauce and gratin Dauphinoise (p.178) also go well. Serve hot-smoked venison like this too.

400 g (14 oz) sliced tjälknöl

$^1/_2$ teaspoon fennel seeds

4 tablespoons pale soft brown sugar

6 tablespoons Swedish mustard

2–3 tablespoons olive or vegetable oil

1 large bunch fresh dill

Crush the fennel seeds as finely as you can. Stir the sugar into the mustard until it has dissolved. Stir in the fennel powder and 1 tablespoon of the oil and beat it hard. Chop the fresh dill finely, then add lots (2 heaped tablespoons at least) to the sauce and stir it in. This will be quite stiff; if you want it thinner, add more oil. Serve this with the tjälknöl.

The beginning of chapter 7 gives general tips on cooking steaks, including a timing chart on p.108.

Venison steak salad with spiced pumpkin seeds
Serves 2

You can increase the amount of steak for a more substantial meal: this is a starter-size. Almonds work just as well as pumpkin seeds here. The Roman writer Plutarch wrote that you only need to eat five or six almonds a day in order to acquire the ability to drink astonishingly. Whether he meant that you would not become intoxicated easily or that you wanted to drink astonishingly because the almonds were salty remains ambiguous. Whatever he meant, almonds are one of my favourite ingredients.

300 g (11 oz) venison steak

Butter/oil to fry it

2 portions interesting salad/herb leaves

Rounded teaspoon of ras-el-hanout (tagine spices)

50 g (2 oz) pumpkin seeds (or almonds)

Oil and lemon juice to dress the salad

12 large basil leaves

Divide the salad leaves between two plates. Fry the steak over a fierce heat till nicely browned on both sides. Lower the heat and cook for about 4 minutes for a 1.5 cm (½ inch) thick steak. It should be pretty rare at this stage. Scatter the spices over the meat and into the pan. Turn the steak over once or twice, then remove from the pan and keep warm. Add the pumpkin seeds and fry them lightly in the spicy pan. Remove and keep warm. Add a drop of cold water to the pan and scrape up the spicy brownings. Add the juice of half a lemon and some fragrant oil (olive, walnut or argan oil are all good) to the pan and then use this to dress the salad leaves. Slice the steak into thin slices across the grain and divide these between the two plates. Scatter over the pumpkin seeds and dress with the basil.

Minature venison brochettes with yoghurt and cucumber sauce

Cut the steak into cubes and thread 3-4 cubes onto each cocktail stick. Dust these miniature brochettes with half the spices and cook as above, though bear in mind they will cook fast - use a very hot pan and as soon as they are browned all over, they are done. Serve quickly - they make great finger food. Make a dipping sauce out of 5cm (2 ins) finely chopped cucumber stirred into 2 tablespoons plain yoghurt and 2 tablespoons mayonnaise with 1 tablespoon freshly chopped mint stirred in.

Venison steak salad with watercress and pomegranate

Serves 2

Genuine aged Modena balsamic vinegar is an expensive luxury, viscous and deep-flavoured. But there are a few excellent balsamic syrups and thickened vinegars available now – Belazu make a good one.

300 g (11 oz) venison steak

80 g (3 oz) watercress

1 pomegranate

Syrupy balsamic vinegar

Butter and oil to cook steak

Wash and dry the watercress. Break it up into bite-sized pieces and divide between the four plates. Cut the pomegranate into quarters and remove the seeds, discarding all the bitter yellow connecting skin. Scatter seeds over the watercress. Drizzle some balsamic vinegar sparingly over the watercress.

Cook the steak rare, and allow it to cool down slightly for a minute or so. Slice finely into nice pink strips, and drape these over the salad. Serve at once.

Winter steak salad with blood orange and chicory
Serves 2

Sicilian blood (ruby) oranges are only in season for a short while in the late winter. If they are not available, use Valencia or navel oranges, especially if they come from Morocco. Alternatively use three clementines. If you don't have any ras-el-hanout, use a pinch of nutmeg and a pinch of ground cumin instead. And if you like chilli, chop some tiny pieces of bright red ones to add zing, though I prefer it without.

200 g (7 oz) venison steak

$\frac{1}{2}$ teaspoon ras-el-hanout (tagine spices)

1 large head chicory

1 very sweet orange

Walnut or olive oil

Coarse black pepper

Butter and oil to cook steak

$\frac{1}{2}$ teaspoon finely chopped fresh red chilli (optional)

Dust the steak with the spices. Trim the chicory and slice the leaves into pieces about 4 cm (1 $\frac{1}{2}$ ins) wide. Peel the orange, removing all the pith, and slice it into rounds, removing the pips. Toss the chicory and orange together, dredging them with oil and some coarse black pepper. Divide between two plates or bowls. Heat up a frying pan with the butter and oil, and fry the steak over a high heat till browned on both sides. Remove the pan from the heat and allow the steak to rest for a minute or two before slicing it thinly and serving the slices on top of the salad. The steak should be nice and rare and the salad at room temperature.

Venison chunks with Persian herb salad
Serves 2

Persian summer salads are made of pungent herbs from the garden: marjoram, chervil, lemon verbena, thyme, chives, chive flowers, wild garlic, sorrel, rocket, any peppery or spicy leaves that are available, a small amount of mint, and dredged with pot marigold petals. If the weather is hot and the herbs are very strong, some crisp plain lettuce leaves are sometimes needed to dilute the barrage of heady flavours.

300 g (11 oz) diced haunch or loin

Butter or oil to cook it

$1/2$ teaspoon turmeric

1 tablespoon tomato purée

1–2 teaspoons honey

1 lemon or lime

Black pepper, Malden salt

Walnut or olive oil

200 g (7 oz) herbs for salad, *see above*

Prepare the salad first: scatter some Malden salt and some coarse ground black pepper, a squeeze of lemon juice and generous helpings of walnut or olive oil onto the leaves. Then work the salad thoroughly until the leaves are slightly crushed and absorbing the oil – when you eat it with the venison, they will absorb some of the gravy too and be extra savoury and cooling.

To cook the venison, brown it very quickly all over using a hot pan. Scatter in the turmeric and stir in the tomato purée, honey and the juice of half of the lemon or lime. Lower the heat and as soon as the honey and tomato purée are dissolved, check the seasoning and serve immediately with the salad.

Venison steak with warm fennel

Serves 2

As well as being lightly cooked, bulb fennel is also lovely sliced and served completely raw, dressed only with walnut or olive oil, salt, pepper, and a squeeze of lemon juice. The flavour goes particularly well with venison. The timings here are for steaks of 2 cm (1 in) thickness, cooked rare. If the steaks are thicker or thinner, or if you want them cooked differently, use the timing chart on p.108.

300 g (11 oz) venison steak

Butter and oil for cooking

1 head of bulb fennel

Juice of 1 orange

2 teaspoons soy sauce

1 teaspoon balsamic syrup

Slice the fennel into rounds, discarding the core and reserving the green feathery leaves in the middle. Heat some butter and oil in a large frying pan and brown the steaks briskly all over (about $1^1/_2$ minutes per side). Reduce the heat and add the orange juice, soy sauce and balsamic syrup. Turn the steaks around in the liquid for 2 minutes (or according to thickness) until they are nicely coated, then remove them to a warm dish to finish their cooking. Add all the fennel and stir it around in the sauce (add a tiny splash of water if it has become too dry) until is well moistened with the syrupy pan juices, hot but still nice and crisp – 3 or 4 minutes is enough. Quickly stir in the chopped green feathery fennel tops and serve with the steaks. If the steaks are very thick, slice them up before serving with the warmed fennel.

Variation

Chunky venison steak with warm chicory

Serves 2

Substitute 2 small heads of chicory for the fennel. It softens much more quickly than fennel so rest the steaks for a couple of minutes before adding the chicory.

STIR-FRYING VENISON

The essence of stir-frying is to cook all the ingredients quickly and to have them all ready at the same time. Stir-fry recipes using chicken and pork tend to advise cutting the meat into thin strips. By the time the vegetables are cooked to crunchy perfection, the meat is cooked through which is what you want for chicken and pork – but not with venison as it becomes too dry. So there are two options. One is to cut it in very thin strips but to make the sauce a little sticky so that the meat has a smooth coating that lubricates it. The other is to cut the venison into thicker strips of about 2 cm (³/₄ in). The object here is to leave the meat nicely pink inside. Make sure the oil in your wok or pan is very hot so that it gets a lovely brown crisp outside very quickly. Then have a warm dish standing by and remove the venison so that it finishes off cooking as it rests. Add more oil if necessary, and cook the vegetables and sauce as normal, adding back the venison at the last minute.

Spicy thick-cut venison stir-fry
Serves 2

350 g (12 oz) venison steak

1 carrot

1 small red bell pepper

1 large handful curly kale or spring greens

2 tablespoons wok or light sesame oil

1 heaped teaspoon grated fresh ginger

1 teaspoon finely chopped fresh chilli

2 teaspoons soy sauce

Juice of 1 orange

Salt and pepper to season

Cut the venison steak into 2 cm (³/₄ in) strips. Cut the carrot and red pepper into thin matchsticks. Shred the curly kale or spring greens very fine. Swirl 1 tablespoon oil round a heated wok or very large, deep frying pan. Once the oil is very hot, add the venison and fry very quickly till brown. Don't stir it too much so that it gets a chance to brown. Remove venison to a warm plate to rest and finish cooking.

Using the other tablespoon of oil, stir-fry the carrot and pepper for two minutes, keeping them moving all the time. Add the grated ginger and chilli and stir-fry for another minute. Then add the shredded greens, the soy sauce and the orange juice. Season with pepper, more soy, and salt to taste and as soon as the kale has wilted, return the venison to the pan, stir quickly into the vegetables, and serve at once.

Mild thick-cut venison stir-fry with chicory

Serves 2

350 g (12 oz) venison steak

1 large shallot

3 spring onions

1 carrot

1 small sweet bell pepper

1 clove garlic

6 juniper berries

1 head of chicory

2 tablespoons olive or light sesame oil

1 tablespoon soy sauce

Pepper, salt

Cut the venison into 2 cm (³/₄ in) strips. Slice the shallot and spring onions and cut the carrot and pepper into matchsticks. Crush the garlic and the juniper berries. Cut the chicory leaves into 5 cm (2 in) pieces. Have a warm plate ready for the venison. Heat 1 tablespoon of oil in a wok or large deep pan and once it is really hot, add the meat and brown it quickly. As soon as it is browned, remove it from the wok and leave to rest and finish cooking on the warm plate. Add another tablespoon of oil and stir-fry the shallot and spring onions for a minute. Add the carrot and sweet pepper, garlic and juniper berries and continue to stir-fry for another two minutes. Add the chicory and stir it is well. Add the soy sauce, pepper, and salt or more soy sauce if necessary. Serve immediately; the chicory should still be crunchy.

Stir-fried chunky venison with fennel and coriander

Serves 2

350 g (12 oz) venison steak

2 tablespoons light olive or sesame oil

1 red (sweet) onion

1 bulb fennel

$^1/_2$ teaspoon caraway or fennel seed

2 tablespoons pine nuts or chopped walnuts

Juice of 1 lemon

2 teaspoons soy sauce

Salt and pepper to season

Handful of fresh coriander leaves

Prepare the meat and vegetables and follow the same procedure as above, stir-frying the meat and removing it to rest, then the onion, then the fennel, caraway seed and nuts. Cook for one minute, then add the lemon juice and soy sauce. Season to taste, stir in the venison and fresh coriander leaves and serve straight away.

Thin-cut venison stir-fry with sweet and sour sauce

Serves 2

350 g (12 oz) venison steak

2 teaspoons soy sauce

3 spring onions

1 sweet bell pepper

2–3 tablespoons light olive or sesame oil

1 teaspoon chopped fresh ginger

1 clove crushed garlic

2 teaspoons brown sugar

1 tablespoon vinegar

Juice of $^1/_2$ orange

Pepper, oyster sauce

8 sweet cherry tomatoes

Cut the venison into thin slices of just under 1 cm ($^1/_2$ in) thick and soak it in the 2 teaspoons of soy sauce for $^1/_2$ hour, then dry it off. Slice the spring onions and pepper into thin strips. Heat the oil in a wok or large frying pan and when really hot, fry the venison very quickly for about half a minute. Then add the pepper and spring onion and continue to cook for two minutes. Then add the ginger, garlic and sugar and cook for a further minute. Finally, add the vinegar, orange juice, and season with pepper, oyster sauce. At the last moment, cut the cherry tomatoes in half and stir in so that they are warm but not cooked. Serve at once.

6. Venison mince

Mince dishes, meatballs and burgers

6. Venison mince

Mince dishes, meatballs and burgers

> *'Breakfast on most excellent minced stag, the only form I thought that animal good in.'*
>
> *Thomas Pennant*

Increasingly, people are using the cheaper cuts of venison for everyday dishes. If children's diets include venison, they will enjoy it all their lives, as well as being provided with essential nutrients to build a healthy brain and body. They will also discover that venison is good in forms other than minced stag.

Venison mince may be used in any dish using beef or lamb mince: sauces for pasta dishes like lasagne and ravioli, moussaka, shepherd's pie, burgers, extra good meatballs, sausage rolls, samosas and so on. Simply substitute with venison and relish the improved flavour. Recipes for terrines and raised pies are in chapter 11.

Fatty meats tend to exude fat from mince, which keeps the meat grains separate as well as browning them. Venison is so lean that mince can stick together when you brown it, so use a little oil or fat, and keep separating it with the spatula as it browns. As long as the pan is hot, the grains will eventually separate and brown. Use your largest pan so there is plenty of room – if too much goes in at once, it starts to bubble and stew instead of browning and will not produce that delicious flavour. Another way to keep venison mince separate is to put it into a small bowl and work some oil into it. Once it is browned, simply add some liquid and cook it gently for about 45 minutes. If the mince is from an old animal, it may take longer to become tender.

Stalker's pie with a cheese curd topping

Serves 4–6

A stalker's pie is traditionally topped with mashed potato, and very good it is too. But I like this even better – the curdy texture is lovely with venison . . . and cheese with slowly cooked meat? Heaven. You can put sliced tomatoes, fresh herbs or cooked aubergine under the cheese curd if you like.

900 g (2 lbs) venison mince

2 onions, chopped

Butter or oil for frying

1 tablespoon tomato purée

2–3 tablespoons flour

600 ml (1 pt) stock or water

Salt, pepper, nutmeg

For the cheese topping

2 tablespoons flour

50 g (2 oz) butter

900 ml (1½ pts) milk

80 g (3 oz) grated cheese

3 eggs

Fry the chopped onions gently in oil or butter till golden and softened, then remove them from the pan. Heat up the pan again and add the venison mince. Brown it well, keeping the mince grains separate and well spread out. When it is all browned, add back the onions, and stir in the tomato purée. Scatter 2 tablespoons of the flour over the top and stir it in. If there looks to be surplus oil, stir in the remaining flour. Then add the stock or water, bring to a simmer and cook for 30 minutes, stirring from time to time to prevent it sticking. Season to taste with salt, pepper and a pinch of nutmeg. Put it into an ovenproof dish that has plenty of room for the topping.

While the mince cooks, make the topping. Stir the flour into the melted butter, cook for a few minutes until beginning to brown, then whisk in the milk, beating hard to remove any lumps, to make a smooth but fairly thin sauce. Add the cheese and stir till melted, then remove from the heat. Whisk the eggs and stir them in, then pour this over the mince in its ovenproof dish, and bake in a moderate oven (Gas 5, 190ºC, 375ºF) for about 35–45 minutes, by which time the sauce should have thickened into a curd and browned on top.

Venison ragù (pasta sauce)

Serves 4-6

Venison is particularly good for pasta dishes, partly because it makes them so tasty and partly because it is an excellent way of introducing venison to children (or anyone else who thinks they don't like venison). Use this sauce as a base and add a chopped pepper, celery or other herbs and spices to suit your taste. To make it more adult, use 150 ml (¼ pt) red wine for half of the liquid.

500 g (1 lb+) venison mince

Olive oil

2 onions, finely chopped

1 carrot, finely diced

2 cloves garlic, crushed

125 g (4 oz) bacon or pancetta, finely diced

2 tablespoons tomato paste

400 g (14 oz) tin chopped tomatoes

½ teaspoon nutmeg

½ teaspoon dried mixed herbs

Pepper

300ml (½ pt) water or stock

Salt

Brown the onion, carrot, garlic, and any other vegetables used, in 3 tablespoons olive oil, then remove them from the pan. Brown the bacon and remove from the pan. Brown the venison mince, breaking up any lumps that form. Add back the vegetables and bacon, stir in the tomato paste and chopped tomatoes, and finally add the herbs and nutmeg as well as some pepper. Add the liquid, cover, and allow it to cook slowly for about 45 minutes. Stir it from time to time and top up with water if necessary. Season before serving.

Venison sausage rolls

Great cocktail nibbles, and children's party food. Use this basic recipe or try any of the sausage mixtures in Chapter 13 or in the burger recipes below. Allow roughly the same weight of pastry to meat – if anything, allow more meat than pastry.

1 kg (2^1/$_4$ lb) minced venison

200 g (7 oz) minced fatty bacon or lamb

2 teaspoons salt

^{1}/$_2$ teaspoon pepper

^{1}/$_2$ teaspoon nutmeg

^{1}/$_2$ teaspoon rubbed sage

^{1}/$_4$ teaspoon ground ginger

^{1}/$_4$ teaspoon ground cloves

Fresh herbs to taste

1 kg (2^1/$_4$ lb) pastry

Beaten egg to glaze the pastry

Mix all the spices together. Mix the venison and other mince together, scatter the spices thinly over them and mix everything together thoroughly. Roll out the pastry 3–4 mm (^{1}/$_8$ in) thick and about 13 cm (5 in) wide. On a lightly floured board and with floured hands, form the sausage meat into rolls of 2^1/$_2$ – 3cm (1 in +) diameter. Lay the sausage meat along the pastry strips and brush the edge of the pastry strip with beaten egg or water. Roll up so the join is underneath and slice into desired lengths.

Venison meatballs: basic recipe

Serves 4 (28 small meatballs)

Because venison is so lean, it is best to keep meatballs small (3 cm or 1¼ inch diameter) so there is lots of outside to get coated in sauce. That way you don't need to add any fat. If you prefer large meatballs, it is better to add some soaked breadcrumbs, moist vegetables (mushrooms, aubergine, etc.) or fat (e.g. minced belly pork or fatty lamb) to keep them moist inside.

600 g (1¼ lb) venison mince

Oil

1 onion, finely chopped

1 tablespoon finely chopped parsley

Salt, pepper

Butter/oil

1 egg, beaten

flour

Fry the onion gently until soft and golden brown. Remove from the heat and when slightly cooled, add it to the mince with the parsley, salt and pepper, and the beaten egg. Mix everything well together. Form the mixture into 28 meatballs, squeezing them tightly in your hand so they stay together when cooking. When ready to cook them, roll them in flour and fry quickly in a generous quantity of butter and oil till nicely browned all over. Then lower the heat and add any of the sauces below. Continue to cook gently for a further 10–15 minutes, turning them over in the sauce from time to time until they are cooked through.

Gingery venison meatballs with a dark wine gravy
Serves 4

Ingredients for the basic recipe plus:

1 tablespoon grated fresh ginger

1 clove garlic, crushed

Sauce

500 ml (17 fl oz) red wine

1 litre (1¾ pts) rich venison stock (p.48)

1 dessertspoon tart jelly

1 tablespoon soy sauce

Pepper

25 g (1 oz) butter (optional)

1 tablespoon flour (optional)

Add the raw, grated ginger and garlic to the basic mixture on p.88 before forming the meatballs.

Start off the sauce first as it takes a while to boil down. Boil the red wine, stock and jelly rapidly together until they have reduced to about 450 ml (¾ pt). It should be fairly dark. Add the soy sauce and some pepper, then taste, adding more if necessary. If you would like the gravy a little thicker, then mash together the butter and flour to make a smooth paste (soften butter in the microwave if it is too hard). Whisk this into the gravy and it will give it a glossy thickness. Once this is ready it doesn't need much extra cooking, so fry the meatballs on their own gently for 15–20 minutes, and only roll them around in the sauce for about 5 minutes before serving.

Venison meatballs with paprika and sour cream

Serves 4

Ingredients for basic recipe on p.88 plus:

1 tablespoon paprika (mild or hot, to taste)

Sauce

1 onion or 2 shallots

1 large clove garlic

1 hot chilli pepper (optional)

75 g (3 oz) butter

500 g (1 lb+) tomatoes

Salt and pepper

1 small carton of soured cream

Fresh basil leaves (optional)

Make the meatballs as in the basic recipe, adding the paprika to the mixture before cooking it.

Make a simple tomato sauce: peel and chop the onions and garlic. De-seed and chop the chilli if used. Peel and chop the tomatoes. Melt the butter in a small saucepan and add the onions and garlic (and chilli if used) and gently cook until soft and golden. Then add the tomatoes and simmer for 5 minutes. Add this to the browned meatballs and continue to simmer until the tomatoes are well softened, the sauce has thickened a bit, and the meatballs are cooked through. Add salt and pepper to taste before serving with a dollop of sour cream and torn basil leaves. A tiny dusting of paprika on the cream looks appetising.

Venison meatballs with Mediterranean sauce

Serves 4

Soft vegetables cooked in oil make a good foil for the venison. This is more of a stew than a sauce and it goes really well with polenta, plain or fried. Reserve a little of the oregano to scatter over at the end. If you use dried oregano, reduce by half.

Ingredients for basic recipe, plus:

1 heaped tablespoon fresh oregano, chopped

Sauce

150 ml (¼ pt) olive oil

1 aubergine, chopped

1 onion, chopped

1 small red bell pepper, deseeded

1 small yellow pepper, de-seeded

1 courgette, sliced in chunks

2 large tomatoes, chopped

Salt and pepper

Make the sauce before you start to cook the meatballs. Heat the oil in a large saucepan and fry the aubergine and onion over a brisk heat. When they are beginning to brown, add the peppers, both chopped into chunks. Toss them in the oil until they are beginning to soften, then turn the heat down to a simmer, cover with a lid, and simmer for 20 minutes, stirring occasionally so that it doesn't stick. Then add the courgette and tomatoes and simmer for another 10–15 minutes. By this time the vegetables should be nearly soft. Season with salt and pepper. Fry the meatballs until browned all over, then add them to the sauce and cook for a further 10–15 minutes till cooked through.

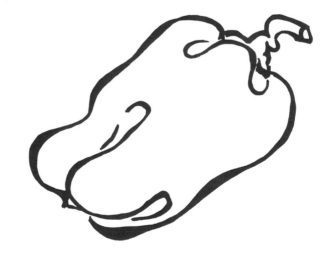

Venison meatballs with walnut and pomegranate sauce

Serves 4

This unusual sauce is one of my favourites. It comes from Persia (Iran), courtesy of Margaret Shaida. It is a sumptuous balance of sweet and tart. Instead of boiling down pure pomegranate juice, two tablespoons of pomegranate paste or a really tart fruit jelly may be used instead. The result is magnificent; the walnuts exude their oil which coats the venison lusciously, and walnut oil is very good for you.

600 g (1¼ lb) venison mince

8 pitted prunes or dried apricots

1 teaspoon turmeric

Flour to coat the meatballs

Salt and pepper

Oil for browning

For the sauce

500 ml (¾ pt+) pomegranate juice (or 1–2 tablespoons pomegranate paste or tart jelly)

100 g (4 oz) freshly shelled walnuts

Oil

500 ml (¾ pt+) venison or other stock

2 onions, finely chopped

Juice of 1 lemon or lime (optional).

Reduce the pomegranate juice first: boil it rapidly with the lemon juice until only about two tablespoons of thick syrup remain. It takes about 30 minutes to reduce.

For the sauce, chop the walnuts into small crumbs. Fry them gently in a little oil, stirring all the time until they darken (about 15 minutes). Add enough stock to generously cover the walnuts, cover the pan, and simmer gently for 30 minutes. Meanwhile, fry the onions in oil till soft and golden. Add half to the walnuts, reserving the rest for the meatballs. Stir in the reduced pomegranate juice, paste or jelly and continue simmering for a further 20 minutes, topping up with more stock if necessary. Then season with salt and pepper and adjust the sweet/sour if necessary with lemon juice, jelly or sugar.

While the sauce cooks, make the meatballs. Chop the prunes or apricots finely and mix into the mince with the turmeric and remaining onion. Season with salt and pepper and form into 24 small meatballs, squeezing them hard so they don't break up. Roll them in flour then brown them all over. Drain off any excess oil, then pour in the walnut sauce and cook gently for another 10–15 minutes until the meatballs are cooked through. Serve with rice and steamed spinach or salad.

Venison satays with a fragrant dipping sauce

Makes up to 50

When I made these for a cooking demonstration, one man asked if he could drink the remaining dipping sauce, he liked it so much. Credit here must go to New Zealand chef Graham Brown, as the sauce is inspired by one of his fusion recipes. Try it also with thin strips or chunks of venison or drizzled over thin slices of roast venison for a starter.

The mince mixture can be pressed onto sticks for satays, or formed into tiny meatballs for serving on cocktail sticks as a pre-dinner nibble. The aubergine and prunes help to lubricate the mixture so there is no need to add fat. If using thin strips of venison, soak them in soy sauce and oil for half an hour before threading them onto satay sticks.

450g (1 lb) venison mince

$^1/_2$ aubergine

8 pitted prunes or dried apricots

4 teaspoons turmeric

Salt, pepper

Flour

Butter and oil for cooking

Dipping sauce:

1 tablespoon miso paste

1 teaspoon Thai yellow curry paste

1 large egg yolk

2 teaspoons soy sauce

2 teaspoons clear honey

2 tablespoons dry wine or rice wine vinegar

3 tablespoons grape seed or light olive oil

To make the dipping sauce, whisk together the miso, curry paste, egg yolk, soy, and honey. Then whisk in the wine vinegar and oil. Serve in little bowls with the hot satays. The sauce will keep up to two weeks in the fridge.

To make the satays, cut the aubergine lengthways into two quarters and microwave on full power for 5 minutes or until the flesh is soft. When cool enough, skin and dice. Chop the prunes. Put both in a blender with the mince, turmeric and salt and pepper. Blend till fine, then squeeze the mixture onto satay sticks. For tiny meatballs, form the mixture into small balls, roll them in flour, and then lightly pinch them in your fingers to give them a flat bottom so that they stand upright when you press cocktail sticks into them after cooking. If using strips of venison, thread them onto the sticks, folding the meat so that it is tightly packed. Fry all over in hot butter and oil and serve with the dipping sauce.

Poached venison frikadellar

Frikadellar (meatballs) are popular all over Scandinavia, particularly in Sweden, though this recipe is Norwegian. Elk or reindeer are the commonly used species there. Although many are served in a sauce like the recipes above, this one is a bit different, pounding the meat ultra-fine and poaching the meatballs – a version of quenelles. They are light and moist, not unlike a French *boudin blanc* without the skin. The optional pinch of sugar is so little as to be barely discernable and makes me wonder if a few hundred years ago, there would have been much more, rather like the popular medieval dish of *blanc manger.*

500 g (1 lb+) venison with all sinew removed

4 tablespoons fresh white breadcrumbs

2 eggs, separated into yolks and whites

300 – 450 ml ($^{1}/_{2}$– $^{3}/_{4}$ pt) single cream

Pinch of salt

$^{1}/_{2}$ teaspoon white pepper

1 teaspoon mild (sweet) paprika

(optional) a pinch of caster sugar

Chop the venison as small as you can, then blend it to a paste in a food processor. Add the breadcrumbs, egg yolks, a good dash of the cream to moisten it, the seasonings, and blend till well mixed. Then beat the egg whites till stiff and fold them into the mixture, adding more cream of necessary to make it just stiff enough not to drop off a spoon. Form the mixture into ovals with two wetted spoons and slide the frikadellars into simmering water. Allow them to cook gently for 15 minutes, then carefully remove them and serve as quickly as possible, either in the consommé (p.62) or with a light creamy sauce, such as a green herb sauce or a light mushroom sauce.

SUPERIOR VENISON BURGERS[1]

Burgers are an excellent way of introducing newcomers to venison. Make them as simple or as elaborate as the fancy takes you. If you make burgers for sale (uncooked or cooked, and even for a charity event), you should be aware of the hygiene and ingredient regulations for selling meat products. For home consumption, you can buy small burger moulds and papers in kitchen shops, you can use a large pastry cutter to form them, or simply form them with your hands. They bunch up a bit when cooking, so flatten them out well first. At home, I grill freshly made burgers over a brisk fire and have them slightly pink in the middle. However, anyone selling burgers is not allowed to recommend this practice, so there has to be a trade off: either you accept the risk that customers will cook your burgers pink, or you include other ingredients in your burgers so that they are still delicious when cooked through to the recommended internal temperature of 75°C (165°F).

Venison has little to lubricate it except its moisture (pinkness), so burgers made with no fat and then cooked to well done will be crumbly and dry. So, like sausages, other ingredients need to be added to keep them moist, and because burgers are not encased in a skin, a binder is also helpful to prevent them falling to bits. Generally speaking, though, burgers have less fat in them (10–20%) than sausages. If you don't want to add fat, use some of the suggestions below to increase succulence.

Ingredients that add succulence include: minced lamb or pork belly, olive oil, nut oils, cooked mushrooms, cooked aubergine, cooked onion, prunes, etc. You can also add brown breadcrumbs or oatmeal. Beaten eggs help to bind the meat together. Here are a few tried and tested suggestions you can adapt to your taste.

Unless it says otherwise, simply mix all the ingredients and form into burgers, pressing them as hard as possible so that they stay together during the cooking. The low-fat ones at the end are best cooked medium rare immediately after being made.

[1] At the time of writing, the word 'Veniburgers' is a Registered Trade Mark so should not be used to sell venison burgers unless with the Trade Mark owner's permission

Venison burgers

675 g (1½ lb) minced venison

225 g (8 oz) minced belly pork, or lamb

100 g (4 oz) medium oatmeal

1 teaspoon ground nutmeg

1 teaspoon ground ginger

2 teaspoons juniper berries, crushed

1 handful parsley, chopped

Salt, black pepper

4 tablespoons red wine vinegar

1 small egg, beaten

Mix all the ingredients together and form into burgers, pressing them as hard as possible to prevent them breaking up during the cooking.

Venison burgers with mushrooms

600 g (1½ lb) minced venison

100 g (4 oz) butter

250 g (9 oz) fresh mushrooms or fungi

4 cloves garlic, crushed

25 g (1 oz) dried ceps, crushed (optional)

1 tablespoon fresh thyme leaves (or 1 teaspoon dried thyme)

Zest of ½ lemon, grated

Salt, pepper

1 small egg, beaten

Chop the fresh mushrooms or fungi and fry them gently in the butter with the crushed garlic. When they are softened and shrunk down, allow them to cool before mixing thoroughly into the other ingredients. Then form into burgers and chill before cooking.

Venison burgers with paprika

800 g (1³/₄ lb) minced venison

100 g (4 oz) minced streaky bacon

1 heaped tablespoon paprika (sweet or hot to taste)

1 teaspoon caraway seeds

1 teaspoon ground nutmeg

Salt, pepper

Low-fat venison burgers

Because these have no fat other than the walnut oil, they are nicest cooked pink. If you want to cook them more than that, add 200 g (9 oz) chopped mushrooms, gently softened in the walnut oil first.

900 g (2 lb) minced venison

Salt, black pepper

2 teaspoons juniper berries

2 tablespoons walnut oil

1 egg, beaten

Low-fat venison burgers with ginger

900 g (2 lb) minced
venison

5 cm (2 in) fresh ginger,
grated

6 small shallots or spring
onions

2 cloves garlic, crushed

Handful of parsley,
chopped

1 tablespoon walnut oil

Salt, black pepper

7. Venison steaks

Cooking information, grilling, frying and barbecuing

7. Venison steaks

Cooking information, grilling, frying and barbecuing

> *'A chap who likes his potatoes sautéed in goose fat, who knows where to find the best goat's cheese and enjoys his steak rare will be a killer in the sack.'*
>
> *1990s feature headline*

Anyone who can already cook venison steaks successfully can skip this part. But for everyone else, it is the most important section. The most common mistake is to overcook venison, and it is easy to overcook small pieces of meat when they are being cooked by fierce methods like grilling and frying. So I have taken the most common questions we are asked and given a quick answer followed by a fuller explanation for those interested in the detail. The recipes refer to the general techniques to avoid repeating them each time. Some recipes are just serving suggestions for sauces and vegetable dishes: many of these can be served just as well with roast or stewed venison, so do use them creatively.

What are the best cuts for grilling and frying?
Starting with the most tender – from the saddle: fillet (filet mignon), loin (sirloin). From the haunch: rump, topside. Silverside and thick flank if from young deer and if well-trimmed. Shoulder steaks if from young deer.

Why do venison steaks dry out so easily?
Venison is a lean meat with less fat than skinless chicken – and it is denser. It cooks more quickly than beef, so always slightly undercook venison steaks and allow them to rest.

Good beef has fat marbled through it: this keeps it succulent even when cooked past the pink stage, because melting fat makes the red meat (the protein) slippery and pleasant to eat. Very lean beef and other lean meats like some cuts of pork, have the same problem as venison, i.e. no matter how young and tender it may be, without a marbling of fat there is nothing to make it succulent except the moisture in the meat. If a lean steak is cooked too long, the protein and blood coagulates, the moisture (water) is driven off and the steak shrinks, becoming increasingly grey, fuzzy textured and hard. The only way to make an overcooked steak pleasant to swallow is to smother it in creamy, slippery sauces and to vow fervently not to cook it so long the next time.

Do you have to marinate venison steaks?
Not at all. Good venison has a distinct flavour of its own and marinades sometimes interfere with other flavours. See chapter 4 for a detailed discussion on marinating and some marinade recipes.

How do you prevent venison steaks from being dry?
Never cook them beyond medium rare because pink meat cannot be dry. The best way to achieve this is to undercook them, then let them rest to finish their cooking so they remain rare or pink – as long as there are still some red juices left in the meat, it is physically impossible for it to be dry. Beware of supermarket advice that tells you to cook steaks too long.

Venison has a high moisture content – the secret is to retain it. The redness in rare and medium steaks is moisture and the redder the meat, the more succulent and tender it will be. Even if you had intended to cook the steak quite rare in the first place, remember that venison continues to cook even after being removed from the heat, so that what should have been a perfect steak has turned into an overcooked barely pink one when it is served up. Fortunately there is a very simple solution: this is to undercook the steak, then remove it from the intense heat and keep it warm for a few minutes to rest the meat while any sauce or vegetables are being finished. The advantage of this method is that you can really brown the outside of the meat to give that delicious caramelised flavour but yet not overcook the inside. During the short resting period, the meat (and chef) relaxes, the heat on the outside of the steak continues towards the middle, and the juices in the underdone centre are drawn back towards the more cooked outside. And when you cut it, instead of having a grey, over-cooked outside ring and a nearly raw centre, the steak will be evenly pink and fabulously moist throughout – altogether a more mouthwatering prospect.

Is it safe to eat rare venison?

For the majority of people, yes, it is perfectly safe to eat venison rare and even raw. But if you are pregnant or immunosuppressed, read below.

Pregnant women and immunosuppressed people are vulnerable to a number of infections. For example, toxoplasmosis is caused by a single celled parasite passed in cats' faeces and is infectious to all animals (including humans), where it can persist in the muscles (meat) of farm animals (particularly sheep, goats and pigs). Humans usually catch it either from eating lightly cooked lamb, goat meat or pork, or from eating unwashed vegetables from soil contaminated by cats. However the available evidence indicates that the risk from beef and venison is negligible. In healthy people, Toxoplasma usually causes no noticeable illness, although in some it may trigger a mild flu-like episode. However, if contracted by a woman for the first time while she is pregnant, then it can cause serious illness in the unborn baby. The very old, young, or immunosuppressed are also advised not to eat any kind of lightly cooked meat.

Why does my supermarket advise cooking venison thoroughly before serving?

Lack of understanding about infections such as toxoplasmosis (above) may explain why some supermarkets advise cooking all kinds of meat until it is very well done (in the case of venison, ruined) which is tragic for the great majority who can safely enjoy eating their venison and beef rare. Supermarket instructions to bake 1½ cm (¾ in)thick venison steaks at Gas 5, 190ºC, 375ºF for 30–35 minutes produces dry, shrivelled-up steaks. It is difficult to conceive of a better way to put people off eating venison.

What if you don't like rare or pink meat?

Accept that the texture will be 'bready', but try the undercook/rest method (see p.101), only resting it for longer so that the pink juices have just disappeared. Then serve it with a creamy sauce. Also, the loin and fillet are more tender than any other cut if cooked past the pink stage.

Those who reject the idea of any pinkness in their meat will be used to the texture of well-done meat. But I still advise undercooking venison steaks and leaving them to rest. As already explained, there is no fat to lubricate a well-done venison steak, so it is best to cook them till just past the medium stage and then rest the steaks. The pinkness will virtually disappear, but the steaks will not dry out so badly. It is, though, worth trying a slightly less well-done venison steak, because I have encountered so many people who claim not to like pink meat, but yet when offered some lightly rosy pink venison were surprised and delighted to find it really delicious and tender and very much to their liking. If you still prefer well-done steaks, serve them with some clear gravy plus a succulent sauce to lubricate the drier texture of the meat.

What kind of fat or oil is best?
My preference is for a mixture of butter and oil. The butter browns the meat quickly (this is helpful for thin steaks) and tastes good; the oil prevents it from burning too quickly.

For browning, choose oil with a high smoking point to brown the meat quickly – grape seed, rapeseed (canola) or light virgin olive oil, for example, or a mixture of these. Nut oils are delicious in salads, but unsuitable for frying because they burn at a low temperature and then taste horrible. If not using butter, rub a little salt into the meat before frying to help it brown. Many margarines and hydrogenated fats denature at high temperatures, so are not suitable for frying; natural oils and butter are far safer.

Some people cannot use fat for health reasons: in this case use a non-stick frying pan or grill, and heat it up till fiercely hot. Rub a thin film of oil and a sprinkling of salt into the steaks to stop it sticking and help it to brown. Remember that venison is remarkably lean compared to other meats so the minute amount of oil needed to lubricate the steaks is of little consequence.

How long does it take to cook steaks?
See the chart on p.108; it varies with the thickness and temperature of your steak, how hot your pan or grill is, and how rare or pink you like it.

Cooking any kind of steak is not an exact science. But once you understand the variables, cooking venison or any other meat becomes simple. So these are the things to think about when deciding how long to cook steaks:

• The temperature of steaks before you cook them. This affects the cooking time, especially with thick pieces of meat. The inside of a fridge could be 10–15 degrees colder than room temperature or of any steaks warming in the sunshine next to a barbecue.

• How many steaks you are cooking at a time. When you place steaks in a frying pan, they cool the pan down momentarily, especially if they come straight from the fridge. Before turning them over, you must allow the pan to come back up to temperature before it will brown the steaks. More steaks in the pan will cool it down for longer.

• The heat over (or under) which it is cooked. The temperature of a barbecue, for instance, can vary hugely; some domestic grills never get hot enough to brown the meat before it has overcooked in the centre; gas hobs in some circumstances (e.g. caravans or portable stoves) can take a very long time to heat up a pan or grill.

• Thickness of the steak. Thick steaks obviously take longer to cook and need longer to rest. Fillet steaks are usually thicker than slices of haunch – they are almost like a tiny roast.

• Thickness of your pan. If your pan is heavy, it cools down less than a thin one does when you put in the steaks. It also retains the heat longer when you draw the pan off the heat to rest the steaks.

• Personal preference: one person's idea of medium rare is another's idea of raw.

So in assessing cooking times, use your own judgement. If in doubt, err on the side of shorter cooking because if necessary you can always rest it for longer or even put it back to cook a little more. You can't reverse overcooked meat. I have included a timing chart, but it is only a starting-off guide.

HOW TO COOK VENISON STEAKS

FIRST, THINK AHEAD Venison steaks should not be kept waiting once ready, so make sure everything else is ready, and if a sauce needs advance preparation, make sure this is done. If the sauce is to be made quickly in the pan while the steaks are resting, have all the ingredients prepared and ready. This may sound obvious but it is surprising how often people don't do this.

There are three stages in cooking steaks: browning, cooking and resting. The thinner the piece of meat, the more care is needed and the less time it will need to rest after being browned. Indeed, with very thin pieces – (like steaks only half a centimetre (quarter of an inch) thick, or tiny cubes threaded onto a skewer, or snippets tossed in a wok for a stir-fry) – the cooking and resting time will be so short as to have disappeared. All they need is browning– no further cooking or resting is needed. By the time they are on the table they will be perfect.

On the other hand, plump steaks (e.g. a whole fillet of red deer, a loin fillet of roe, or a thick slice of loin or haunch 3–4 cm 1¼ – 1½ inches thick) will need several minutes cooking after their initial browning, and several minutes resting after that. In between those two extremes lie all the variations of pinkness.

To brown the steaks Get your grill, barbecue or frying pan really hot. Because there will be no fat coming out of the venison, you need to use something to prevent the meat sticking to the cooking surface and, very importantly, to produce the caramelisation on the surface of the meat which is what makes it taste delicious. Use butter and oil, or just oil if preferred. If steaks are cut ultra-thin (about 5mm ¼ inch), then quick browning is all they need. One to two minutes per side is enough and no further cooking or resting is necessary.

To cook the steaks Lower the temperature although thin steaks of about 1 cm (½ in) will not need this stage; they can simply be browned well and then rested. Thick steaks and whole fillets will need several minutes of cooking while turning them over a few times to distribute the heat. When they are still underdone, they should then be rested. See the timing chart on page 108 as a guide.

Resting the steaks Important for two reasons: Firstly, when meat is cooked at high temperatures, the outside – the more cooked part – stiffens a little. Resting meat allows the muscle fibres to relax again, making them tender. Secondly, at this stage of cooking, the steaks are underdone in the middle. If you sliced them open, the outside would be quite well done while the centre would be almost raw. The resting process allows the heat from the outside to be transferred into the centre, and it allows the juices in the centre to be drawn back to the outside, a bit like a sponge. The result is uniformly pink meat – beautifully juicy and tender.

SHALLOW FRYING (PAN-FRYING) AND STIR-FRYING I think frying is the best way to cook venison steaks because it is easiest to get a pan hot enough, and then you can use the pan juices as the basis for a sauce or gravy afterwards. Use about 2 teaspoons of butter and the same of oil, though just oil can be used. Heat the pan till the butter has stopped frothing and is starting to turn brown. If using oil only, heat till swirling in the heat but not smoking. Add the steaks and allow them to brown. Large steaks reduce the heat of the pan, especially if taken straight from the fridge, so leave them untouched for a few minutes to allow the pan to heat up again and brown the steaks before turning them over. Brown on the other side, then reduce the heat a little and continue to cook them, turning them over once or twice until ready to rest.

Very thin steaks or small pieces of stir-fry venison need a hotter pan because the meat must brown really quickly to avoid drying the centre. Here, the oil or butter/oil needs to be starting to smoke and the pieces cooked immediately. They need only very quick all-over browning before being removed from the pan; they will have finished their cooking by the time they have got to the table. If using the pan brownings and juices to make a sauce, make sure the butter or oil has not burnt. If they have, they may be bitter so strain them off before dissolving the pan juices.

'GEORGE FOREMAN' GRILLS These grills have a hinged lid that closes over the food and grills both sides at once. Venison has no fat, so brush the steaks liberally with oil and heat up the grill on its top setting for 5 minutes before putting them in, otherwise they won't brown. They cook incredibly quickly – a $1^{1}/_{2}$ cm ($^{3}/_{4}$ in) steak is cooked to medium after 3 minutes with no resting, so reduce the cooking times below to less than half, otherwise they start to steam and lose moisture drastically. Let thick steaks rest before serving.

LOW-FAT FRYING AND RIDGED GRILL-PANS If using a ridged grill-pan or non-stick frying pan, brush the surface with oil or butter to taste. If fat cannot be used for health reasons use a butter-substitute that has natural statin in it to reduce cholesterol, or, if permitted, a very thin film or spray of olive oil will stop the meat from sticking and allow it to brown. Proceed as for pan-frying. Remember that these very heavy cast-iron pans take a while to heat up but they retain their heat once they are hot. Watch out that they don't continue to heat up and burn the fat. So unless you are cooking a lot of steaks at once – which lowers the heat a bit – you will want to reduce the heat almost as soon as you have turned the steaks over.

GRILLING By this I mean a grill that delivers heat from above. Preheat the grill till very hot. Thick steaks cook most successfully – the thinner the steak the hotter it must be, otherwise the steak will not have time to brown before the inside has overcooked. Brush the steak with butter or oil and brown on both sides. Remembering that the steak should be undercooked, reduce the heat and cook till it is ready for resting. Remove from the heat to a warm plate and rest according to thickness. Very thin steaks are not easy to grill successfully as they cook through very quickly, (often before the outside is browned) and they won't need resting.

Barbecuing, broiling and charcoal grilling Either marinate the steaks in oil and pungent herbs beforehand, or brush them well with oil before and/or rub them in spices (see p.52). If possible, have ready a warm dish to rest the steaks briefly before serving: in windy weather a lid stops them cooling off. If cooking for large numbers, try to make sure the steaks are not left to dry up. If you undercook them as discussed above, they will yield some juice as they rest which helps to keep them moist. If you want to put the steaks straight onto bread or plates without resting, try to make use of the hotter part of the barbecue for the initial browning and then the cooler edges for finishing off thick steaks; thin steaks can go straight into rolls or onto plates without resting.

Fondues and pierrades (hot-stone cooking) Proceed as for other meats, remembering to cook venison less rather than more for the most succulent results. Venison cut into chunks for fondues can be 'rested' on your plate if necessary. For hot-stone cooking, cut the meat thinly so that it cooks very fast and needs no resting.

Baked steaks Some people like to cover their steaks with a sauce and cook them in the oven rather than frying or grilling them. I advise browning them first for better flavour and colour. At Gas 5, 190ºC, 350ºF, the timing is about 2 minutes longer than the chart on the next page for frying, e.g. a $1^{1}/_{2}$ cm ($^{1}/_{2}$ in) thick steak will be medium after 10 minutes.

Quick-poaching This is not the same as braising or stewing, because the meat is served rosy pink. It is a good method for anyone wanting to cut down on fat and oils. It is gentler than frying and grilling, and surprisingly quick. The venison is gently simmered in stock or a thin sauce. Ideally, brown the meat first to make it taste better. The stock or sauce should be brought to the boil, then the heat turned down so that the liquid is just moving but not bubbling at all. Make sure the meat is completely covered, but it doesn't matter if the pieces touch each other as they cook. The thicker cuts cook about 3–4 minutes more quickly than in the frying table below if you include the time taken to brown it. Most of the sauces in this chapter will work fine with poached steaks but bear in mind that the flavour of the meat will be milder than fried steaks.

1 cm

2 cm

3 cm

4 cm

5 cm

6 cm

7 cm

8 cm

9 cm

10 cm

11 cm

12 cm

13 cm

14 cm

15 cm

16 cm

17 cm

18 cm

19 cm

FRYING (PAN-FRYING) VENISON STEAKS

Approx total cooking times *including resting*, allowing 1– 2 minutes per side for browning and then removing to rest about halfway through. These times are approximate as it depends on the temperature of both frying pan and steaks. For example: for a 3 cm (1$^1/_4$ in) steak served rare, it would have 2 x 1$^1/_2$ minutes to brown both sides, 3 minutes cooking time, and 5 minutes for resting =11 minutes. For a 1$^1/_2$ cm ($^3/_4$ in) steak served rare, it would have 2 x 1 minute to brown both sides, 2 minutes cooking and 3 minutes resting = 7 minutes total. If in doubt, always undercook steaks. it's easy to cook them some more if need be.

THICKNEESS	RARE	MEDIUM
5 cm (2 in)	15	18
4 cm (1$^1/_2$ in)	13	16
3 cm (1$^1/_4$ in)	11	14
2 cm (1 in)	8	10
1$^1/_2$ cm ($^3/_4$ in)	7	8
1 cm ($^1/_2$ in)	5	6 (no resting)
0.5 cm ($^1/_4$ in)	3	4 (no resting)

Venison steaks with horseradish Hollandaise sauce and pan jus

Serves 4

This is one of the simplest and best of combinations: the creamy sauce with its slight sharpness makes the perfect foil for venison. Ready-made Hollandaise sauce can be bought, but it is not difficult to make. You can leave it as the classic Hollandaise or you can add other flavours. I have suggested horseradish, but tarragon turns the sauce into Béarnaise which goes well with venison in the summertime. A teaspoon of crushed fennel or caraway seeds added to the vinegar as it is reducing lends an aniseed flavour. A teaspoon of concentrated tomato purée works well too. Make sure that whatever you add doesn't thin the sauce too much.

4 x 180 g (6 oz) thick venison steaks

Butter and oil to pan-fry

Hollandaise sauce

180 g (6 oz) chilled butter

3 tablespoons white wine vinegar

1 small shallot or 2 fat cloves garlic, finely diced

2 egg yolks

1 tablespoon fresh horseradish

Pan jus

12 crushed juniper berries

1 tablespoon rowan or redcurrant jelly

250 ml (8 fl oz) stock/wine

Black pepper, salt

First make the hollandaise sauce. Chill the butter thoroughly and cut into cubes. Put the wine vinegar and shallot into a small pan. Boil until it has reduced to about a tablespoon, then scoop it into a small heatproof bowl that will fit over the little pan. Put 2–3 cm (1–1½ in) water into the pan and bring to simmering point. Place the bowl over the pan so that the steam rather than the water warms it, otherwise it will get too hot. Add the egg yolks and one cube of butter to the shallot and reduced vinegar, and stir with a wooden spoon to break the yolks.

Don't stop in the middle of making this sauce, for if the egg becomes overheated, it will coagulate rather than thickening, producing melted butter with scrambled egg in it. As soon as the first piece of butter starts to melt, keep stirring and add another. Continue this process until nearly all the butter is incorporated and the sauce thickened. Add your chosen flavouring, if used, and keep the sauce warm but not cooking any more.

Next cook the steaks as desired (p.104). While they rest, add the crushed juniper berries and jelly to the pan. As soon as the jelly has melted, add the stock/wine. Bubble it quickly till syrupy and season to taste with salt and black pepper. There will only be a small amount per person, but less is more in this case.

Venison with morels and saffron mashed potatoes

Serves 4

The texture of mushrooms and other fungi goes particularly well with venison. Fresh morels are a springtime treat as they appear around April and May. They are an expensive luxury, being about the only wild fungi to be found in the spring; their characteristic honeycomb texture and deep flavour makes them very distinctive. You can also buy them dried. In the autumn, apricot yellow chanterelles may also be substituted – also excellent with venison.

4 x 180 g (6 oz) venison steaks

30 g (2 oz) dried morels

300 ml (¹/₂ pt) venison stock

300 ml (¹/₂ pt) red wine

1 tablespoon fresh thyme leaves

2 tablespoons olive oil

4 tablespoons red vermouth or port

10 crushed juniper berries

1 clove garlic, crushed

Salt and pepper

For the saffron mash

900 g (2 lb) potatoes

150 ml (¹/₄ pt) warm milk

Good pinch saffron strands

Salt

50 g (2 oz) butter

If you use dried morels, soak them in the stock or water; they need at least 4 hours, though more is better. When they are soft, drain off the juice and put it into a pan with the wine, stock and thyme. Mix together the oil, vermouth or port, juniper berries and garlic, then add the steaks and leave them for 2 hours, turning them occasionally. Remove the steaks and pat dry. Add the marinade to the wine and stock and boil hard to reduce it all to strong gravy. Add the morels and simmer gently till they are cooked. Season at the end, and serve with the steaks, fried or grilled to taste, and the saffron mash below.

To make the saffron mash, soak the saffron strands in the warm milk for at least half an hour. Boil the potatoes, drain when soft, mash them with the butter, then beat in the saffron milk and a good pinch of salt. If it is not creamy enough, add more butter or more milk according to taste. Keep warm while the steaks cook.

Venison steaks with St George's mushrooms and ramsons

St George's mushrooms appear around 23rd April, St George's day; they are large mushrooms with a slight aniseed flavour. About this time, wild garlic (ramsons) springs up all over the countryside. Its leaves are wonderful for salads, being only gently garlic-flavoured, and they go really well with both mushrooms and venison. Proceed as before, using about 350 g (12 oz) of mushrooms; these need to be gently sweated in butter and oil to reduce and intensify them before being added to the sauce. The ramsons can either be steamed like spinach or the leaves torn and served as a small side-salad.

Minute steaks with ceps, garlic and lemon thyme

This is my favourite autumn dish that sends me every year out into the woods to seek out boletus. Some people hate their slimy texture, but I think it perfect with venison.

Cooked like this, ceps (boletus) keep very well in the freezer and to my mind are much better than dried ones. I refuse to put quantities here as I could eat four portions without blinking. A small amount makes a great garnish. Just enjoy what there is. Melt a good knob of butter in a saucepan and add some crushed garlic, as much as you like. Then add the sliced boletus and cook them briskly with the lemon thyme. Eventually they reduce down to about a third of their volume. Now you can add salt and pepper and eat them, but don't forget to cook your steaks first. Minute steaks, cut only 5 mm ($\frac{1}{4}$ in) thick, are cooked in seconds, and need no resting. The ceps have a powerful flavour, so a simple salad is nice with it.

Surf and turf: Venison fillet with oysters or anchovies

Serves 4

The oyster version of this dish was Angela Jaques' signature dish when she was chef at the Scotch Malt Whisky Society in Edinburgh: this is adapted from her idea. The anchovies work well as long as only a subtle hint is used. For large species of deer, use the filet mignon, for small species, use the loin fillet. The julienne of vegetables can be your choice – use parsnips or celery if you prefer.

2 x 350 g (12 oz) trimmed pieces of fillet

2 carrots, 1 bell pepper, $^{1}/_{4}$ celeriac

8 oysters (or 25 g / 1 oz anchovy fillets)

200 ml very reduced venison stock

Small wineglass port or red wine

1 dessertspoon soy or oyster sauce

Squeeze of lemon

To serve

Steamed baby spinach

Oil

Cut the vegetables into thin julienne strips and reserve. Using a long, sharp knife, make a slit all the way down the fillets to form a tube. Stuff the oysters into the cavities and secure the open end with a cocktail stick. (If using anchovies, place them carefully down the centre, trying to distribute them as evenly as possible.) Sear the fillet in hot butter/oil, then roast in a very hot oven (Gas 8, 230ºC, 450ºF) for 5 minutes. Then allow the fillets to rest according to thickness – about10 minutes – the flavours work best between rare and medium.

While the fillets rest, add the stock, wine, soy sauce and lemon to the pan and allow it to bubble till syrupy. Steam the spinach; stir-fry the vegetables in hot oil until just beginning to soften. When the fillets are done, slice them into rounds, and serve on top of the stir-fried vegetables with the sauce poured over them and the steamed spinach with a squeeze of lemon on it.

Summer steaks with a warm ginger dressing

Serves 4

A simple but tangy way of enjoying a steak. The dressing is a vinaigrette that goes well with the lovely fresh salad leaves available in the summer. Really good new potatoes or bread are the only other thing needed here.

4 x 180 g (6 oz) haunch or loin steaks

Butter/oil to pan-fry

Mixed salad leaves and herbs

Dressing

Grated rind and juice of a lime

2 cm (¼ in) root ginger

1 teaspoon honey

3 tablespoons water

1 tablespoon balsamic vinegar (or 2 of wine vinegar)

6 tablespoons olive oil

Salt and pepper

Put the lime rind, root ginger (chopped), honey and water into a small pan and simmer for a few minutes to infuse, then whisk them into the rest of the dressing ingredients. It should be served slightly warm with the steaks. Once cooled, this dressing will keep for weeks.

Fry the steaks very quickly in very hot butter/oil, then remove them from the heat to rest (see p.104). Place each steak onto the salad leaves. Pour the dressing into the frying pan and amalgamate the brownings, then drizzle this nice warm dressing over the steaks and salad.

Venison with Thai yellow curry sauce and fragrant jasmin rice
Serves 4

This recipe comes from New Zealand chef Hamish Brown with whom I shared a demonstration. It has that vibrant combination of flavours that characterise fusion food, in this case a 'curry' with pink meat. Palm sugar (jaggery) is moist brown sugar made from the sap of the palm tree, widely used in Asian cooking; you can substitute honey. Makrut lime leaves are the Asian equivalent of bay leaves, which can be used instead. This is a delicate, quite sweet dish, and I think also works well without the sugar.

700 g (1½ lb) venison haunch cut into 2 cm (¾ in) dice

1 tablespoon vegetable oil

2–3 tablespoons Thai yellow curry paste

1 tablespoon palm (or soft brown) sugar

2 cloves garlic, crushed

1 tablespoon chopped ginger

2 sticks lemongrass, chopped

4 Makrut lime leaves (or bay leaves)

750 ml (1¼ pt) coconut cream

400 ml (¾ pt) chicken stock

1 tablespoon chopped fresh basil

2 tablespoons chopped fresh coriander

50 g (2 oz) jasmin rice per person

To serve: mango chutney

First make the yellow curry sauce: heat the oil and add half of the curry paste, sugar, garlic and ginger and stir over a medium heat for 5 minutes. Add the lemon grass, lime (or bay) leaves and coconut cream and bring to a gentle simmer, then add the chicken stock and taste. Add more curry paste if wished. Allow it to simmer for 5 minutes. Remove from the heat, purée it and pass it through a sieve. Add the chopped herbs and reserve.

Cook the jasmin rice and keep warm.

Fry the venison cubes to caramelise all sides of the meat. It is important not to overcook the venison or it will toughen, so make the pan very hot and brown the meat quickly, leaving it rare; it completes its cooking as the sauce warms through. Reduce the heat a little, then add the yellow curry sauce and heat through quickly but without boiling it. Adjust seasoning to taste and serve with the Jasmine rice and mango chutney. The meat should still be rosy pink and moist inside.

Venison steaks with Lanark blue cheese
Serves 4

This extremely easy recipe isn't much use for anyone concerned about their cholesterol, but luckily lots of us aren't as it is a firm favourite. Caramelised or roasted baby onions or shallots go well – see p.71. Originally I used Roquefort cheese since the suggestion came from Catherine Souef, a deer producer near Carcassonne. However, there are so many excellent British blue cheeses now that I now use whatever is local: Wensleydale Blue, Stilton, Shropshire Blue, Caithness Blue and many more. Lanark Blue is made by Humphrey Errington, and I give the title to his cheese as a mark of respect for his long, difficult, expensive, but finally successful battle against the Lanarkshire cheese police who threatened the life of not only Humphrey's enterprise, but the whole future of artisan cheese-making in Britain.

4 x 180 g (6 oz) haunch steaks, thick cut

Oil

100 g (4 oz) Lanark or other blue cheese

150 ml (¹/₄ pt) cream

Pepper

Fresh chives

Pan-fry the steaks to taste, though undercook them and leave them to rest (p.104). Mash together the Lanark Blue and the cream. Drain excess fat from the pan and add the cream/cheese mixture, scraping up all the brownings from the pan, and allowing the cheese to melt. If it looks too dry, moisten the sauce with milk. Lanark Blue is a salty cheese, so the sauce probably needs no more salt, but a little pepper is good. If any juices have come out of the steaks, stir these into the sauce. Tip the sauce over the steaks, sprinkle with fresh chives.

Venison steak with red and green grapes

Serves 4

This simple recipe relies on really flavourful, additive-free stock. It is better to have a little good stock than a lot of watery stock. You can either serve the meat as steaks (1 large or 2 small per person), or cut it into chunks and thread these onto skewers. It's a nice combination, the freshly cooked venison with the deep venison stock, and the fresh grapes with the rich red wine, all married together. It's a recipe I make with pheasant as well.

4 x 180 g (6 oz) portions venison steak

Butter and oil

20 large red seedless grapes

20 large white seedless grapes

2 glasses red wine

150 ml (¼ pt) reduced venison or beef stock

Salt and pepper

Cut the grapes in half and set aside. Cook the steaks in butter and oil, undercooking them, and then taking them out of the pan to a warm place to rest (See p.104–105). While they rest, pour the fat out of the frying pan and add the reduced stock and wine to the pan. Boil hard till reduced by half. It should be syrupy by this stage, and almost crinkling on the surface. Season to taste. Add the halved grapes to the pan to warm through. Don't let them actually cook or they will turn to a mush – they are nicest still crisp. Add any juices from the rested meat to the sauce, and serve with the steaks, either whole or sliced.

Variation

Skewers of venison with plums

Serves 4

Use the ingredients above, replacing the grapes with plums. Halve the plums. Cut the steaks into chunks and thread them onto skewers (pre-soaked if wooden), alternating each piece of venison with half a plum. Prepare the sauce by adding the wine to the stock and reducing by half. Melt some butter and oil in a large pan and fry the brochettes swiftly, turning them as soon as they are browned. As soon as they are browned all over, they can be served with the sauce; there is no need to rest them for more than a moment or two.

Venison fillets with fresh spring risotto

Serves 4

This refreshing risotto goes well with pink-roasted venison as well; the fragrant spiciness of lime zest complementing the spring treats of baby broad beans, asparagus and new peas. The fillets can be filet mignon or trimmed log-shapes from the haunch. If you use precooked risotto rice, follow the recommendations for liquid and cooking times on the pack, and adjust the stock accordingly. You may wish to use the zest from only one of the limes, though I like to use both.

4 x 180 g (6 oz) venison fillets

1–2 unwaxed limes

300 g (11 oz) asparagus spears

1 litre (1³/₄ pts) venison beef or chicken stock

100 g (4 oz) butter

4 shallots, chopped

300 g (11 oz) risotto rice

200 ml (¹/₃ pt) dry white wine

100 g (4 oz) baby broad beans

100 g (4 oz) baby peas

Salt and pepper

80 g (3 oz) grated Parmesan (optional)

Grate the rind off the limes and reserve. Trim the asparagus and chop into 2 cm (1 in) lengths. Heat up the stock. Melt the butter in a large, deep frying pan, and gently fry the shallots till transparent. Add the rice and fry it gently for five minutes, then add the wine and the lime juice. Increase the heat and add a quarter of the stock and the lower ends of the chopped asparagus. Once it has been absorbed, add another quarter and keep stirring. Now start to fry the steaks (see p.104), keeping an eye on the risotto as you cook them. When the third quarter of stock is added, put in the middle parts of the asparagus as well.

When the last quarter of stock is added to the risotto, put in the broad beans, peas, asparagus tips and lime zest. Check the seasoning and add salt, pepper and more lime zest if wished. Finally, stir in the grated Parmesan if wished – it makes the risotto creamier but is not essential.

Medallions of venison with red wine and juniper sauce

Serves 2

This is about the easiest recipe of all as long as you have some concentrated, additive-free stock. The better the stock, the better the sauce will taste. Redcurrants are optional but they are a classic accompaniment to venison.

4 x 80 g (3 oz) venison loin steaks

Butter and oil to pan-fry

10 crushed juniper berries

1 tablespoon rowan or redcurrant jelly

1 small glass red wine

100 ml (4 fl oz) concentrated venison stock

Salt and pepper

2 large sprigs redcurrants (optional)

Heat the butter and oil in a heavy frying pan till very hot. Brown the steaks on both sides, turn down the heat and continue as on p.104-105. Remove steaks to a warm plate to rest.

Pour off any surplus oil. Add the juniper berries and jelly to the pan. When the jelly has melted, add the red wine and stock, boil and reduce until syrupy, season to taste, then strain the sauce and serve with the steaks. The redcurrants can either be used as a garnish, looking like bunches of rubies, or they can be removed from the stalk and warmed through in the sauce before serving.

Venison steaks with rhubarb sauce
Serves 4

Rhubarb works really well with venison, but never use cast iron pans to cook it as rhubarb makes the sauce taste tinny. You can also use gooseberries but the colour isn't so rich. Really good additive-free stock makes all the difference to the sauce.

4 x 180 g (6 oz) venison steaks

Butter and oil to cook them in

350 g (12 oz) rhubarb

300 ml (¹/₂ pt) concentrated venison or beef stock

1–2 tablespoons rowan jelly, or other tart fruit jelly

Salt and pepper to taste

Chop the rhubarb and boil it in the venison stock until pulped. Rub it through a sieve and return the purée to the pan. Add rowan jelly and salt to taste - use a strong, tart jelly rather than one made insipid with apples. A recipe for rowan jelly is on p.46; it's very easy to do.

Heat some butter and oil in a large frying pan until really hot. Cook your steaks to taste (see p.104). Then while the steaks are resting, add the rhubarb sauce to the frying pan to dissolve the pan juices before serving with the steaks.

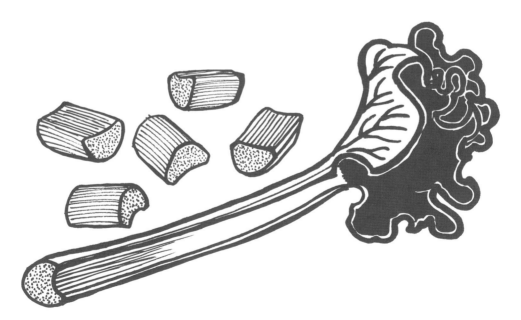

Venison steaks with chocolate and chilli dipping sauce

Serves 6

The Spanish chocolate makers, Cacao Sampaka make a large range of chocolates that are barely sweet at all and can be eaten as tiny tapas. Their flavourings include curry, chilli, balsamic vinegar, cloves, anchovies, olives, garlic, saffron and cardamom. I wasn't so keen on the Parmesan-flavoured ones but the rest were magical combinations. When chocolate first came to Europe, it was served as a spicy savoury pick-me-up drink, just as it still is in South America, so its use in savoury meat sauces is not so peculiar. It's a long-standing ingredient of Italian game dishes.

Chocolate in meat sauces needs careful handling, as it can be overpowering. I prefer unsweetened cocoa powder to bitter chocolate. Though luscious, it is best used sparingly, which is why I recommend these as dipping sauces though you could serve just a tiny dribble of sauce with the steaks. Choose the strength of chilli that suits you: if you use chilli powder, 1 teaspoonful should be plenty to start with, for chilli paste start with a tablespoon. This gives about 300 ml ($^1/_2$ pt) of sauce so could in fact serve more than 6.

6 x 180 g (6 oz) steaks

2 fresh or pickled chilli peppers

1 large clove garlic, crushed

Oil or butter for frying

200 g (7 oz) tomatoes, peeled and chopped

300 ml ($^1/_2$ pt) venison or beef stock

150 ml ($^1/_4$ pt) wine

1–2 tablespoons tart jelly

2 teaspoons cocoa powder

Chop the chilli peppers finely and gently fry them with the garlic in oil or butter till soft. Add the finely chopped tomatoes and simmer to thicken them a little, then add the stock, the wine and half of the jelly, then boil it down to a good sauce consistency. Stir in the cocoa powder and season with salt, pepper, and the rest of the jelly if wished. For a completely smooth sauce, strain it through a small sieve. Cook the steaks to taste, and serve the chocolate sauce in tiny individual bowls.

Venison steaks with chocolate and cardamom dipping sauce

As above, but replace the chilli with 2 teaspoons of crushed whole cardamom pods, and increase the jelly to 3 tablespoons. It may not need any pepper. Add the cardamom with the stock and when it has boiled down, strain the sauce to avoid the cardamom becoming overpowering.

Venison steaks with chocolate and clove dipping sauce

As above, but replace the chilli with $^1/_4 - ^1/_2$ teaspoon of ground cloves, scattering it over the garlic before adding the stock and wine. Since basil smells very similar to cloves, you may like to use some in a salad or as a garnish. Even people who say they don't like cloves love this sauce.

Venison steaks with chocolate, balsamic and ginger dipping sauce

As above, but replace the chilli with 1 tablespoon of grated fresh ginger, and the fresh tomatoes with 1 tablespoon tomato purée. Fry the ginger and garlic gently, then stir in the tomato purée, the stock and the wine. Add 2 teaspoons of thick balsamic vinegar or syrup (or to taste – balsamic varies so much), and finish as above.

Venison Stroganoff with spätzli

Serves 4

This was a favourite dish of our chef at the Scottish Deer Centre in its early days. It was Tom who told me that you could keep meat fresh for a week to ten days submerged in oil in the fridge. Since there is no need for any other oil to cook it in, the finer the oil the better. Spätsli are a family favourite, going well with this or any stew. However, fresh pappardelli or tagliatelli are also good. You can make the spätzli a few days in advance before the final frying stage; they also freeze well. They are a little time-consuming to make but a treat worth the effort. A bright green vegetable is good here: either steamed spinach or spring greens, briefly cooked in very salty water so they are still slightly bitter-sweet.

700 g (1¹/₂ lb) venison haunch

At least 300 ml (¹/₂ pt) good quality oil

2 teaspoons juniper berries, crushed

1 small onion, sliced

1 bay leaf, crushed

2 cloves garlic, crushed

250 g (4 oz) mushrooms, sliced

¹/₄ teaspoon caraway seeds, crushed

200 ml (¹/₂ pt) double cream

Salt and pepper

Spätzli

300 g (11 oz) plain flour

Prepare the oil by gently warming it with the juniper berries, onion, bay leaf and garlic. This brings out their flavours into the oil. Allow it to cool completely. Slice the meat into thin strips rather less than 1 cm (¹/₂ inch) cross-section and stir them around in the oil. Make sure the meat is completely submerged in oil – top up with more if necessary. Leave it for several days, ideally.

Make the spätzli in advance: beat all the ingredients together thoroughly until the thick batter is bubbling, then leave for an hour to rest. Boil a large pan of salty water and also fill a large basin with cold water. Using a rubber spatula, push the batter though the holes of a colander into the boiling water; it will dribble through forming curious shapes that sink and then bob up to the surface. Lift them out with a slotted spoon or sieve and plunge them into a basin of cold water. Drain them thoroughly, then keep aside. The final stage is to fry them. Do this in batches rather than overcrowd the pan. Heat some butter and oil till golden brown, scatter in the drained spätzli (and bacon if used) and fry till golden

3 eggs

150 ml (¼ pt) water

1 teaspoon salt

Butter

50 g (2 oz) finely chopped bacon (optional)

brown and crisp all over. It can take a while, so get this going before you cook the venison.

When ready to cook the venison, drain all the oil off through a sieve, pressing out as much as you can. Heat a large frying pan and brown the venison strips – do them in batches so that it browns quickly and doesn't crowd the pan. As soon as each batch is browned, remove it to a warm dish. Add the mushrooms and caraway seed and stir-fry quickly till they have reduced and cooked a bit. Then add the cream and scrape up the pan brownings. Return the meat to the pan along with any juices that have emerged, season to taste, and allow the meat to warm through without allowing the sauce to bubble as that would toughen the nicely relaxed meat. The whole procedure should only take about 15 minutes.

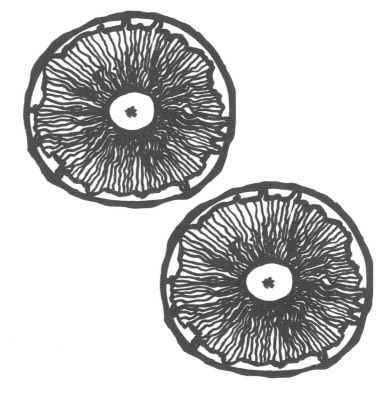

Barbecued venison steaks with salsa verde

Serves 4

Salsas are served cold as a contrast to hot steaks and are lovely for outdoor eating in sizzling hot weather, so this is one for the barbecue and goes well with home-made burgers as well as steaks. It is best made fresh so the herbs don't wilt. The herbs can be changed to suit personal tastes. I know one of my daughters will be replacing the parsley. The piquant anchovies are rather good here but by no means essential.

4 x 180 g (6 oz) steaks or burgers

4 sprigs flat-leaf parsley

2 long sprigs mint

2 long sprigs basil or coriander

2 anchovy fillets (optional)

1 dessertspoon capers or chopped gherkins

1 clove garlic

1 dessertspoon wholegrain or Dijon mustard

Juice of $\frac{1}{2}$ lemon

2–3 tablespoons good olive oil

Salt and pepper

Chop the herbs, anchovies, capers and garlic finely. Whisk together the mustard, lemon juice and 2 tablespoons of oil and add the chopped ingredients. Season with salt and pepper, and if necessary, add more oil. Keep this cool and serve it with your perfectly barbecued steaks – see page 107.

Piquant salsa verde for barbecued steaks

Serves 4

Mexican salsa verde is usually made from tomatillos (green tomatoes) and usually has chilli in it. Again, it's excellent for barbecued and grilled venison.

350 g (12 oz) green tomatoes

1–2 small fresh or pickled chillies

3 cloves garlic, crushed

Large handful fresh coriander

Salt, pepper

Remove the husks from the green tomatoes, then chop them. Deseed and chop the chillies. Either chop everything very finely by hand, or put the ingredients in a blender to chop, but don't blend it to a paste: it should be in recognisable pieces. Mix and season to taste with salt and pepper.

Venison steaks with tart grape purée

Serves 4

This purée (not unlike gooseberry purée) has just the right balance of tart to sweet; it is really more of a relish than a sauce as you don't need very much, so it's another good one for barbecues. For once, grapes that are unripe work well. They make a good contrast to crisp sauté potatoes or home-made chips. Any sort of steak may be used but I favour plump ones here. Use either thick-cut slices of haunch or loin, or whole fillets.

700 g (1½ lbs) thick-cut venison steaks

Oil or butter

2 small shallots, finely chopped

350 g (12 oz) green grapes, chopped

3 tablespoons white wine vinegar

1 small glass (100 ml) dry white wine

1 tablespoon chopped fresh coriander or parsley (optional)

To make the purée, soften the shallots in a very small amount of oil, and once softened, drain off any excess oil and add the chopped grapes, wine vinegar and wine. Boil them until the liquid has almost disappeared, then rub them though a small metal sieve, leaving only the grape skins and pips behind. This can be made ahead and kept warm if wished.

To cook the steaks, heat some butter and oil in a frying pan and brown them all over briskly. Lower the heat and continue to cook for a further 10 minutes, then remove from the heat and rest them for a further five minutes or to taste. Serve with chips or sauté potatoes, glazed carrots and a small pool of the green grape purée.

Honey-glazed venison steaks

Serves 4

Dead simple and good eating. I'm not sure I would use this recipe if I rarely had venison, as it can overwhelm the delicate flavour a little, but it's a very good foil for strong venison, and for those of us who eat it regularly and want a change, it gets the thumbs up. Carrot and parsnip mash goes well with it, being also slightly sweet; for a contrast have steamed spinach. This is also a good way to cook venison sausages.

4 x 180 g (6 oz) steaks

Butter and oil to cook

4 teaspoons honey

4 teaspoons wholegrain mustard

Juice of ¹/₂ a lemon

Heat the butter and oil in a large frying pan till the butter is mid-brown, then put in the steaks and brown them for 2 minutes per side. Then turn the heat down and add the honey, mustard and lemon juice and keep turning them over in this mixture until they are well coated and cooked as desired.

Quick-poached venison with dark wine sauce

Serves 4

Quick-poached venison suits many other sauces as well as this one – try the rowan and rhubarb or the grape purée, the chocolate sauces, or some colourful ratatouille. If you are not worried about butter or cream, then the Hollandaise, mushroom or blue cheese sauces also make a nice contrast. If you don't have any stock to poach the venison (remember it can be frozen for later use after this poaching), use some Miso soup or a bouillon cube.

4 x 180 g (6 oz) thick-cut venison steaks

600 ml (1 pt) stock (enough to cover steaks)

Oil or butter

Sauce

Oil

2 cloves garlic

1 teaspoon grated ginger

Juice of 2 oranges

1 tablespoon light soy sauce

2 teaspoons balsamic syrup

Salt and pepper

First make the sauce. Using a small amount of oil, gently sweat the garlic and ginger till golden. Then add the orange juice, soy and balsamic syrup. Bring to the boil and reduce to a nice syrupy texture which will coat the steaks. Season to taste, and keep warm.

Bring the stock to the boil in a small pan, then reduce the heat till it is not quite bubbling. Brown the steaks all over in hot oil (or butter and oil if wished). If they are thick (3–4 cm, $1^{1}/_{4}$–$1^{3}/_{4}$ in) they may need browning on four sides – this will take a couple of minutes if the oil is hot. Then put them into the stock and simmer for a further 8 minutes or so which will make them rare. You can test by cutting through a steak if you are not sure. If it is not done enough, simply pop it back in. If you prefer to cook them without browning first, they will take a few minutes longer to cook.

Cover them with the sauce before serving.

8. Roasting venison

Cooking information, preparation, carving and cooking

8. Roasting venison

Cooking information, preparation, carving and cooking

> *'I am sure it is a Lordes Dysshe ... It is a meate for great men'*
>
> *Andrew Boorde 1542*

HAUNCH OF VENISON

'May be decidedly called the second great pedestal; turtle soup and haunch of venison being the two great pedestals, or Gog and Magog of English cookery. It is appreciated from the independent citizen to the throne; for where is there a citizen of taste, a man of wealth, or a gourmet, who does not pay homage to this delicious and recherché joint, which ever has, and ever will be in vogue; but even after all that nature has done in point of flavour, should it fall into the hands of some inexperienced person to dress, and be too much done, its appearance and flavour would be entirely spoilt; its delicious and delicate fat melted, and the gravy lost; of the two it would be preferred underdone, but that is very bad and hardly excusable, when it requires nothing but attention to serve this glorious dish in perfection.'

Alexis Soyer, *The Gastronomic Regenerator*, 1846

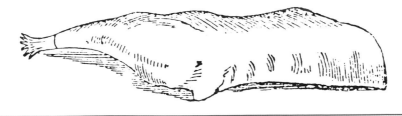

HOW TO COOK PERFECT ROAST VENISON

The words 'a haunch of venison' or 'saddle of venison' conjure up something really special, and so they should. When perfectly cooked, there is little to beat them. But roasting venison gives rise to more questions and more anxiety than any other cooking method. This is not surprising since roasting joints are expensive cuts and usually served for a dinner party or special occasion. Below are the questions I am most frequently asked. There is a short answer followed by a fuller explanation for those who like to understand the background. After that come four basic methods of roasting venison so that you can cook any recipe, even if your joint is a different size or shape. Some of the flavours, sauces and vegetable dishes in this section can be used equally well with steaks or stews.

All you need to roast venison to perfection is

- A suitable piece of venison (see p.31 for the cuts, p.13 for the different species and sizes of deer, and chapter 2 for aspects affecting the flavour and eating quality of venison.)
- A meat thermometer (see below)
- Ten minutes to read this section

How much do I need?

About three-quarters the amount of domestic meats, as venison is filling. For a small roast for 2–3 people, allow 180–225 g (6–8 oz) boneless venison per portion for a main course. For venison on the bone, 225–350 g (8–12 oz) per portion, depending on the cut. However, in recipes using larger joints, I would allow 225–350 g (8–12 oz) for boneless joints and 350–450 g (12 oz–16 oz) for joints on the bone, because when sharing a roast, people usually like to offer second helpings or eat more the next day. Be more generous if you wish – I am sure everyone will be grateful. Or decrease it if you want to finish it all at once. See p.40 for more detail on portioning.

What's your best tip for roasting venison?

I have two. Firstly, always undercook it and then let it rest (see below). The second and best tip is to beg, borrow or buy a meat thermometer. A cheap one will do.

A meat thermometer removes all the anxiety because you can see exactly how the meat is cooking. A simple dial thermometer costs only the price of a portion of venison – far less than a kitchen knife – surely this is money well spent. Even though I have roasted venison countless times, I wouldn't dream of cooking a large or unusual shaped joint without my meat thermometer.

A dial thermometer spike is inserted into the centre of the thickest part of the muscle – avoiding the bone if there is one – and it stays in the joint as it cooks. Digital probe thermometers are used to check progress from time to time. Remove the undercooked meat from the hot oven when the thermometer reads 10ºC (20ºF) below your final desired cooked temperature – see the chart on p.137, or use beef cooking recommendations. The commonest mistake is to overcook venison, so err on the undercooked side. By the time it is on the table it will have cooked a little more.

I don't have a meat thermometer. How do I know it is cooked?

If you are familiar with roasting beef pink, then cook venison almost the same way, but undercook it and then leave it to rest and finish off to your liking. Alternatively, use the thickness chart below.

Only a meat thermometer tells you exactly how 'done' your roast is, so it is unquestionably the most fool-proof system. The cooking chart below gives a guide but there are many variables, like temperature of both the meat and the oven. If you use a skewer to test the colour of the juices, remember that venison juices are redder than beef, so don't be afraid to serve it when the juices are still quite dark– by the time it is served up it will have dispersed a lot.

Which cuts are best for roasting?

Saddle, loin, haunch (leg). Reserve the shoulder for braising unless the venison is from a young deer as there will be too much sinew.

The saddle (or loin) is the most reliable cut, whatever the age of the animal. For most people buying venison, it will be younger and tender, in which case the haunch also makes a wonderful tender roast. For large numbers of people, a haunch is the one to use. The shoulder of a young animal can be roasted, but it has more sinews and it is less easy to carve into good slices so I would reserve it for some of the lovely braised dishes instead.

Do you have to marinate venison?

Not at all. It is not necessary to marinate venison (and many children don't like the taste of marinades), but by all means do so if you like the richer flavour of marinated meat. See chapter 4 for more information on marinating and some recipes, and p.26 for tenderising venison without marinating if yours is old.

Does it have to be larded, or barded?

Not if you want to eat low-fat meat, and not if you serve it rare or medium rare. It is physically impossible for pink meat to be dry. You only need to lard it when you cook it to well-done.

Barding means wrapping fat round the meat. Larding is inserting fat deep into the meat. Neatly barded joints look attractive, but since the fat is on the outside of the meat, it doesn't help to keep the interior succulent. The role of barding was to prevent the outside surface of large, lean joints from hardening into leather when they were being spit-roasted in front of a fire. This was also the reason for wrapping large joints in a paste that was discarded afterwards. With smaller joints cooked quickly in the oven and served pink, neither paste nor barding is necessary. But if you like the taste and texture of fat (and why not?) then do bard your venison. Wrap it up in fat, bacon or pancetta, but beware it isn't so strong that it drowns out the flavour of venison.

Larding is not necessary when venison is cooked pink. Young or old, extra fat is not needed as the pinkness - the 'red gravy' as my father used to call it - keeps the joint beautifully moist. So venison served rosy-red is about as low fat and succulent a meat as you can get. However, larding is advisable when venison joints are cooked past the pink stage, because at this point they start to dry up. Soft fats like butter, lard, dripping, solidified oils, will melt slowly out as the meat cooks and can be skimmed off the gravy afterwards if wished. Hard fats like sticks of venison, lamb, pork, beef or bacon fat will remain in the cooked meat when it is sliced. You can 'lard' venison with other things at the same time: garlic, mustard, even mushroom or aubergine strips for succulence. Or you can roll the fat in herbs or spices to introduce extra flavours.

Do you need a larding needle?

No. I don't have one either. If you want to lard meat with any kind of fat, cut it into sticks and freeze them for half an hour or so until hard. Then take a small sharp knife and make holes deep into the meat, about 3 cm (1½ in) apart. The hard sticks of fat can now be easily pressed down into the holes.

Should roast venison be served pink, or well-done?

If you are roasting venison, it should be served rare to medium rare. Well-done venison should be cooked more slowly. See below.

Alexis Soyer, the famous nineteenth century chef, wrote, 'Venison must be underdone, red in the middle, and full of gravy, but not raw.' I agree. There is a move afoot to advise cooking red meat for so long that it is ruined. The uncut muscle meat of venison is virtually sterile and therefore safe to eat rare, even raw, so long as the outside of the meat is sterilised by cooking at a high temperature. Browning and roasting involve high temperatures. So it is perfectly safe to eat underdone venison (and beef), though there is a risk to some people in eating underdone lamb, pork or goat meat. See p.102 for details.

Venison roasted to well-done turns grey and dry with a texture like blotting paper; and if from an old animal the slices curl up and it sometimes actually squeaks when you try to carve it. Don't do it. Please. If you really don't like pinkness in meat, read below for instructions on how to gently braise it to a wonderful succulence that is so different from pink roasted venison that they might almost be different meats.

I like it really pink but my partner likes theirs well-done...

This is a common situation. Bar cooking two separate joints or finding a new partner, the following may help.

1. Choose a joint that has one part thinner than the rest – the thin parts will be less pink. Bone-in joints often have widely varying thicknesses which should suit differing tastes.
2. Carve off some slices and pop them in the microwave for 20 seconds on 'low' (or to taste) until they lose their pinkness.
3. Give the non-pink eater the outside slices, which are usually more cooked. Give him/her a very hot plate, carve theirs onto it first but hand it to them last. It will have become less pink by then.
4. For larger numbers, use two small joints and cook one for longer than the other.
5. Give up the idea of roast venison and follow cooking methods below, which cook joints slowly to well-done.

My venison is from an old animal and I like pink meat. I suppose I should cook it for longer?

If it is to be served pink, cook it less, not more, and carve the slices as thin as possible. Roasting is a fierce way of cooking, and venison roasted past the pink stage turns dry and very tough. If you don't want it pink, don't roast it. Pot-roast or braise it (see below) and when braising, yes, you do cook old venison more slowly and for longer.

The tougher and leaner your meat is, the less tolerant it is of fierce cooking like grilling and roasting. So before you cook your venison joint, decide whether you want it pink or well-done. Even really old venison, if cooked rare or pink and then sliced thinly, makes good eating, especially if as much sinew as possible is removed first. Use the advice below but roast it a bit less and rest it a bit more. For well-done meat, see the two slow-cooking methods which advise long slow cooking together with some larding to keep the meat succulent.

I want to use a particular recipe but my joint is bigger/smaller. How do I calculate the cooking time?

Multiply up/down the other ingredients as required, then use the general cooking times below because it is the thickness of the joint that most affects the cooking time.

Is it better on the bone or off the bone?

Both are good, though bones don't have time to improve small joints when cooked pink.

Roe, Chinese water deer and muntjac haunches, being so small, are good left on the bone, and a saddle is always bone-in. The shape of a large piece of saddle or haunch on the bone is a glorious sight, and since it will be in the oven for longer, leaving the bone in makes more sense, particularly if the bone has been cut to allow the marrow fat to escape. However, small slices of bone-in venison are not in the oven long enough for the bones to do anything other than get in the way of the carver. Bones lend succulence to joints that are braised, although they do make carving some cuts (like shoulder) rather more awkward.

Help! The thermometer is reading 70ºC (160ºF) or more – how do I rescue my overcooked venison?

Make sure your sauce or gravy is thinner than usual, and carve the slices straight into the gravy so the slices soak up the juice at once.

If venison is overdone, withdraw the meat from the oven and put it, covered, on a plate or wooden board so it does not cook any more. There will be some juices in the roasting dish; quickly add a little water to them and dissolve all the precious browning so that it has maximum flavour. If you have made a clear gravy or thin sauce to go with the meat, strain this extra gravy into it, making it thinner than usual. If the juices are almost tasteless and you don't want to thin your sauce, add a little something to give it a mild flavour, perhaps a teaspoon of culinary jelly or a few drops of soy sauce or stock if you have any. Use a warmed shallow dish rather than a plate to carve the joint, and pour the thin gravy into the dish. Carve the joint so the slices fall immediately into the gravy to soak up the precious liquid like blotting paper – the slices will become moist even if they are not pink. If you carve it first and add the sauce later, the slices quickly dry out and once that happens it is difficult to get them to absorb anything.

How long do I cook it for?

It depends on the thickness of the joint, whether or not it has been in a cold fridge, how accurate your oven temperature is. So the timings in the chart are a guide only. However, it is always safer to undercook it rather than overcook it.

After browning the joint in a frying pan, roasting times are in the chart below. It is far better to calculate the roasting time using the thickness of the meat rather than just its weight. For example, a 350 g (12 oz) and a 900 g (2 lb) piece of loin both only need 8–10 minutes in a preheated hot oven (Gas 8, 230ºC, 450ºF) followed by 4–6 minutes resting for rare meat. However, a chunky 900 g (2 lb) rolled haunch joint may need 15–20 minutes in the hot oven followed by 15 minutes resting time. A huge joint lowers the oven temperature more, and being thicker, will obviously take much longer but it often takes fewer minutes per kg or lb of meat. If using a meat thermometer, remove the meat from the hot oven when the internal temperature is 45–50ºC (110–120ºF), then allow it to rest while the temperature rises to rare or medium as desired.

The chart gives cooking times according to the thickness of the joint. It can only be a guide, since ovens vary considerably in their actual temperatures. Fan ovens cook much more quickly than standard ovens, so reduce temperatures by 25ºC (75ºF). Measure the thickness of the joint, not the length.

COOKING TIMES FOR ROASTING VENISON

Roasting times at Gas 8, 230°C, 450°F

Fan ovens should reduce temperatures by 25°C (75°F). Ideal resting temperature is approximately 80°C (175°F).

Rough guide: minutes per cm (inch) thickness

Rare: 2–3 minutes per cm (5–7$^1/_2$ per inch) then rest for 2–3 minutes per cm (5–7$^1/_2$ per inch)

Medium: 3 minutes per cm (7$^1/_2$ per inch) then rest for 3–4 minutes per cm (7$^1/_2$–10 per inch)

Using a meat thermometer

Remove from hot oven when thermometer reads:		Finished internal temperature for roast venison.	
Rare	45–50°C (115–120°F)	55–60°C (130–140°F)	
Medium	50–55°C (120–130°F)	60–65°C (140–150°F)	
Well-done	55–60°C (130–140°F)	70°C (160°F)	

After 70°C, (160°F) venison will be dry. Ideally do not roast it beyond 65° C (150°F).

Some actual results: This demonstrates that the timing chart works well for the more every-day sizes. But the huge whole red deer haunch needed a little longer per cm (inch) thickness since it cooled the oven down more.

A bone-in red deer haunch (shank off) weighing 9.5 kg (21 lb) and 20 cm (8 in) thick took 1$^1/_4$ hours at Gas 8, 230°C, 450°F, plus 1$^1/_4$ hours resting at Gas $^1/_2$, 80 °C, 175 °F, and was medium rare.

2 whole bone-in fallow deer haunches, 10 cm (4 in) thick weighing 2.5kg (5 lb) each, were cooked together for 30 min at Gas 8, 230°C, 450°F, plus 40 minutes resting at Gas $^1/_2$, 80°C, 175°F and were rare-medium.

1 whole roe haunch (ex rump & shin), 7 cm (3 in) thick weighing 1.2 kg (2 lb 12 oz) had 18 minutes roasting at Gas 7, 220°C, 425°F plus 18 minutes resting at Gas $^1/_2$, 80°C, 175°F and was rare.

1 cm

2 cm

3 cm

4 cm

5 cm

6 cm

7 cm

8 cm

9 cm

10 cm

11 cm

12 cm

13 cm

14 cm

15 cm

16 cm

17 cm

18 cm

19 cm

HOW TO ROAST VENISON, SERVED PINK

Both of the following two basic methods avoid the danger of last-minute overcooking. Larding is unnecessary because the juices in rare meat make it impossible for the venison to be dry. You don't get much gravy because all the juice is still in the meat, so prepare a sauce in advance; the delicious but small amount of juices that come from resting the joint can be added at the last minute to enrich your sauce.

---

1) PRE-HEAT YOUR OVEN SO IT IS READY WHEN YOU NEED IT
IF YOU HAVE A FAN OVEN, REDUCE ALL TEMPERATURES BY 25°C OR 75°F.
2) IF YOUR JOINT IS SMALL, MAKE YOUR SAUCE BEFOREHAND

HIGH TEMPERATURE ROAST VENISON

BROWN THE JOINT First brown it all over in a frying pan, using a mixture of oil and butter. Use oil with a high burning point (olive or grape seed oil). The butter makes it brown faster and adds flavour. The browning process takes 6–10 minutes depending on the size of joint. Next, if you have one, insert the meat thermometer into the thickest part of the meat, avoiding touching any bones.

PART-ROAST IT This can be done in an open roasting dish. Partially cook it in a very hot oven (Gas 8, 230ºC, 450ºF) leaving it undercooked at this stage. Give it 3 minutes per cm (7¹/₂ per inch), when the meat thermometer should read 45ºC (115ºF) The needle on a dial type will usually point straight down, at half-past six.

REST IT Always rest the meat in a warm place to complete the cooking, relax the meat and distribute the juices evenly. A plate warming drawer or cool oven of about 80ºC (175ºF) is best, but if you have to leave it on the stove top, cover it with foil and a thick cloth to keep the heat in. During this period, the heat continues to travel to the centre of the joint, while the underdone juices in the middle are drawn back towards the more cooked, drier edges. Use the beef readings on the meat thermometer to determine whether it is rare or medium, and don't let the internal temperature go above 65°C (150°F). At the end of the process the venison is evenly pink and succulent thoughout. Utterly delicious.

SLOW BUT PINK METHOD

This way of slowly cooking joints was pioneered by Count Rumford about 200 years ago. It was revived in Switzerland in the 1970s where it was taught in the Betti Bossi cookery school. Use the best cuts: loin or slim joints of haunch up to 7 cm (3 inches) diameter if young and tender. There is no reason at all why larger joints should not be cooked in this way too – it is simply the browning period followed by a very long resting time. Again, a meat thermometer tells you how it is cooking. The big advantage is that you don't need to hover over the joint while your guests are eating a first course.

BROWN Brown the joint all over including both ends. Thorough browning is vital because otherwise the meat has no colour on the outside and lacks flavour. It also sterilizes the outside.

COOK VERY SLOWLY This must be done at Gas ¹/₂, 80°C, 175°F until the meat thermometer reaches 55–60°C (130–140°F). No more. The time this takes will depend on thickness and will take under an hour for a loin roast of 5 cm (2 inches) and up to two hours or more for a plumper rolled haunch joint. If the temperature seems to be rising too quickly this may be because your oven is running hotter than the controls say (quite common at low temperatures), and fan ovens cook more quickly. If you want to delay the cooking a bit, turn the oven down to 70 or even 60°C (160 or even 140°F).

WELL-DONE BRAISED VENISON

Braising is suitable for any cut, because it is not roasting. Well-done braised venison is cooked slowly with a little liquid. Joints with the bone in are particularly good. You get marvellous, ready-made gravy, and it doesn't need such careful timing as does the fast method. To prevent it from drying out, the meat is first larded, then browned, then cooked in a covered dish with about 5 cm (2 inches) liquid (water, wine, orange juice, cider, ale etc.) and vegetables if wished. The flavour of the liquid will alter the rich gravy, and any fat used in larding can be skimmed off afterwards.

LARD the meat (see p.133-4). Then BROWN it, add your preferred liquid, cover, and BRAISE at Gas 4, 180ºC, 350ºF for 2–4 hours until tender. Cooking time depends upon the tenderness of the meat: shoulder needs longer than haunch or saddle, and if the animal is old, longer still. The method is similar to making a stew in that it takes as long to cook 1 kg (2¹/₄ lbs) as it does to cook 2 kg (4 lbs). Baste from time to time, and if it is a large joint, turn it over at least once during the cooking. When the joint is cooked, skim off any excess fat from the gravy if wished; there will be little or none left in the meat. If the meat is ready before you want to serve it, keep it warm in a cool oven and baste with the juices occasionally. If necessary, boil down the juices to intensify the flavour, then season and thicken as desired.

ANTIQUE WELL-DONE 'ROAST' VENISON

This is a very old-fashioned method and it's a terrific way to tenderise really tough cuts – even shanks – yet present them as moist but well-done roast venison, even though it is only 'roasted' for about 10 minutes. There are just four easy steps: larding, browning, simmering, roasting. You need a large frying pan, a large lidded pan deep enough to be able to submerge the joint in water, and a roasting tin at the end. For ingredients, you need fat (see below), butter and oil, and a selection of vegetables like carrots, leeks, celery, onions, plus herbs and spices of your choice.

LARDING is essential. This time soft fats like butter are not enough. You need to use actual strips of raw fat. Beef or lamb fat are alright, but pork belly or back fat works best, for not only do you get the fat but you also get the skin which melts down into a luscious jelly which is still there at the end to lubricate the joint. Get a thin piece of pork skin with the fat attached, about ¹/₃ skin to ²/₃ fat, smoked or unsmoked. Cut this into long strips about 1 cm (¹/₂ inch) square in cross-section. Freeze them till hard, unless you have a larding needle. Then, using a small knife, make deep slits all over the joint not more than 2 cm (1 inch) apart, and insert the strips of fat. Finally, bind the joint up with string, especially if it is on the bone, because it shrinks off the bone and may fall off altogether when you lift it out. Don't worry what it looks like, as you snip the string off before serving.

BROWN THE JOINT Do this thoroughly and put it in your large pot. Peel the vegetables, cut them into generous chunks and brown them also. Add to the pot and fill it with enough water to cover the meat. Add some black peppercorns, crushed juniper berries, a bunch of thyme, a few bay leaves, but no salt.

BRING IT SLOWLY TO THE BOIL When this has been done, reduce the heat so that it barely simmers – it should just give the occasional bubble. Put the lid on and allow it to simmer for around four hours so that it is completely tender all the way through. Some of the lardons may stick out, but don't worry about that. Draw the pan off the heat but leave the meat immersed. If you want to do this part in advance and let it cool down in the meantime, you will need to heat it up – nice and slowly – all the way through before carrying onto the next stage. The bonus here is plenty of lovely stock for making soup and sauces.

FINISH IT IN THE OVEN When almost ready to serve, heat the oven as hot as it will go. Carefully lift the hot meat out of its liquid onto a rack to drain for a moment, then put it in the roasting tin. Smear any protruding bits of lard all over the surface of the meat. If there are none, smear butter over the top instead. Then put it in the oven until the surface is brown and crisp – like a roasted joint. Because the meat is already hot, this happens very quickly – in a fan oven it may only need five minutes; in a conventional oven 10–15 minutes depending how hot you can get it. This final stage should be done as quickly as possible so that all the moisture you have so carefully preserved inside the meat doesn't dry up. As soon as it is brown, serve it up so it doesn't dry out. Remove the strings before serving. When you slice it, there will still be little pieces of the pork skin dotted through the slices. These will have turned to a succulent jelly that gives a lovely texture to the meat. The slices will not be too neat, but the taste makes up for it.

CARVING VENISON ON THE BONE

THE SADDLE: The saddle is symmetrical – the diagram shows where the bones lie. Ideally, the fillets are removed whole and everyone is given some fillet and some loin. To carve the loin, run the knife down either side of the backbone as in the

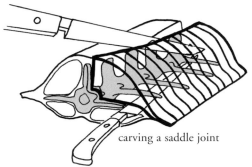
carving a saddle joint

diagram. Take note of the small bumps of bone that stick out above the ribs. Then carve slices as in the diagram, and separate them from the base afterwards. Alternatively, remove both loins from the bone and carve into slices.

THE HAUNCH: The way to carve a haunch depends on whether it is a whole haunch or a slice of it (more likely with the large species). The diagram shows you where the bones lie, and the only difficult part is negotiating around the pelvic bone if it has not been removed. Meat is more tender if it is carved across the grain of the meat – this is most important in older animals. With young venison, this is less important so a slim slice of the centre of the haunch may be carved in either direction. A whole haunch should be carved like a leg of lamb, starting in the centre and working out to both ends.

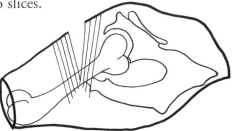
carving a whole haunch

carving a section of haunch

A SHOULDER: A whole or part shoulder from young deer may be roasted and carved like shoulder of lamb. Take off the meat each side of the bladebone (A), noting the diagonal ridge. Then separate it from the leg bone (B), remove bladebone, and slice the remaining meat across the grain. Due to the number of muscles, the slices are never as neat as those from haunch and saddle.

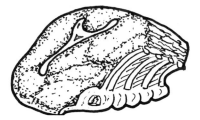
carving a shoulder on the bone

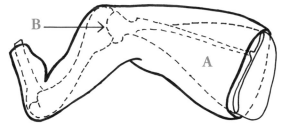

Roast loin of venison with red wine sauce

Serves 4

This is pretty well my signature dish as I have cooked it so many times on television: it is easy and a good example of quickly cooked tender venison. Allow 25% extra if the loin is not trimmed; use trimmings to make the stock. You can substitute haunch (leg), though alter cooking times (see p.137) if it is thinner or thicker than 5 cm (2 inches). Good rowan jelly should be punchy. If it is insipid add zing with lemon juice. It is possible to buy meat stock nowadays, though it may need reducing to intensify its flavour. Real gluttons appreciate a hollandaise sauce as well (p.150). This is sumptuous, but takes away from the elegant simplicity of a dish that is as good in summer as in winter.

700 g (1½ lb) trimmed venison loin

Butter and oil for browning

1 heaped tablespoon rowan jelly

12 juniper berries, crushed

200 ml (7 fl oz) dry red wine

150 ml (¼ pt) reduced venison stock

Salt and pepper to season

Preheat the oven to Gas 7, 220ºC, 425ºF. Heat the butter and oil in a large pan until the butter is golden, and brown the meat thoroughly all over. Turn it into a small roasting pan and tip the hot fat over the top. Do not wash the pan. Roast the venison for 10–12 minutes, then remove it to rest for 12–15 minutes. This will be quite pink – if you want it more done, let it rest for another 10 minutes – the meat must not actually cook further, merely be kept warm so that the meat relaxes and ends up evenly pink throughout.

While the meat rests, add the rowan jelly, crushed juniper berries and red wine to the frying pan and deglaze the pan juices. When the jelly has dissolved, add the stock and then reduce until you have a small amount of exquisite ruby-coloured sauce. Leave it like this till the meat is ready, so that the juniper berries can infuse, then strain the sauce to remove the juniper.

When the meat has rested, add the juices that came out of the joint to the sauce, give it a quick boil, and adjust the seasoning before straining it. Cut the meat into thick chunks or thin slices according to taste, and serve with the sauce.

Roast venison with raspberry sauce

Serves 4

This is based on a recipe that John Tovey cooked at the Royal Highland Show as part of a healthy eating demonstration: hence his choice of venison, garlic, olive oil and raspberries. It's a delightful combination, perfect for light, summery cooking. Raspberries vary in acidity, so if necessary adjust the sweetness with the sugar and lemon juice. Using chilli-flavoured oil lends an interesting kick to the sauce. The optional splash of whisky goes well with raspberries.

700 g (1½ lb) venison loin, or slim rolled haunch

4 tablespoons olive oil

6 cloves garlic

300 g (12 oz) raspberries

1 tablespoon whisky (optional)

Icing sugar and/or lemon to taste (optional)

12 juniper berries, crushed

Crush or chop the garlic, press it onto the meat and place in a dish with the oil, turning it till covered in oil. Leave to marinate for 24 hours, turning occasionally.

Then prepare the purée. Gently heat the raspberries until they break down into a pulp, but don't overheat them or they will discolour. Rub them through a sieve into a tiny pan, using a wooden spoon to press all the fruit pulp, leaving behind only the pips. Add the whisky and then some icing sugar if you think it lacks sweetness. It should be only just sweet or it will become sickly. If it is bland, add a squeeze of lemon juice.

Brown the meat in a small ovenproof pan using the oil from the marinade. Remove most of the garlic as it may burn. Add the crushed juniper berries and roast in a hot oven (Gas 7, 220ºC, 425ºF) for 8–10 minutes. Rest for 10–15 minutes or use your meat thermometer to decide when it is cooked to your liking.

Sieve the juices from the rested meat into the raspberry purée, then adjust the seasoning before serving.

Eighty degrees venison with blackberry sauce

This slow method avoids any last-minute cooking of the meat, so is preferred by some people. Use the ingredients as above, replacing the raspberries with blackberries or blueberries. Soak the meat and make the sauce as above. Then use the 80-degree cooking method on p.139. Cultivated blackberries and blueberries are sometimes insipid; if the sauce lacks sharpness, squeeze a little lemon juice into it.

Roast venison with a fragrant dipping sauce

Serves 4

This is roast venison with a contemporary twist. It's a lovely light dish, perfect for warm weather or perhaps in smaller quantities for a starter. It uses the dipping sauce on p.93. Fragrant rice, polenta or cous cous with stir-fried vegetables would go well with this.

700g (1½ lbs) boneless venison loin or haunch

Butter and oil for browning

Dipping sauce
See ingredients on p.93

Brown, roast and rest the venison according to the guidelines on pages 137-8.
Whisk together the sauce ingredients and prepare the rice / polenta / cous cous.

When the venison has been rested, slice it very thinly and drizzle the sauce over it. Serve the rest in a bowl to hand round.

Thin-sliced venison with a mushroom 'tarte Tatin'
Serves 4

Although you can, of course, serve these with any shape or size of roast venison, the timing here is for a small, log-shaped piece of about 6 cm (2 in) diameter which cooks in about the same time as the tarts. Choose either a large whole red deer fillet, or a slim piece of loin, or a tender piece of haunch muscle trimmed of all sinew. Try to get thyme with a strong punchy flavour. If it is insipid, use extra. Chanterelles grow all around here in the autumn and I dry them, but other dried wild fungi may be used instead. Depending on the season, buttered spinach, steamed kale, or a root vegetable purée all go well with this. For a sauce to go with it, try the thin gravy from the next recipe. Gluttons might even go for the hollandaise sauce as well.

The idea of an upside down mushroom tart came from Graham Brown, a New Zealand chef who has spent years enthusiastically promoting venison to chefs all over the world. It was Graham and his team who coined the 'Denver cut', a term widely used in the wholesale venison trade (p.263). These tarts are very filling, and also make a delicious vegetarian dish (though you'd have to substitute a vegetarian stock - perhaps made from miso paste - instead).

700 g (1 1/2 lbs) slim roasting venison

4 tablespoons dried chanterelles

4 huge flat-cap mushrooms

150 g shallots, peeled and chopped

2 tablespoons fresh thyme leaves

300 ml (1/2 pint) concentrated venison stock

4 x 8-10 cm (3-4 in.) circles puff pastry

Butter, oil, seasoning

Ingredients for a sauce (see p.149)

Soak the dried chanterelles in water for 30 - 45 minutes, then chop finely and reserve the juice. Cut out the stalks from the the flat cap mushrooms and dry them out in a hot oven (Gas 7, 220ºC, 425ºF) for about half an hour, till they are much reduced and leathery. This concentrates the flavour as they are very watery. Soften the shallots and chanterelles in butter, then add the stock and chanterelle liquid and reduce to a syrup, then stir in the thyme leaves. Slice the mushrooms into segments (not essential, but it makes them easier to eat) and place them, black side down, into greased tartlet tins of about 4 x 8-10 cm (3-4 in.) diameter. Spoon the shallot mixture over the top and cover with puff pastry circles.

Now brown the venison quickly all over in hot butter and oil, then part-roast it in a hot oven (Gas 7, 220ºC, 425ºF). Put the mushroom tarts in the oven at the same time. Remove the venison after 10-12 minutes and allow it to rest for a further 10 minutes or so, by which time the puff pastry should be risen and golden brown.

While they cook, make a sauce if wished. To serve, slice the venison thinly. Turn out the mushroom tarts, pastry side downwards, and serve with the venison and sauce.

Roast haunch of venison with rowan and rhubarb sauce

Serves 6

With its tart sweetness, rhubarb makes a marvellous accompaniment to game meats. Most country dwellers have a clump in the garden and can enjoy both early forced rhubarb and the fuller flavoured open-to-the elements version that comes later in the year. If you have plenty, it is well worth freezing some – it goes well with a lot of game. Most commercial rhubarb is grown around Wakefield in Yorkshire where it is produced in huge, warm forcing sheds that exclude all light so that the rhubarb is rosy-pink, tender and sweet. Some years ago, BBC's *Food Programme* went there and actually managed to record the sound of a crinkled leaf unfurling in the darkness – a memorable piece of radio.

The venison can be roasted and served pink and juicy, or braised till well-done. See pages 138-9. The type of rhubarb and rowan jelly used alters the sweet/tart balance, so if adjustment at the end is necessary, add lemon juice if it is insipid or sugar if too tart. The stock should be additive-free and the richer it is (see p.48), the better the sauce will be. Don't use a cast iron pan for this recipe as the acid in the rhubarb corrodes it and makes the sauce taste metallic.

1–1.5 kg (2–3 lb) rolled haunch

450 g (1 lb) rhubarb

300 ml (¹/₂ pt) concentrated venison or beef stock

1–2 tablespoons rowan jelly

Small pinch of ground ginger (optional)

Salt, pepper, sugar, lemon juice to taste

Brown the venison, and roast it to taste using the guide on p.138 for pink, or p.139 for well-done.

Chop the rhubarb and boil it with the stock until pulped. Rub it through a sieve and return the smooth purée to the pan. If it is too thin, boil it till thicker. Dissolve the rowan jelly in this purée, season with salt and pepper, and a tiny pinch of ginger if wished, then adjust the taste with sugar and/or lemon juice if necessary. This makes quite a thick, rich sauce. After the venison has rested or been braised, there will be some precious juices which should be added to the sauce before serving.

Spice-rubbed venison with lime risotto

Serves 4

You can use any combination of spices you fancy – see p.52 for other suggestions, but these ones go well with the lime risotto. To make it into a winter risotto, use pearl barley instead of rice, and wintry vegetables like celery, carrots and red peppers.

750–900 g (1½–2 lb) venison haunch, saddle or loin

3 tablespoons coarsely chopped fresh coriander

For the spice rub

3 cardamon pods

½ teaspoon green peppercorns

½ teaspoon freshly grated nutmeg

1 teaspoon coriander seeds

For the lime risotto

1-2 unwaxed limes

4 shallots, chopped

100 g (4 oz) butter

300 g (11 oz) risotto rice

200 ml (⅓ pt) dry white wine

1 litre (1½ pts) venison beef or chicken stock

300 g (11 oz) asparagus spears

100 g (4 oz) baby broad beans

100 g (4 oz) baby peas

80 g (3 oz) grated Parmesan (optional)

Heat up a pan without any oil and toast the spices for 3–4 minutes. Cool, then grind coarsely. Roll the venison in the spices, wrap it in clingfilm and leave for 2 hours.

Check the cooking times for your joint on p.137 so that you start to cook it at the right time. If you prefer milder spices, scrape most of them off before cooking; for a more spicy flavour leave them on.

The risotto will take 30-40 minutes to cook. Grate the zest off the limes and reserve. Trim the asparagus and chop into 2 cm (1 in) lengths. Heat up the stock. Melt the butter in a large, deep frying pan, and gently fry the shallots till transparent. Add the rice and fry it gently for five minutes, then add the wine and the lime juice. Increase the heat and add a quarter of the stock and the lower ends of the chopped asparagus. Once it has been absorbed, add another quarter and keep stirring.

When the third quarter of stock is added, put in the middle parts of the asparagus. With the final quarter of stock add the broad beans, peas, asparagus tips, and lime zest. Add salt, pepper, and more lime zest ifwished. Finally, stir in the grated Parmesan if used – it makes the risotto more creamy but is not essential. Scatter the fresh coriander over the risotto before serving with the venison.

Roast saddle of venison with hollandaise sauce and thin gravy
Serves 8-10

This is the dish for the birthday celebration, for Christmas, New Year or some other festival – the ultimate roast venison. I make no apology for including the same sauce in both roast and steak sections. It would be too sad for it to be left out of either. You can, of course, use a lovely haunch joint instead. Use the cooking guidelines on p.137-9. The timing here is for a red deer saddle of about 12 cm (4¹/₂ inch) thickness. As explained on p.32, saddle is always a bone-in cut.

3.25 kg (7 lb) whole saddle (or 2 smaller ones)

Butter and oil for cooking

Good venison stock for gravy

Hollandaise sauce

6 tablespoons white wine vinegar

2 small shallots or 4 fat cloves garlic

4 egg yolks

350 g (12 oz) chilled butter

Salt and pepper

Roast the venison according to taste. While it cooks, make the gravy by adding the venison stock to the pan in which you browned the joint and boil it down until it is a nice deep brown. If it looks thin and flavourless, fry a chopped onion till deep brown, and add that to the stock. After the joint has rested, remove it to its serving dish and keep warm. Add the reduced stock to the roasting pan and incorporate all the juices, then season to taste and strain before serving. It is better to have a small amount of well-flavoured gravy than lots of poor gravy.

Allow about 20 minutes to make the hollandaise sauce. Make sure the butter is thoroughly chilled and cut into cubes. Put the wine vinegar and chopped shallot into a small pan. Boil until it has reduced to about a tablespoon, then scoop it all into a small heatproof bowl that will fit over the little pan. Put 3 cm (1¹/₄ inches) water into the pan and bring to simmering point. Place the bowl over the pan so that the steam not the water warms it, otherwise it will get too hot. Add the egg yolk and one cube of butter to the shallot and reduced vinegar, and stir with a wooden spoon to break the yolks.

It is important not to stop in the middle of making this sauce, for if the egg is overheated, it coagulates rather than thickens to give melted butter with scrambled egg in it. That is why the butter should be chilled. As soon as the first piece of butter starts to melt, keep stirring and add another. (If it happens alarmingly quickly, the bowl is getting too hot. Quickly take it off the water, throw in several pieces of cold butter and stir quickly before returning it to the pan.) Continue until nearly all the butter is melted and the sauce has thickened. If you need to leave it standing before serving, stop the cooking just before the sauce has completely thickened. Take the bowl off the steam and put it in a cold surface for a few minutes to cool the bowl and stop the cooking. Season, then keep it just warm (not hot) until you need it. It usually thickens up during this process.

Roasted saddle with chocolate-enriched sauce

Serves 4

This is inspired by John Wood's recipe for saddle of hare: an Italian tradition. The sauce was so dark and rich and mysterious that I adapted it for venison. Only a few hundred years ago, hare was also referred to as venison. Use a neatly trimmed up saddle from roe or muntjac, or trimmed loin from the larger species, otherwise adapt the cooking times. The ingredients list is long but if you don't have absolutely everything on the list it will still taste good, simply different. For example, if you don't have port, use red wine enriched with a tablespoon of redcurrant or rowan jelly instead. And if you don't enjoy presenting plated dishes to your friends, then don't. Serve it up any way you like – flavour is the important thing.

700 g (1^{1}/$_2$ lb) venison loin or 1 kg (2^{1}/$_4$ lb) saddle

250 g (8 oz) potato

250 g (8 oz) celeriac

2 carrots

1 small yellow-fleshed turnip

2 parsnips

Olive oil and/or butter

4 slices streaky smoked bacon or pancetta

3 cloves garlic, chopped

200 ml (7 fl oz) red wine

400 ml (^{3}/$_4$ pt) port

200 ml (7 fl oz) concentrated venison stock

2 sprigs rosemary

2 sprigs thyme

Preheat the oven to Gas 8, 230ºC, 450 ºF. Boil the potatoes, adding the celeriac after five minutes. When cooked, drain and mash them together with a little oil or butter and keep aside, covered, in a warm place. Peel and dice the carrots, turnip and parsnip. Brush some olive oil onto them, then roast or grill them, turning them once to brown evenly. Meanwhile, brown the loin quickly all over, remove from the frying pan and, when cool enough to handle, wrap the four bacon slices round it (secure with cocktail sticks) leaving three narrow gaps so that it can be cut into four portions later.

Add the garlic, red wine and port to the browned vegetables and reduce by a third, then add the stock, rosemary, and thyme. Place the loin or saddle on top and roast in the hot oven for 8–15 minutes according to thickness (see p.137). When the venison is ready to rest, remove it and keep it in a warm place to relax. Drain the sauce off the vegetables, squeezing them well, then reduce the sauce until syrupy and melt the chocolate into it. Add salt and pepper to taste.

Black pepper

80 g (3 oz) 70% dark chocolate

4 small sprigs each of fresh thyme and rosemary to garnish

To serve, mix the warm mashed potato and celeriac, season, and divide into four servings. For a smart presentation, press the potato/celeriac into large round cakes, using pastry cutters, in the centre of each plate. Slice the venison into four portions, each wrapped in its bacon slice, and place one onto each round of potato, rosy side uppermost. Decorate with the thyme and rosemary sprigs and spoon the deep dark sauce round the edge.

Venison Wellington (Venison en croûte)

Serves 4

This is a wonderful classic: we served it at our daughter's wedding, giving each of the nineteen tables its own individual joint to carve, which made a good ice-breaker. The only tricky part is the timing – it's a balancing act between not overcooking the venison and yet allowing the pastry to cook – a particularly good use for a meat thermometer. I have used both haunch and loin. The meat should be cut into an even log shape of about 4–5cm (1½–2 inches) minimum diameter, so if using roe or small fallow loins, bind two together so they stay in place during the initial roasting – remove the ties before wrapping them in pastry. Remove every scrap of silver skin from the meat so it doesn't curl up when cooking. The two most favoured fillings are finely chopped mushrooms or a smooth pâté. I have added a couple more underneath. If you can mix wild mushrooms with the plain ones, so much the better. Truffles are wasted here, but a few drops of truffle-flavoured brandy or oil add extra wooded tones.

900 g (2 lb) venison loin or haunch

Butter, oil

2 cloves garlic

350 g (12 oz) mushrooms/fungi

80 g (3 oz) butter

Salt, black pepper

2 tablespoons parsley, chopped

1 tablespoon fresh thyme leaves

450 g (1 lb) puff pastry

Beaten egg to glaze

Heat some butter and oil in a large frying pan and thoroughly brown the meat on all four sides, keeping it nice and flat. Then either roast it in a hot oven (Gas 8, 230ºC, 450ºF) for 5 minutes, or reduce the heat in the frying pan and keep turning the meat for 5 minutes. Remove and allow it to cool completely (45–60 minutes).

Make the mushroom filling by chopping the garlic and mushrooms finely. Heat the butter in the pan you browned the meat in, and add the garlic, and the minute it starts to brown, add the mushrooms. Allow these to cook and reduce until they are looking buttery rather than watery. Season with salt and pepper, and stir in the parsley and thyme. Allow this to cool as well.

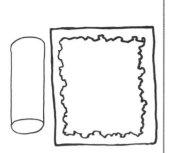

1.. Roll out pastry big enough to cover meat and overlap.

Brush edges with egg and spread out mushroom paté over pastry

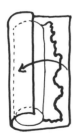

2. Fold first edge over meat

Preheat the oven to Gas 7, 220°C, 425°F. Roll out the pastry to 0.5 cm ($^1/_4$ inch) in a rectangle big enough to wrap your joint – it needs to overlap by 3cm ($1^1/_2$ inches) and to cover the ends. Brush a band 3 cm ($1^1/_2$ inches +) round the edge of the pastry with beaten egg. Spread the mushroom mixture over the rest of it (see fig. 1). Then wrap the meat in the pastry (see figs. 2,3,4). Turn the meat so that the sealed edge is underneath (see fig. 5). Seal the ends like a parcel, removing excess pastry, and press it firmly all over to make sure it is well sealed (see fig.6).

Decorate the top if wished, and glaze with the remaining egg. (If preparing in advance, don't glaze the pastry till you are ready to cook it because if it dries hard it prevents the pastry from rising). Insert the meat thermometer in one end. Bake in the oven for 15 minutes, or until the pastry is golden and puffed. Then reduce the heat to moderate (Gas 3, 160°C, 325°F) and cook for another 10–15 minutes, depending on the thickness of the meat and the degree of rare-medium desired. Your meat thermometer will tell you when it is perfect.

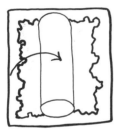

3. Fold second edge over meat so that it overlaps

4. Press edge to seal

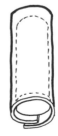

5. Turn it over so seal is underneath

6. Fold edges to seal (remove excess pastry). Insert meat thermometer

Venison en croûte with smooth pâté

Replace the mushroom mixture in the main recipe with 350 g (12 oz) of smooth liver pâté. Ideally it would be venison pâté (see recipe on p.214), but any really good one will do.

Venison en croûte with juniper and coriander

Replace the mushroom mixture in the main recipe with a mixture of: 2 onions and 2 cloves of garlic, finely chopped and gently softened till golden, 2 teaspoons of juniper berries and 2 teaspoons coriander seeds, all finely crushed; 1 tablespoon really well-flavoured oil. Mix all the ingredients and spread the mixture over the pastry and proceed as above.

Venison en croûte with green herbs and horseradish

Replace the mushroom mixture in the main recipe with the following, all chopped finely: 1 small onion, 1 clove garlic, a handful of spinach leaves, a handful of parsley and a handful of pungent herbs (rosemary, oregano, thyme, lovage, etc). Cook the onion and garlic in butter till soft and golden, then add the spinach, parsley and herbs and allow them to wilt and reduce. Then add 3 tablespoons double cream and 1 whisked egg. Stir until it starts to thicken, then allow it to cool before spreading on the pastry. When this has cooked under the pastry, it forms a herb-flavoured curd. Serve with horseradish sauce.

Venison in an oatmeal, garlic and juniper crust

Serves 4

This punchy version suits hungry people who have been out all day; it has remained a favourite with us. All meat cooked in pastry needs plenty of gravy or sauce to go with it (try the recipe on p.150) and choose vegetables that are juicy rather than starchy. The crust should be as thin as possible so that the top is crisp without overcooking the inside. The oatmeal pastry is a little fragile to handle but is worth the effort.

The cooking times here are calculated for loin with a cross-section of about 8 x 5 cm (3 x 2 inches). If using roe deer loin you may need to tie two pieces of loin together to make a plump enough piece of meat to prevent overcooking. A slim log-shaped piece of rolled haunch will do too – remove all strings before rolling it into the crust. A meat thermometer helps enormously.

650 g (1½ lb) venison loin or slim boneless haunch

Butter/oil for browning

Oatmeal crust

150 g (6 oz) plain flour

80 g (3 oz) medium oatmeal

40 g (1½ oz) butter

40 g (1½ oz) lard

2 plump cloves garlic, crushed or chopped finely

1 teaspoon juniper berries, crushed finely

Beaten egg to glaze

Heat butter and oil till starting to colour and fry the meat all over until nicely browned. Remove it from the pan onto a cold plate and leave to cool completely. Once the joint has cooled down, remove any strings from the meat.

Preheat the oven to Gas 8, 230ºC, 450ºF. Mix the flour and oatmeal and rub in the butter and lard, then the crushed garlic and juniper berries. Make a workable dough using the minimum water you can manage. Roll out thinly to 0.5 cm (¼ inch). Working carefully to avoid cracking the crust, completely encase the cold meat ensuring the join is underneath. If there should be any small cracks, pinch them together with your fingers. Brush with beaten egg to seal it, and decorate if wished. Cook in the hot oven until the crust is crisp and pale golden (15–20 minutes), then rest it for another 10 minutes.

Blackened rack of venison with gratin of fennel

Serves 4

So far as I am concerned, the combination of creamy fennel gratin and roast venison is a marriage made in heaven. You can serve it with any roast, steak or casserole, but I have chosen a rack this time for a treat. A rack is the forward part of a saddle that has been split down the backbone, i.e. a row of chops joined together. For four people you want an eight-rib rack off large deer or two eight-rib racks off small deer. Remove the chine bone so that only the rib bones remain. When carving a rack from a smaller deer, slice between every other rib to make thicker portions. The cheese for the gratin can be Parmesan, grana panada, Gruyère or mature Cheddar.

Approximately 800 g (1¾ lb) venison rack

1 tablespoon thick balsamic vinegar

2 tablespoon soy sauce

2 teaspoons clear honey

4 shallots, finely chopped

2 bay leaves

1 teaspoon juniper berries, crushed

½ teaspoon red peppercorns, crushed

600 ml (1 pt) strong venison stock

Salt and pepper

Butter/oil for browning

Mix together the balsamic, soy sauce and honey and rub this mixture into the meat. Allow it to steep for 2–3 hours before cooking it. In the meantime, make the gravy. If your stock is very rich, then it may only need reducing and seasoning. If it is less rich, brown the shallots, add the bay leaves, juniper and peppercorns and cook for a minute or two, then pour the stock over them. Boil until reduced by half, then strain into a clean pan. Season to taste. If it is still not strong enough, add, very cautiously, a little of the honey/soy mixture.

To make the gratin, slice the fennel thinly, barely cover with water and boil for a few minutes until it is nearly tender. Drain off the water and keep this. Melt the butter in a pan and stir in the flour, allowing it to cook but not brown. Add the fennel water bit by bit, beating well to prevent lumps forming. When it is a smooth creamy consistency allow it to cook gently for about 10 minutes to cook the flour. Season to taste, then stir in the cooked fennel, pour it into a shallow ovenproof dish, and sprinkle the cheese on the

For the fennel gratin

3 heads bulb (Florence) fennel

30 g (1 oz) butter

1 heaped tablespoon flour

80 g (3 oz) cheese, grated

top. Bake in a hot oven (Gas 7, 220°C, 425°F) for about 15 minutes until the top is well browned.

To cook the venison, remove it from its marinade and pat dry. Sear it in a hot roasting pan with butter and oil, then roast it in a hot oven (Gas 7, 220°C, 425°F) for 10 minutes for a large rack and 5 minutes for small ones. Then remove to a warm oven to rest for a further 10 minutes or until the meat thermometer reads 50–55°C (125–130°F). The meat should have a well-blackened outside and bright rosy-red interior. Serve with the gravy and gratin of fennel.

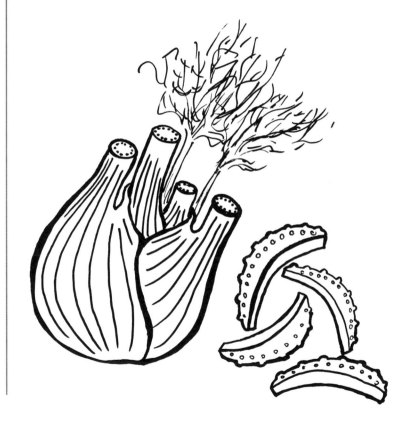

Roast haunch of venison with roast figs and sauce grand veneur
Serves 6

Sauce Grand Veneur is the classic French sauce for roast venison: it is also called Sauce Chasseur. Both mean the hunter's sauce, though the term veneur is usually reserved for red deer. However, roe deer are favoured by French chefs, probably because they are not chased around so much before shooting as red deer often are in France. If the haunch is marinated, then usually some is added to the sauce; it should be slightly piquant with a sweetness added by the redcurrant jelly. The secret of making a really velvety sauce is the stock. If it is made with shin bones, it will have plenty of gelatine. The haunch is roasted nice and pink, and often served with little pastry boats filled with mushroom purée.

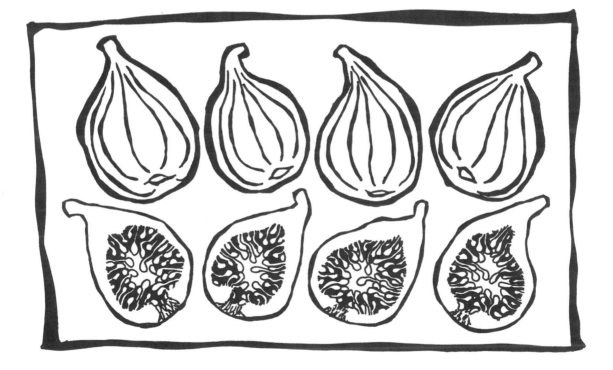

2 kg (4¹/₂ lb) haunch on the bone

Marinade (optional - see chapter 4)

Butter/oil

8 figs

For the sauce

2 carrots, chopped

2 onions, chopped

1 stick celery, chopped

75 g (3 oz) butter

2 tablespoons flour

150 ml (¹/₄ pt) white wine

100 ml wine vinegar

1.2 litres (2 pts) good stock

1 bouquet garni

1 tablespoon redcurrant jelly

Salt

Pinch of cayenne pepper

Crème fraîche (optional)

Lemon juice (if needed)

The joint can be marinated if wished (see chapter 4) for a couple of days. When ready to cook it, lift the haunch from its marinade and pat dry. Heat some butter/oil in a large pan and brown the joint all over. Part-roast it in a hot oven (Gas 8, 450ºF, 230ºC) then rest in a cool oven until medium rare – see p.138.

To make the sauce, gently soften and brown the carrots, onions and celery in a little oil. In another pan make a roux with the butter and flour and cook gently till it is turning brown. Stir the wine and wine vinegar into the roux and add the browned vegetables. Add the stock and the bouquet garni and 300 ml (¹/₂ pt) of the marinade if used, and let the stock simmer very gently for two hours. Strain the sauce into another pan and add the redcurrant jelly, some salt and the cayenne pepper. If necessary, reduce to 600 ml (1 pt). You may need to adjust the sweet/tart balance using either more jelly or some lemon juice. Some people like to stir in some crème fraîche just before serving. The sauce should be velvety smooth.

To cook the figs, cut in half lengthways, brush with oil, and roast in a hot oven or under the grill for 10–15 minutes. Serve with the venison and its sauce.

Sticky-braised venison with grilled vegetables
Serves 6

A sticky black coating makes a contrast with the colourful vegetables. The joint is turned around in the liquid as it cooks to help the dark juices to form their delicious surface. Serve with steamed spinach drizzled with walnut oil and scattered with toasted pine nuts.

2 kg (4¹/₂ lb) venison haunch or shoulder

Butter, lard or bacon fat to lard

Dark coating sauce

1 litre (1³/₄ pts) mango juice

2 tablespoons black treacle

1 tablespoon dark soy sauce

1 tablespoon honey

1 tablespoon wholegrain mustard

4 cloves garlic, crushed

1 teaspoon coriander seed, crushed

Small pinch of ground cloves

Thyme, bay, sage

2 teaspoons grated ginger

Roast vegetables

900 g (2 lb) mixed vegetables, e.g. red onions, bulb fennel, aubergine, courgettes, celeriac, parsnip, asparagus

Olive or grapeseed oil

Handful of fresh basil or marjoram

Lard the joint (see p.140), then brown it in a frying pan. Remove the joint to an ovenproof dish that neatly holds it. Mix together all the sauce ingredients in a pan, bring to the boil and pour them over the joint. Cook in a medium oven (Gas 4, 180ºC, 350ºF) for 2¹/₂– 3 hours or until tender, turning the meat over every half hour or so. If the bottom is getting dry, add a splash of water. When the meat is cooked, there should be some rich, dark gravy to accompany it. Check the seasoning and add salt, pepper or more mango juice to taste.

While the meat cooks, prepare the vegetables. Peel and quarter the onions and flake them into 'petals'. Do the same with the bulb fennel. Cut the rest into bite-sized chunks and toss them in oil. When the meat is cooked, fry or grill the vegetables swiftly until just cooked and nicely coloured. Serve at once, scattered with the fresh herbs.

Duo of fillet and ossobuco with carrot and celeriac mash
Serves 4

This is the sort of dish you love or loathe. I enjoy the contrast between the rich gelatinous ossobuco and the pink and juicy fillet, tender but with a bit more bite. The quickly cooked piece can either be *filet mignon* from red deer, a loin fillet from the small species, or a slim single muscle from the haunch.

4 slices venison ossobuco

375 g (12 oz) whole venison *filet mignon* or haunch fillet

500 g (1 lb+) mix of onion, carrot, parsnip, chopped

250 g (8 oz) stoneless prunes, chopped

6 juniper berries

300 ml (½ pt) red wine

400 ml (¾ pt) strong venison stock

2 tablespoons rowan or other tart jelly

400 g (14 oz) carrots

400 g (14 oz) celeriac

Butter

Brown the ossobuco and mixed vegetables, then place in a casserole dish with the chopped prunes, crushed juniper berries, the red wine, the stock and the jelly. Bring to simmering, then cook at Gas 3, 160º, 325ºF till tender (about 4-5 hours). Then strain off the sauce and reduce till syrupy. Season and reserve, and keep the ossobuco covered and warm.

Boil the carrots and celeriac together, drain and mash with some butter. Season and keep warm.

Heat the oven to Gas 8, 230ºC, 450ºF. Brown the fillet in butter so that it is really crisp on the outside, roast for 5 minutes, then leave to rest for 6–7 minutes. Slice the fillet into medallions. Put some carrot and celeriac mash in the centre of each plate, arrange the loin slices on top, place a piece of ossobuco beside it, and add the rich, dark sauce.

Braised haunch of venison with Hungarian red cabbage

Serves 8

Red cabbage is one of the few brassicas that goes well with venison (spring greens and kale are the others). It can be prepared in advance or cooked while the meat is braising. I would also serve good creamy mashed potato with some crushed juniper berries stirred though it.

2.5–3 kg (6–7 lb) bone-in haunch

Fat for larding

10 cloves garlic (optional)

600 ml (1 pt) sweet stout or wine

150 ml (5 fl oz) smetana (sour cream)

Sweet paprika

For the red cabbage

2 firm heads red cabbage, shredded

80 g (3 oz) smoked bacon, diced

Lard for frying

1 large onion, chopped

2 cloves garlic, crushed

1 tablespoon caraway seed

1 teaspoon salt

1/2 teaspoon cayenne pepper or hot paprika

2 large ripe apples, peeled and chopped

To make the red cabbage, brown the bacon pieces in a large pan till golden brown. Add the onions and fry gently till they are translucent. Add the cabbage, garlic, caraway seed and 120 ml (4 fl oz) water. Cover, and cook till the cabbage starts to soften (about 8–10 minutes). Add the salt, the cayenne pepper or hot paprika, the apples, lemon, red wine and vinegar. Cover, and cook for another 10 minutes. Then add the honey, and turn the heat down very low to prevent burning. After half an hour, check the level of liquid. If the cabbage is well covered with liquid, remove the lid and allow it to reduce till it is just able to bubble gently. Now take out the lemon halves and taste the cabbage. Add about 2 teaspoons of brown sugar if necessary to achieve the right sweet/sour balance. Cover, and continue cooking until the cabbage has reduced to about one-third of its original bulk, by which time the apple will have dissolved completely. Adjust the salt if necessary before serving.

To cook the haunch, brown it quickly in a large frying pan or under the grill. Let it cool before larding with the fat (and garlic if used) as described on pages 133-4. Put it in a deep dish and add the stout or wine. Cover the dish and cook in a medium low oven (Gas 3, 300ºF, 150ºC) for 2–3 hours. During this time, baste the joint from time to time with the cooking liquid, and top it up with

1 lemon, halved

2 large glasses red wine

3 tablespoons wine vinegar

4 tablepoons honey

Brown sugar, to taste

water if necessary. When the joint is cooked, remove it to a warm serving dish and keep it covered so that it doesn't dry out. Skim fat off the gravy, strain it and boil it down to reduce to half. Stir in the sweet paprika and sour cream, and season to taste. Serve with the red cabbage.

Shoulder of venison with barley risotto

Serves 4-6

> In 1460, the chef John Russell wrote, *'Fatt venesoun with frumenty hit is a gay plesewre your souerayne to serve with in season to his honowre.'*

Risotto is the modern equivalent of frumenty – a universal favourite in medieval times before potatoes had arrived to fill hungry stomachs. Frumenty is slowly simmered whole grains, usually of wheat, but it can also be made from pearl barley. Both are good, the slow cooking turning them into a gelatinous foil to the venison.

If your venison is young and tender, use the shoulder. If it is from older beasts, use the haunch. Light ale can be used instead of stock or water, if wished. I sometimes use one brewed with gooseberries that gives a nice tingle.

1 kg (2¼ lb) rolled venison shoulder or haunch

Fat for larding

2 onions, chopped

4 sticks celery, chopped

750 ml (1¼ pt) stock or ale

180 g (6 oz) pearl barley or wheat grains

Seasoning

Lard the venison (see page 140). Heat up some oil or fat in a fireproof dish and brown the meat well all over. Remove it, add the vegetables and brown them as well. Add the stock or ale and dissolve the brownings on the bottom of the dish. Rinse the pearl barley or wheat and stir it into the liquid. Add a good pinch of salt and some black pepper. Replace the meat and nestle it into the grains.

Bring to a slow simmer, cover the dish and then either keep it simmering over the stove top or else transfer it to a medium low oven (Gas 3, 160ºC, 325ºF) for 2–3 hours or until the meat is tender and the grains have swelled. Check the liquid after about 1½ hours in case it needs topping up, especially if cooking on the stove top, and stir the grains to make sure they are not sticking on the bottom of the dish.

9. Comfort food: slow-cooked venison

Stewing, braising, venison pies

9. Comfort food: slow-cooked venison

Stewing, braising, venison pies

This section sums up many peoples' perception of venison: slowly cooked, cold-weather, comfort food. It is here that you find the greatest variety of flavours, from deep dark spicy ones to light clear broths; from simple, homely dishes to the sumptuous flavour and texture of long-simmered walnuts and pomegranate. Slow-cooked joints are dealt with in the roasting section; this one deals with diced venison and smaller cuts like shanks or ossobuco.

There are four basic ways to cook venison stews. They can be cooked in a medium to slow oven, or simmered very gently on the stove-top – a method I prefer for tough cuts like shanks. You can also use a slow cooker (use beef guidelines) or you can speed things up with a pressure cooker. Venison shoulder cooks approximately 2 minutes more quickly than beef guidelines in a pressure cooker, though old venison or shin could need 2 minutes more.

I am often asked what to serve with venison. Many of the recipes include accompaniments, most will go equally well with other recipes. Here are some general suggestions for slow cooked dishes:

CRISP TEXTURES Precooked potatoes fried to dark brown in lovely oil or duck fat; also roast potatoes and home-made chips (French fries), hasselback potatoes (p.172); rösti (p.182); fried spätzli (p.122); fried dumplings (p.180); root vegetables roasted and almost blackened (p.162); toasted pine nuts or sliced almonds scattered over vegetables like steamed spinach or curly kale.

CREAMY, SUCCULENT OR MOIST TEXTURES Mashed potatoes, especially with herbs or crushed spices mashed into it: try juniper berries, saffron, fresh horseradish, fresh rosemary, lovage or thyme; carrots mashed with celeriac or parsnips, carrot purée; mushrooms, potatoes cooked as a gratin dauphinoise (p.178); herb dumplings cooked in the stew; vegetables cooked in a white (béchamel) or light cheese sauce, especially bulb fennel; aubergines, either stewed or fried in batter; braised chicory or braised celery.

Rich 'marinated' venison casserole

Serves 4-6

Marinade flavours lend great richness to slowly cooked dishes. However, marinating beforehand is unnecessary here since the long, slow cooking tenderises the meat and brings out the flavours. Also, you don't have to pat each individual chunk dry before browning it. See chapter 4 for more about marinating and other marinade recipes. Serve this with roasted root vegetables on p.162 or mashed root vegetables (p.172).

900 g (2 lbs) diced venison shoulder

2 medium onions

4 sticks of celery, chopped

Butter

$^1/_2$ bottle red wine

2 tablespoons mild wine vinegar

2 tablespoons rowan jelly

2 tablespoons olive oil

1 teaspoon ground ginger

1 teaspoon ground nutmeg

$^1/_2$ teaspoon ground black pepper

12 juniper berries, crushed

225 g (8 oz) mushrooms, cubed

Salt to taste

Dice the onions and celery and soften them in butter. Remove them to a casserole. Turn up the heat and brown the diced venison in batches, making sure it browns quickly all over. Add the meat to the casserole along with all the other ingredients except the mushrooms. Bring to simmering point, cover and cook in a medium oven (Gas 5, 190°C, 375°F) for $1^1/_2$ hours. Add the mushrooms and cook for a further $^1/_2$ hour; even longer and more slowly if the venison is from an old animal. Add salt to taste at the end. It improves by being kept till the next day.

Tagine of venison

Serves 4

A tagine is both the name of the recipe and the name of the vessel in which it is slowly cooked in North Africa: an earthenware dish with a conical lid specially designed to conserve every drip of moisture so precious in a dry country. An ordinary lidded casserole dish can also be used. Venison makes a particularly good tagine to enjoy in the summer as well as in winter. You may of course use venison shoulder for this dish but it needs longer to cook. Although I prefer the texture and bright colour of dried apricots, destoned prunes may be successfully substituted or added as well. If you haven't presoaked the fruit add it at the beginning of the cooking process.

You could write a book about *ras-el-hanout*, the spices for tagine. Some recipes claim medicinal and aphrodisiac properties in addition to their culinary ones since they increase circulation by warming the blood. Recipes include anything from eight to thirty different spices, the common denominators being cinnamon, chilli pepper, cumin seed, coriander, cloves, ginger, nutmeg and turmeric. So there is no correct recipe – the more spices you use the more complex the flavour and perfume will be, and if you dislike a particular spice, leave it out. Salted lemons and limes are common ingredients in the Middle East and lend subtlety to lots of dishes. To make some, pack lemon slices into a jar with lots of coarse sea salt between the layers and leave for a few weeks until they produce a wonderful salty 'jam'. It keeps forever.

700 g (1¹/₂ lb) venison haunch, trimmed and cubed

1 large onion, chopped

2 tablespoons olive oil

1 red pepper, deseeded and cut into chunks

¹/₂ head of garlic cloves, peeled and halved

Heat the oil in a pan and toss the onion and meat in it till a little brown. Add the red pepper and garlic and then the spices and fry them too for a minute. Add enough water to cover, bring to simmering point and either simmer gently or cook in a medium oven (Gas 5, 190°C, 375°F) for about an hour. Then add the apricots and cook for a further ¹/₂ hour or until the meat is tender. Add preserved lemon or salt to taste.

1 teaspoon cumin

1 teaspoon ground ginger

1 teaspoon turmeric

1 teaspoon nutmeg

¹/₂ teaspoon ground
coriander seed

¹/₂ teaspoon cinnamon

¹/₂ teaspoon saffron

¹/₂ teaspoon ground black
pepper

¹/₄ teaspoon chilli powder

¹/₄ teaspoon ground cloves

125 g (4 oz or 12) dried
apricots, presoaked

2 slices of chopped salted
lemon (optional)

Handful of fresh parsley,
chopped

Handful of fresh coriander,
chopped

Couscous

300 g (10 oz) couscous

2 tablespoons oil

300 ml (¹/₂ pt) water

To cook the couscous, heat the oil in a saucepan and fry the couscous till just beginning to brown. This gives a nutty flavour and prevents it sticking together. Then add the water, though be careful as it will spit. Withdraw from the heat and cover for 3–4 minutes until the water is taken up, stirring the couscous to fluff it up. Serve with the tagine, adding the freshly chopped herbs just before serving.

Venison ossobuco, hasselback potatoes and carrot and fennel mash
Serves 4

Ossobuco is a thick slice of shin that include the bone. It is one of the toughest parts of any animal and requires very long slow cooking. Try and hurry it up and you will end up with a texture akin to knicker elastic or worse. Leave it to simmer for hours though, and the cartilaginous parts turn into a heavenly jelly which, with the bone marrow, lubricates the meat to produce a voluptuous dish with a silky sauce. This is one of the occasions when it pays to have lots of ingredients to produce a dark, rich, sauce. Like oxtail, slices of shin vary greatly in size. This dish may also be made as a casserole using 65g (1½ lbs) diced venison shoulder or shin but the cooking time for shoulder can be reduced to 2–2½ hours.

1 kg (2¼ lbs) venison ossobuco cut into 8 or 12 slices

250 g (8 oz) diced root vegetables (carrot, parsnip, turnip, celeriac)

Butter or oil

1 large onion

3 cloves garlic

250 g (8 oz) stoned plums, prunes or apricots

300 ml (½ pt) red wine

150 ml (¼ pt) port or red vermouth

150 ml (¼ pt) stock or water

1 teaspoon balsamic vinegar

2 tablespoons rowan or redcurrant jelly

8 juniper berries, crushed

Brown the root vegetables, onion and garlic, and place in a large casserole dish. Brown the slices of ossobuco over a fierce heat and add them to the casserole with the plums, red wine, port, stock, balsamic vinegar, jelly, crushed juniper berries, spices and fresh herbs. Bring to simmering point in a hot oven, then cover tightly and cook very slowly indeed at a low temperature (Gas 3, 160°C, 325°F) till tender, about 4 hours.

Allow 1½ hours to prepare and cook the potatoes. Either peel, or scrub them thoroughly. Sit each potato in a deep wooden spoon. Then, with a sharp knife, make cuts about 5 mm (¼ inch) wide all the way along, as though you were partially slicing a loaf of bread. Continue with the rest of the potatoes. Smear the tops with butter and/or drizzle with oil, sprinkle with sea salt and grind some pepper over them. Bake in a fairly hot oven (Gas 6, 200° C, 400°F) for about ¾ – 1 hour depending on size. When done, the potatoes will have opened out slightly, like a fan, crisp on top and moist in the centre.

½ teaspoon ground nutmeg

½ teaspoon ground ginger

Bunch of fresh herbs (thyme, fennel, rosemary)

Hasselback potatoes

4 large or 8 medium potatoes

Butter or oil

Coarse ground or flaked sea salt

Pepper

Carrot and fennel mash

650 g (1½ lbs) carrots

1 tablespoon butter

150 ml (¼ pt) cream

Pinch of coriander or caraway seeds

Handful of fresh fennel

Seasoning

While these cook, make the carrot mash. Peel and chop the carrots, boil for about 20 minutes till soft, then mash them coarsely with the butter and cream. Season with salt and pepper, and stir in the fresh fennel leaves, snipped finely. Keep warm.

When the ossobuco is cooked, carefully remove the slices and divide them between four warmed plates. Strain the sauce from the vegetables, check its seasoning and spoon it round the meat. Serve with the hasselback potatoes and carrot mash.

Autumnal venison casserole

Serves 20–25 or 4–6

A casserole is an easy way of feeding large numbers of people, and this is a lovely rich one that we make for large gatherings of friends after searching the autumn woodlands for wild fungi. I have put the larger quantity for 20 on the left hand side. On the right are the ingredients for 4–6 people. You can use the formula to multiply up other recipes.

Dried mushrooms give an intense flavour to the stew – if they are fresh use more. Dried fungi are expensive, so buy the cheaper broken pieces, which are perfect here. I am a great tea drinker and make my own blend with Lapsang Souchong. There is always a pot of tea standing by the stove, ready to add a smoky, tannic element to sauces, and in casseroles it adds another layer to a complex flavour. If making tea seems a fiddle just to enhance a casserole, then leave it out and use a drop more wine.

For 20 people		*For 4–6 people*
3 kg (7 lb)	Diced venison shoulder or haunch	1 kg (2 $\frac{1}{4}$ lb)
	Seasoned flour	
	Butter/oil	
100 g (4 oz)	Dried fungi (shitake, ceps, etc)	30 g (1–2 oz)
12	smallish onions	4
12	carrots	4
1 head	celery	3 stalks
1 litre (1$\frac{1}{2}$ bottles)	red wine	350 ml ($\frac{1}{2}$ bottle)
300 ml ($\frac{1}{2}$ pint)	strong Lapsang Souchon tea	100 ml (4 fl oz)
2 tablespoons	balsamic vinegar	3 teaspoons
2 tablespoons	rich soy sauce	3 teaspoons
1 tablespoon	juniper berries, crushed	10
	Salt and pepper	

Soak the dried fungi in water as directed, if anything adding more rather than less water. They take at least 30 minutes to reconstitute; keep them under water with a saucer and stir them about once or twice. Add this flavoured water to the casserole.

Dust the diced venison in seasoned flour and brown quickly in small batches, removing it to a casserole. For the larger quantity you will need about 12 litres (20 pints) capacity. Brown the onions, carrots and celery. (If frying space is at a premium, toss these in oil and brown them in the oven or under the grill.) Add these to the cooking pot. Swill out the brownings in the pan with a little water.

Stir in all the other ingredients, chopping the reconstituted fungi if necessary. Bring to simmering point. Cook slowly, either on the stove top if your pot is too big for the oven, or in a medium oven (Gas 5, 190°C, 375°F), for 2–3 hours. Top up with water or extra wine if necessary. If cooking on the stove top, stir from time to time, and top up with water if necessary so that it doesn't stick to the base of the pot. Add the final salt and pepper seasoning at the end.

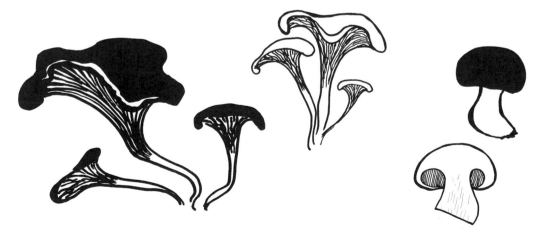

Kiran's venison curry

Serves 4-6

Lots of people ask Kiran Singh Sirah, a Glasgow based artist, for his curry recipe. A great teacher and writer, he points out rightly that Indian cooking does not lend itself to exact amounts, it being more a question of personal preference and intuition. His recipe is from the Indian Punjab – it's a base that can be used with other meats or vegetables, so if you feel you would like more of something, or less, then follow your inclination. The important thing, says Kiran, is to cook it with love and enjoy the perfume and colours of the spices as they cook. He would not normally brown the meat first. His tip for coriander, if you do not use it often, is to buy a big bunch from an Asian grocer, wash it, pat it dry, and then store it in the freezer for future use.

900 g (2 lbs) diced venison

2 onions, finely chopped

Mustard seeds, large pinch

Cumin seeds, large pinch

Oil for frying

6 cloves garlic, finely chopped

1 green chilli, finely chopped

5 cm (2 in) fresh ginger, finely chopped

200 g (7 oz) tin chopped tomatoes

1 teaspoon garam masala

$\frac{1}{2}$ teaspoon turmeric powder

$\frac{1}{2}$ teaspoon of chilli powder

Salt to taste

$\frac{1}{2}$ glass red wine (optional)

2 medium potatoes, cubed (optional)

2 tablespoons fresh coriander

150 ml ($\frac{1}{4}$ pt) cream (optional)

Gently fry the onions, mustard seeds and cumin seeds. Add the garlic, chilli and ginger and continue frying for about 10 minutes over a low heat until the onions have turned reddish brown and the spices release their flavours. Add the tomatoes, the rest of the spices, and 1–2 teaspoons salt (to taste). Stir for 5 minutes, then add 100 ml (4 fl oz) of water, the red wine, and finally the venison.

Cover the pan and simmer gently for about 2 hours, stirring occasionally to stop it sticking. Add the cubed potatoes about halfway through. Right at the end, add the cream and coriander and serve with rice and/or Nan bread.

Pot-au-feu of roe venison with bulb fennel
Serves 6

The general perception of venison is rich dark meat, suited to robust flavours. However, many species, especially when young, can produce quite pale-fleshed meat well suited to more delicate treatment. Pot-au-feu is just that: meat and vegetables slowly simmered in a clear broth in a pot over the fire until tender. The meat can be all in one piece or cut into portions, and if you use shin rather than haunch or shoulder, it doesn't need larding. Some people serve the broth as a first course and the meat and vegetables afterwards. Bulb (Florence) fennel, as well as being gently cooked with the meat, is also lovely sliced and served raw, dressed only with walnut or olive oil, salt, pepper, and a few freshly shelled walnuts.

1.5 kg (3 lb) venison haunch or shoulder on the bone

100 g (4 oz) thick-cut pork belly or fatty bacon

Butter/oil for browning

2 large bulbs of fennel

3 large carrots

3 small Milan (white) turnips

6 tomatoes, peeled

Sprigs of rosemary, thyme, bay leaf

300 ml (¹/₂ pt) white wine (or 2 tablespoons white wine vinegar)

Black pepper and salt

Cut the belly pork into thick strips and freeze. Then use these strips to lard the venison thoroughly (see p.140). Brown it all over in a large pot. Peel the vegetables and cut them all into quarters, then add them to the pot with the herbs and the white wine or vinegar. Season with pepper. Add enough water to nearly cover the meat, then bring it slowly to the boil. Reduce the heat till it is barely simmering (or cook it in a slow oven) and cook gently like this for at least 3 hours, more if it is shoulder from an older animal. Right at the end, season with salt to taste. Any left over broth is useful stock for future use.

Dark-braised roe shanks with gratin dauphinoise

Serves 4

A roe deer shank gives one portion, a fallow deer shank at least two. Larger shanks are best sliced into ossobuco. The sinews turn into a fabulous jelly that makes them succulent beyond words. Use any combination of vegetables and liquid that takes your fancy – below is one suggestion for a very rich version, but they are also delicious very simply braised with just carrots and celery, and water as the liquid, like the pot-au-feu in the next recipe. The only necessity is to cook them slowly and for a long time – speed it up and you might as well try to chew car tyres.

Gratin dauphinoise goes well with venison. There are many versions of it, some with cheese on top, some without. Some use cream, some milk, some half and half, all of which work fine. And the garlic can be decreased if you don't like it too punchy. The most important thing so far as I am concerned is that the potatoes are waxy not floury. Charlotte, Nadine and (of course) Nicola are all good varieties.

4 x 350–500 g (12–16 oz) shanks or slices of shank

450 g (1 lb) diced onions, carrots, celery, parsnip

Butter/oil for browning

1 tablespoon rowan or redcurrant jelly

1 tablespoon tomato purée

300 ml (½ pt) orange juice

300 ml (½ pt) red wine

2 tablespoons soy sauce

2 teaspoons balsamic vinegar

1 teaspoon grated root ginger

Brown the vegetables and place them on the base of an ovenproof dish that neatly contains the shanks. Brown the shanks thoroughly but quickly. Place them, end-to-end, on top of the vegetables. Mix together the jelly, tomato purée, orange juice, red wine, soy sauce, balsamic vinegar, and spices, and pour this over the shanks, which should be at least half covered by the liquid. Cover the dish with tin foil or a lid, bring to simmering point in a hot oven (Gas 7, 220°C, 425°F) then turn it down to Gas 3, 160°C, 325°F, and cook very slowly for 4–5 hours. Alternatively, simmer very gently on the stove-top. Once or twice during the cooking, turn the shanks over so that both sides have been immersed in the juices. Top up the liquid if necessary half way through.

To make the gratin, peel and slice the potatoes thinly and rinse in cold water to remove excess starch. Butter a shallow dish and sprinkle half of the garlic over the base. Arrange the sliced potato

1 teaspoon ground nutmeg

1 teaspoon crushed juniper berries

For the gratin dauphinoise:

500 g (1 lb) waxy potatoes

25 g (1 oz) butter

2 cloves garlic, crushed

300 ml (¹/₂ pt) double cream

Ground nutmeg

Salt and pepper

50 g (2 oz) grated cheddar or Gruyère cheese

in layers, sprinkling a little salt, pepper and nutmeg between each layer, and adding the remaining garlic halfway through. Press the layers down to make the top as level as possible. Pour the cream gently over the top, season with pepper and a sprinkling of nutmeg, and scatter the cheese over the top. Bake in a moderate oven (Gas 6, 180ºC, 325ºF) for about 1¹/₂ hours. The top should be golden brown.

When the shanks are really tender, remove them to a serving dish, cover with tin foil and keep them warm. Add a splash of water to the vegetables in the ovenproof dish to dissolve all the flavoursome brownings round the edge. Then strain the juice through a sieve, pressing the vegetables to yield all the sauce. It should be a lovely deep brown and quite thick. If you wish, purée the vegetables and add them as thickening, but I prefer the clearer sauce. If it is a little too thin, boil it down quickly to reduce it to syrup. Check the seasoning – you may not need salt if the soy sauce was salty.

Venison 'goulash' with fried egg dumplings

Serves 8

According to George Lang, author of *The Cuisine of Hungary*, this is not a goulash (gulyás) but rather paprikás or pörkölt, because the only spice used in a true gulyás is caraway seed, and sour cream is not added. But most people think the essential flavours of goulash are paprika and sour cream. True gulyás can be traced back to the ninth century when roaming shepherds would cook their meat in an iron kettle with onions and caraway until it produced a rich broth. When they had eaten their fill, they spread the rest of the stew/soup out to dry, probably on their sheepskin capes. When they needed a quick meal, all they had to do was to boil up some of their dried meat. If they added more water it was gulyás soup, if less it became gulyás stew, a distinction which remains today in Hungary.

The paprika in this recipe should be hot and Hungarian – some mild paprika is little more than colouring. If you only have mild paprika, mix it with cayenne pepper and a little chilli powder. If you don't like hot spices, use sweet paprika with just a small amount of cayenne or chilli to add a tingle. Steamed spinach or kale is excellent with this.

Dumplings are staple fare all over Eastern Europe; there are dozens of different types made from potatoes, vegetables, meat or just plain flour, egg and seasoning, and then poached, boiled or fried. They can be as fluffy and light as a soufflé or, in the wrong hands, leaden. With a rich stew, I enjoy the contrasting texture of fried dumplings, but I have to admit that they are usually served just boiled.

1.5 kg (3 lbs) cubed venison shoulder or haunch

250 g (8 oz) smoked fatty bacon

2 large onions

1 heaped tablespoon Hungarian paprika

Tiny pinch of caraway seeds

2 green peppers, diced

To make the goulash, chop up the onion and bacon and fry them in a flameproof casserole till lightly browned. Remove them and brown the meat in the same pan (do this in batches so that it browns rather than stews). Replace all the meat, onions, and bacon and reheat them, then stir in the paprika, caraway seed, green peppers and garlic. Add a teaspoon of salt and 300 ml (½ pt) of water. Cook over a very low heat or in a medium to low oven (Gas 4, 180ºC, 350ºF) for 1½ hours. By this time the meat should be nearly cooked.

2 cloves garlic, crushed

1 teaspoon of salt

2 tablespoons smetana (sour cream)

1 tablespoon flour

2 ripe or tinned tomatoes, chopped

2 tablespoons double (heavy) cream

For the dumplings

50 g (2 oz) lard or beef dripping

200 g (7 oz) flour

1 teaspoon salt

2 eggs

Butter and oil or duck fat for frying

Mix the sour cream into the flour and whisk it into the stew. Add the tomatoes and cook for another 30 minutes or so, until the meat is cooked. Just before serving with the fried dumplings, whisk in the double cream.

While the meat cooks, make the dumplings. Rub or chop the fat into the flour with the salt. Lightly beat the eggs and mix them quickly into the flour, just enough to make sure everything is mixed; no more or they will toughen up. Leave the dough to rest for 10 minutes while you boil a large (4 litre/ 7pint) pan of salty water.

Using a dessertspoon, scoop out pieces of the dough and drop them into the boiling water. Do this as quickly as you can. When the dumplings bob up to the top, they are cooked. Remove them with a slotted spoon or small sieve, plunge them into cold water and then drain them. This stops them sticking together.

While the tomatoes and cream are cooking in the stew, fry the dumplings. Heat a large pan with a generous amount of butter and oil or duck fat till it is golden. Fry the dumplings till golden brown and crisp and serve at once with the goulash.

Civet of venison with carrot and celeriac rösti
Serves 6

A civet is a dark, rich stew, often, but not always, made with game and thickened with blood. Originally, it just meant that the dish contained cives (onions), and in France you still encounter a civet of almost anything – I have even been offered a civet of mackerel. The belly of pork adds that desirable fatty succulence. I think venison neck works well here as it has the most open texture. Shin works well too, but will need at least another hour's cooking. If your venison has a little fat on it, then don't trim it off – it will add to the richness. As with all rich stews, don't panic if you don't have every single ingredient. This 'rösti' is almost an omelette – the contrasting texture and flavours go very well with venison stew.

1 kg (2¹/₄ lbs) venison neck or shoulder steaks

Oil for browning

125 g (4 oz) fat belly pork or bacon pieces

125 g (4 oz) baby onions

1 large carrot, chopped

2 sticks celery, chopped

125 g (4 oz) mushrooms or wild fungi, chopped

3 large cloves garlic, chopped

¹/₂ bottle red wine

¹/₂ teaspoon juniper berries, crushed

Sprig of thyme + bay leaf, or a bouquet garni

For the rösti

200 g (7 oz) carrot, grated

200 g (7oz) celeriac, grated

1 dessertspoon grated ginger root

¹/₂ teaspoon caraway or fennel seed

2 small eggs

2 tablespoons milk

Butter and oil to fry

Chop the bacon into small chunks. Brown the bacon, baby onions, carrot and celery, doing this in batches if need be. Remove these to a fireproof casserole. Brown the venison and add that too, then soften the mushrooms and garlic in the same pan. Deglaze the pan with the red wine and scrape up all the brownings, and add this to the casserole with the juniper berries and herbs. Cover the dish and bring to simmering point. Then either simmer gently on the stove-top or cook in a moderate oven (Gas 4, 180ºC, 350ºF) for about 2 hours, or until the venison is tender. Top up with wine or water if it gets too dry. Adjust the seasoning at the end.

To make the rösti, mix the grated carrot, celeriac and ginger together and season with salt and pepper. Whisk the eggs and milk and mix into the grated vegetables. If you are using rings to fry the rösti, oil or butter them. Heat up plenty of butter and oil in a large pan and divide the mixture into 6 portions. Fry them until golden brown and then turn them and do the other sides. Lower the heat and continue to cook until both sides are a deep rich brown. Serve with the venison civet.

VENISON FROM PARADISE

The word 'paradise' comes from *paradisi*, the Persian word for a beautiful pleasure park irrigated with clear mountain water and populated by graceful Persian fallow deer that afforded some strenuous sport from time to time, followed by some luxurious feasting on the quarry. Persian (Iranian) food is a wonderful mixture of sweet and sour, spicy and fragrant. The following two dishes are adapted, with only minor adjustments, from lamb and duck dishes in Margaret Shaida's inspirational book *The Legendary Cuisine of Persia*. If you are having a buffet, they go well together. Serve them with plain rice, or, if you want to be very festive, saffron rice with ruby-like beads of fresh pomegranate stirred into it.

Simmered venison with walnuts and pomegranate
Serves 6

The concentrated pomegranate flavour adds exactly the right balance of sweet and tart so typical of Persian cooking. If you can't get hold of pomegranate juice, use really tart fruit jelly. Walnuts were so highly regarded that they were reserved for the kings of Persia: once they were taken to Greece, they became the food of the gods, so voluptuous is their oil. When minced and slowly simmered, they make a fabulous accompaniment to venison.

900 g (2 lbs) diced venison haunch or shoulder

1 litre pomegranate juice (or 2–3 tablespoons tart jelly)

150 g (5 oz) freshly shelled walnuts

Oil

1 onion

600 ml (1 pt) venison or other stock

Salt and black pepper

Juice of 1 lemon (optional)

If using pomegranate juice, put it in a wide pan and boil it down until only 3 or 4 tablespoons of syrup remain. It will be reduced by the time the meat has cooked. Chop the walnuts into small crumbs. Fry them gently in a teaspoon of oil, stirring for about fifteen minutes until they darken, then draw them off the heat.

Fry the onion in oil till golden brown, then add the meat and brown that too. Add just enough stock to cover the meat, cover with a lid or foil and simmer gently for 30 minutes. Then add the fried walnuts and simmer for another 30 minutes, topping up with stock if necessary.

Then stir in the pomegranate paste (or jelly) and continue to simmer until the meat is tender (about another 30–45 minutes, longer for shoulder). Season with salt and pepper, adding lemon juice if necessary to increase the note of tartness. Serve with steamed spinach and plain or saffron rice.

Venison stew with aubergine sauce

Serves 4

The texture of cooked aubergine is perfect for venison. Shoulder from young animals can be used instead of haunch, but it may need another half hour to cook.

700 g (1½ lb) boneless haunch

1 kg (2¼ lbs) aubergines

2 medium onions, chopped

Oil for browning

1 teaspoon turmeric

3 tablespoons tomato purée

3–4 medium tomatoes, chopped

50 g (2 oz) grapes

Juice of 1 lemon

Salt and pepper.

If you have a microwave, halve the aubergines lengthways and cook in the microwave at full power for four minutes. Turn them over and give them a further 3 minutes. When they are cool enough to handle, cut them into chunks. If you don't have a microwave, bake them in the oven for an hour, or else slice them and fry in oil.

Slice the onions and brown them in oil. Add the meat and fry it till nicely browned. Add the turmeric and then the tomato purée, the chopped tomatoes, grapes and lemon juice. Add enough water to just cover the meat and simmer for 30 minutes. Add the chopped, cooked aubergines and a little more water if necessary. Cover and simmer for a further 30 minutes or until the meat is tender. Season with pepper and salt before serving.

Venison in orange and brandy sauce

Serves 4

Every now and then you hit on a recipe that everyone seems to love. This is one of them, from Jenny Elmhirst of Round Green Farm in Yorkshire. Jenny and Dick have been farming deer almost as long as we have and have done a huge amount of work on promoting venison, both to chefs and the general public.

If your venison is from an old deer, it is worth using diced haunch instead of shoulder for this lovely dish. Roasted or mashed carrots go well with the orangey flavour.

750 g (1 1/2 lbs+) venison shoulder, diced

3 tablespoons oil

225 g (8 oz) baby onions, peeled

1 clove garlic, crushed

2 tablespoons flour

300 ml (1/2 pt) venison or beef stock

2 unwaxed oranges

3 tablespoons brandy

1 tablespoon tomato purée

1 tablespoon black treacle (molasses)

Pinch of ground coriander

25 g (1 oz) butter

110 g (4 oz) mushrooms, thickly sliced

Seasoning

Preheat the oven to Gas 3, 160°C, 325°F. Heat 3 tablespoons of oil in a frying pan and sear the venison. Transfer the meat to a casserole dish. Fry the onions and garlic in the same fat till lightly browned then transfer them to the casserole. Add the flour to the fat in the pan and cook for a minute, then stir in the stock and bring to the boil. Pare the rind from 1 1/2 oranges and cut into thin matchstick strips. Add the rind to the sauce with the juice of both oranges. Add the brandy, tomato purée, treacle, coriander and seasoning. Stir, then pour all this into the casserole dish.

Cover tightly and cook for 1 1/2 hours. Fry the mushrooms in butter for a few minutes, then add to the casserole. Taste, adjust seasoning if necessary, and cook for a further hour or until the meat is tender.

Venison steak pie (venison pasty)

Serves 6

The following three recipes are for dish pies – for a long time known as pasties. Recipes for raised pies are on p.218. Pasties have more luxurious pastry, sometimes enriched with eggs and cream: most had pastry above and below the meat and were unsupported by a dish but most pies now have pastry only on top and are made in a dish. Use twice as much pastry if you want to line the bottom as well. Samuel Pepys was especially fond of pasties: two-thirds of his many diary entries for venison were pasties, though once he describes 'being almost cloyed having been at 5 pasties in 3 days: viz 2 at our own feast and 1 yesterday and 2 today'.

People have firm preferences for pastry. I love crumbly short crust pastry with rich gravy. Others prefer flaky or puff pastry or the connoisseur's suet crust. Below are variations using the three different types. Make sure you have a pie dish the right size. If you line the bottom, about 1¼ litres (2 pints) is about right, if you don't line it, you can use a smaller one. If your dish is a bit big and there is a danger of the pastry dipping down too far, use a pie funnel or egg-cup to keep it up. None of the ingredients are crucial – add other vegetables or spices if you want. You could copy or trace some of the drawings in this book for decorations.

1 kg (2¼ lbs) shoulder or haunch steak

Butter/oil for frying

1 large onion, chopped

Plain flour

1 teaspoon juniper berries, crushed

1 dessertspoon rowan or currant jelly

Cut the steaks, either into small steaks about 80 g (3 oz) each, or into large chunks. Heat some butter/oil in a large frying pan and fry the onion till soft and golden. Remove it to a casserole. Dust the venison pieces in flour and quickly brown them, adding more butter/oil of needed. Do this in batches so that they brown rather than stew, and only dust the meat immediately before it is going to be fried so that it doesn't get too covered in flour – you don't want the gravy to be gloopy. Put the browned meat into the casserole.

1 dessertspoon tomato purée

1 teaspoon Worcestershire sauce (optional)

Leaves from a bunch of fresh thyme

600 ml (1 pt) liquid (stock, ale, stout, water, wine)

Short crust pastry

450 g (1 lb) plain flour

Pinch of salt

180 g (6 oz) lard

180 g (6 oz) butter

Cold water

1 egg yolk or milk to glaze

Add a little of your cooking liquid to the pan and dissolve all the floury brownings, then add this to the meat. Stir in the other ingredients; the liquid should just about cover the meat. Cover and cook at Gas 4, 180°C, 350°F, for 1¹/₂ hours.

While it cooks, make the pastry. Rub the lard and butter into the flour and salt (or use a food processor on pulse). Add the minimum amount of cold water to allow the dough to stick together. Form into a smooth ball and if possible, keep it cool for at least an hour before rolling it out though it's not crucial.

Assemble the pie about 45 minutes before you want to eat it. If you want pastry above and below, roll out the pastry and line the pie dish. Moisten the edge of the pastry. Fill it with the cooked stew, heaping it up in the middle nicely – you may not need all the liquid. Roll out the rest of the pastry and cover the top. Cut off the excess. Press the two layers of pastry together, then pinch back the edges to thicken them. Decorate the top as you like, but leave a little hole somewhere for the steam to escape, otherwise the liquid may burst out of the sides. Glaze the pastry with egg yolk or milk.

Bake the pie in a medium oven (Gas 5, 190°C, 380°F) for about 45 minutes. If it looks as though the top of the pastry is browning too much, put it lower down in the oven, cover with paper and lower the heat a little.

Venison steak and kidney pie

Serves 6

As above, adding at least 125 g (4 oz) venison kidney and reduce the steak accordingly. If wished, add 250 g (8 oz) mushrooms, cut into large pieces. Sauté these in butter till softened, and stir them in just before you put on the pastry crust. Use any of the three types of pastry given here. They are all good, just different. As always with venison kidneys, never, ever, use kidneys from male deer during the rutting (mating) season or for about a month before and after it.

Venison and game pie

Serves 6

Proceed as for the steak pie, but using only 500 g (1 lb+) of venison steak. The rest can be of any boneless game you like: pheasant, rabbit, hare, pigeon, and so on. And I would add 250 g (8 oz) mushrooms, cut into large pieces. Sauté these in butter till softened, and stir them in just before you put on the pastry crust.

Red deer pies, garnished
From *The Accomplisht Cook* by Robert May 1671

Venison surf and turf with flaky pastry
Serves 6

Ingredients as for the steak and kidney pie, except reduce the venison to 750 g (1½ lb+) and add either 6 or 12 fresh oysters. Open them carefully, sieve the salty juices to remove any shell and reserve it to add to the venison stew; you'll need less salt to season it. Wash the oysters quickly to remove any shell. Proceed as for the steak pie, but tuck the oysters into the stew just before you bake it with the crust. They don't need much cooking, and if you like, you can cut them in half.

Flaky (rough puff) pastry

450 g (1 lb) plain flour

225 g (8 oz) butter, chilled

Pinch of salt

Cold water

Keep everything cold to prevent the butter bursting through the flour. If it does, dredge more flour over it. Cut the butter into pieces about the size of big hazelnuts. Mix them into the flour and salt, and use just enough water to make a dough that will stick together. The butter should still be in large lumps. Flour a pastry board well, and cover the lump of dough well in flour too, forming it into a rectangular block with your hands. Do this quickly so you don't warm the butter. Then roll it out away from you about 2 cm (1½ in) thick, into a rectangle three times as long as it is wide. Rub a little flour on top, then fold the top third towards you and the bottom third away from you to form a square block. Turn it round 90 degrees so that the second rolling is in the opposite direction to the first. Repeat the turn, roll, fold procedure at least three more times, the more the merrier as it gets more flaky with each folding. Then rest it for an hour in the fridge before rolling it out for your pie. Cook as before.

Venison steak and kidney steamed pudding

Serves 4

The steamed 'crust' here has a texture more akin to dumplings than pastry, so think of it as that. But it can also be used for the baked dish pies above. As always with venison kidneys, never use them from male deer during the rutting (mating) season or for about a month before and after it. The gratin of fennel on p.158 goes specially well with this.

450 g (1 lb) shoulder or haunch steak

Butter/oil for browning

100 g (4 oz) fatty bacon

1 small onion, chopped

180 g (6 oz) mushrooms, chopped fine

Plain flour

Salt and pepper

100 g (4 oz) venison kidneys

1 teaspoon juniper berries, crushed

$1/2$ tablespoon rowan or currant jelly

$1/2$ tablespoon tomato purée

Scant teaspoon Worcestershire sauce (optional)

200 ml ($1/3$ pt) liquid (stock, ale, stout, water, wine)

Heat some butter and oil in a large frying pan and brown the bacon, then remove it from the pan and gently fry the onion. Remove that, and add the mushroom and fry till it has reduced. Dust the venison steak in flour, add some more butter/oil to the pan and brown the venison in batches so that it browns quickly. Remove from the heat, season with salt and pepper, and stir in all the other ingredients but only half of the liquid.

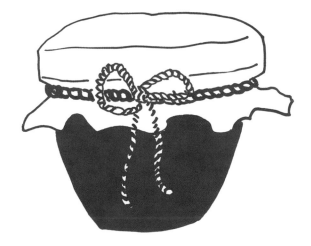

Suet crust

350 g (12 oz) plain flour

150 g (5 oz) venison or beef suet, grated

30 g (1½ oz) butter (optional)

200 ml (⅓ pt) water

Pinch of salt

Now make the suet crust. Rub the suet and butter into the flour. Add enough water to make a soft paste, then roll it out to a bit less than 1 cm (½ in) thick. (If you use this crust for baking instead of steaming, brush it with egg yolk to glaze it.)

Butter a 1.5 litre (2 pint) pudding basin and line it with the suet crust, avoiding trapping air under it. Fill it with the meat mixture, adding more liquid if necessary. Cover the top with more of the crust, excluding any air, and crimp the edges together really firmly so that no gravy can escape. Cover the basin securely with two layers of greased and buttered tin foil. Then stand the basin in a large pan with enough water to come half-way up the basin. Bring almost to the boil, and simmer very gently for 3–4 hours.

Sweet and sour tough to tender venison

Serve 10–12

This was Dorothy Hartley's suggested method of cooking really tough beef. She had an idea that it came back from the Boer War where it was used by some British army cook to cope with Transvaal oxen which when old and stringy, would probably not be unlike tough venison. 'Try it,' she says, 'I believe it would soften a frozen mammoth.'

My contributions are the larding, since venison is so lean, and the sweet and sour coating, as the cooking liquid is not suitable for a sauce. There is no need to restrict this to tough old venison – normal venison can be cooked without the pickle before being finished with the sweet and sour coating.

Use brown ale or sweet stout rather than bitter or lager beer. If you don't have a stainless steel saucepan, bake it in the oven in a covered ceramic dish, as the acid could eat away at aluminium or iron. Pickling spice is a mixture of black and white peppercorns, mustard seed, allspice, coriander seed, mace, whole cloves, and sometimes some garlic, chilli or turmeric.

1.75 kg (4 lb) boneless shoulder or haunch

250 g ($^1/_2$ lb) fatty bacon or belly of pork

150 ml ($^1/_4$ pt) vinegar

1 tablespoon black treacle

1 large onion, chopped

Bunch of fresh herbs

Pinch of pickling spice

1–1$^1/_2$ litres (2–3 pts) mild brown ale

Cut the pork belly into strips. Open out the meat as much as you can and insert the pork or bacon evenly all over it, trying not to break the outer skin. Then roll it up and tie it as tightly and neatly as you can. If the joint has already been rolled and tied, then simply make deep incisions all over it and insert the pork. If you have a larding needle and enjoy using it then lard the joint as deeply as you can.

Place the joint in a saucepan on top of the fresh herbs and the pickling spice. Pour the vinegar over it and then the treacle, and cover it with the chopped onion. Let it stand all day and then gently pour the ale over it till level with the top of the meat. Heat it up gently until it is just about to boil, then turn the heat right down to the barest simmer. Skim the top, then cover the pan and simmer gently for anywhere from 2–4 hours until the venison is

Sweet and sour finish

1 large onion, chopped
finely

50 g (2 oz) butter

1 orange

2 tablespoons tomato
purée

1 teaspoon salt

2 tablespoons wine vinegar

$^1/_2$ teaspoon ground ginger

$^1/_2$ teaspoon allspice

perfectly tender. The length of time will depend on the age and cut of meat used.

At this stage you can either finish off the joint immediately or else allow it to cool in the liquid and finish it later. Don't allow it to cool down out of the liquid or it will dry out.

To make the sweet and sour finish, gently cook the finely chopped onion in the butter till golden and transparent. Peel the orange, and chop it into small pieces, discarding the pips as you go. Add these plus all the other ingredients to the onions, and cook them all together until the mixture is like a thick jam.

When you want to finish the meat, lift it out of the liquid and pat the surface as dry as you can so the sweet and sour coating will stick. Spread the coating all over the joint and bake it in a hot oven (Gas 8, 230ºC, 450ºF) until it becomes luscious, dark and sticky. If you finish the joint off while it is still warm from the first cooking, that is all it needs. If you are finishing it from cold, then after the initial cooking of the coating, turn the oven right down to low (Gas 3, 160°C, 325°F) and continue to cook it until the meat is heated up all the way through, about another 30–45 minutes. The exact time depends on the thickness of the joint, but a meat thermometer will tell you exactly when it is ready. The internal temperature should be 75°C (165°F).

Venison stew with herb dumplings

Serves 4

This is a family favourite on rainy summer days when fresh herbs are abundant and we need cheering up – simple comfort food. In order to cook dumplings in the gravy, it must be thinner than for a normal stew, otherwise the dumplings will be solid instead of puffing up into irresistible fluffy balls. Use a wide pan to cook the dumplings in so that there is enough room for them to swell. They should at least double in girth when cooked. The herbs can be what you have available. I usually include parsley, thyme, lemon mint and marjoram, but use what you like best. They are best served immediately, so have everything else ready.

650 g (1¹/₂ lbs) diced shoulder

2 onions, chopped

Oil

Flour (optional)

4 carrots, chopped large

2 sticks celery, chopped

2 large tomatoes

Stock or water

Salt and black pepper

For the dumplings

120 g (4 oz) plain flour

50 g (2 oz) minced suet

¹/₂ teaspoon baking powder

Large handful of mixed herbs

Brown the onions and venison and place in a fireproof casserole. If you like slightly thickened gravy, roll the venison in flour before browning it. Add the other vegetables and enough water to nearly cover the meat. Bring to the boil and cook in a moderate oven (Gas 5, 190°C, 375°F) for 1¹/₂–2 hours or until the venison is tender. If it is from an older animal, reduce the heat a little and cook it for longer. When the meat is tender, add a little more water to thin the gravy (the meat should be just submerged). Season with salt and pepper and keep warm.

To make the dumplings, mix the suet into the flour with the baking powder, a generous pinch of salt and some pepper. Chop the herbs finely and mix them in. Then add enough cold water to form a soft dough. If it is too dry they won't swell so much. Flour your hands and form balls of 3–4 cm (1¹/₂ inch) diameter. Bring the stew gently to the boil and give it a stir to prevent it sticking to the bottom. Drop the dumplings into the boiling stew and cover the pan. Cook for 3 minutes, then reduce the heat and simmer very gently for a further 20 minutes by which time they should have doubled in size. Serve them immediately so they don't collapse, though it isn't a complete disaster if they do.

10. The fifth quarter

Venison liver, heart, kidneys and more

10. The fifth quarter

Venison liver, heart, kidneys and more

'The fifth quarter' is what butchers call all the parts of an animal that are not cut into steaks, joints, stews and mince. They are the extras that make a carcase profitable: liver, kidney, tripe, tongue, sweetbreads etc. Having been out of favour (though not with me) they are now being recognised as treats and appear on some very classy menus. Americans have two terms: 'organ meats' and 'variety meats', of which the second is good because that is exactly what these cuts do – add variety, especially in terms of texture. You only get a small amount of kidney, tongue or sweetbreads, so savour them. Somehow tender fillet seems just a little boring after these special cuts.

VENISON LIVER

Venison liver is one of life's great gastronomic treats. Deep in colour, one would imagine it would taste strong like ox or pig's liver, but in fact it is as soft and sweet and fine textured as calves' or lambs' liver. No wonder it was the traditional stalker's perk; it was only reluctantly relinquished when regulations came in requiring the liver to be sent to the game dealer for veterinary inspection. Livers act as filters to collect drug residues or pollutants. Venison liver is more likely to be free from chemicals than that of most domesticated animals and test results from the UK's Veterinary Medical Directorate show a healthy set of statistics for venison liver, though interestingly (and contrary to popular belief) farm venison comes out better than wild with, at the time of writing, no residues ever being found. This is probably because wild deer are older, so accumulate more heavy metals. In Scandinavia and Eastern Europe, the liver is not supposed to be eaten at all because of its high cadmium levels. One warning, though: if you shoot your own deer, never, ever, cook liver (or kidneys) from a stag or buck around the time of the rut – it is indescribably awful – chuck it away for even most dogs won't eat it. In a rutted out stag, the liver goes bright yellow. Only use liver from young or female animals, and sniff it first. It should smell sweet.

Liver should either be cooked very quickly or slowly stewed. Cooked quickly, it is pink, sweet, juicy and melt-in-the mouth tender. Cut it fairly thin – 1 cm maximum (¹/₂ inch) – so that it cooks quickly without being raw in the middle. Cooked gently and slowly, it is soft and still sweet. Slow-cooked liver has a more 'bready' texture and needs to be cooked in gravy or sauce to keep it moist. Cooking it in-between these two extremes makes it hard, dark and bitter.

Venison liver for Derek Cooper

Serves 4

This is the simplest, and to my mind, the best way to enjoy venison liver. When the broadcaster Derek Cooper came to our farm to record *The Food Programme* he chose venison liver to eat on the radio. Apparently he had been given it some fifteen years previously and it was our task to recreate this wonderful memory. Derek's appreciative consumption of that liver on the airwaves was responsible for a new wave of enthusiastic venison liver consumers who should remain grateful to this remarkable man. Lightly grilled figs make a wonderful accompaniment.

600 g (1¼ lb) venison liver

Butter and oil for frying

Plain flour

Juice of 1 lemon

Malden salt

1 small bunch of flat-leaved parsley

Another lemon, cut in quarters

Slice the liver no more than 1 cm (½ in) thick. Chop the parsley coarsely. Heat the butter and oil (equal quantities) in a large frying pan. Dip the slices of liver in the flour and shake off excess. When the butter has stopped frothing and is beginning to go golden brown, fry the liver, making sure it is not overcrowded in the pan; it may be necessary to cook it in two batches. Cook for 2 minutes on one side, then turn over and cook for another 2 minutes. Remove from the pan to a warm dish to rest for a few minutes, and add the lemon juice to the pan to make a small amount of piquant sauce with the pan brownings. Scatter a little Malden salt and parsley over the slices, and serve with a dribble of sauce and the lemon quarters.

Sauteéd venison liver with figs and venison jus

Serves 4

The combination of venison and figs is a good one – foie gras is sometimes served with them. You have to have superb venison stock to produce the jus, so if you can't buy it, make it the day beforehand, see p.48.

600 g (1¼ lb) sliced venison liver

Flour

6 fresh figs, halved lengthways

200 ml (7 fl oz) venison jus (see below)

1 teaspoon rowan or redcurrant jelly (optional)

Seasoning

For the jus

1 litre (1¾ pts) meaty venison stock

½ bottle red wine

To make the jus, boil the stock rapidly to reduce it, and when there is room, add the red wine. Continue to reduce it until it is a deep mahogany brown – it should be reduced to the required 200 ml (7 fl oz) by this time. To make the dish, warm the jus in a small pan and season to taste with salt, pepper and a little tart jelly if wished (though not too much as the figs will be sweet). Add the halved figs and allow them to warm through in the jus; they shouldn't actually cook.

Dust the slices of liver in flour and fry them in butter till nicely browned (about 1 minute each side) then remove the pan from the heat and allow the liver to rest and finish cooking for a further 3–4 minutes. When cooked, divide the jus and figs between four plates, and place the slices of liver in the middle of each. A small handful of root vegetable crisps/chips makes a nice crunchy garnish for this dish.

Smooth liver paté

See p. 214

Venison liver with thyme and potato cake
Serves 4

Another starter which uses a small amount of liver to great advantage. Have the liver cut very thin to $1/2$ – 1 cm ($1/4$–$1/2$ in) so that it cooks in seconds. The rösti on p.182 or gratin Savoyard p.207 can also be used instead of these cakes if preferred.

4 x 80 g (3 oz) portions venison liver

20 g (small bunch) fresh thyme

350 g (12 oz) potatoes, peeled

1 large clove garlic, crushed

4 tablespoons olive oil

1 lemon

Reserve four sprigs of thyme for serving and remove the leaves from the stems of the rest. Slice the potatoes thinly, rinse, then toss them in a bowl with the garlic, thyme leaves, olive oil, some coarsely ground black pepper and a pinch of salt. Layer them into four large oiled pastry rings on a dish and bake them in a medium oven (Gas 5, 190ºC, 375ºF) for 45 minutes until golden brown on top.

Brown the liver in a hot pan with butter and oil. Because it is so thin, it only needs about 30 seconds per side if the pan is hot. Remove from the heat. Remove the potato cakes from the rings onto four warmed plates, lay the liver slices on top of the potato, and decorate with a sprig of thyme. Finally, squeeze lemon juice over the liver, sprinkle with sea salt and serve immediately.

VENISON KIDNEYS

Not unlike lamb's kidneys, any recipe can be adapted for venison kidneys. They are great chopped and added to a stew for extra flavour. Or they can be fried or grilled or cooked on a skewer and served, rosy pink, on toast, with a salad, or as a starter. Or, if you happen to have a fat young deer towards the end of the summer, the real connoisseur's treat is to roast them, whole, still enveloped in their kidney fat. The suet that melts off them in the oven makes very superior mincemeat for Christmas mince pies. Above all, as with liver, kidneys should be fresh as can be, and never eat kidneys from a stag or buck anywhere near the rutting season. As a student, my husband ate some from a rutting stag as a bet. He said he could taste and smell them for at least a month afterwards. You have been warned.

Venison kidneys with mushroom sauce
Serves 2

This is a classic way to serve kidney as the texture of the mushrooms is so complementary. Don't worry if the kidneys keep exuding a little blood up to the point of serving – just give it a stir and it will be wonderful. If you are lucky enough to have some wild mushrooms or ceps, then this will be a feast indeed.

2 large or 4 small venison kidneys

250 g (8 oz) mushrooms

2 cloves garlic

50 g (2 oz) butter

2 tablespoons brandy (optional)

150 ml (¼ pt) double cream

Fresh thyme leaves

Cut the kidney into small chunks of 2 cm (¾ in) or less, discarding the white core in the middle. Cut the mushrooms into the same sized pieces. Crush or finely chop the garlic. Heat the butter till turning golden and brown the kidneys quickly. Add the mushrooms and garlic and continue to sauté them until the mushrooms have soaked up the fat. Add the brandy, if used, and the cream, and stir until the sauce is nice and thick and coffee-coloured. Scatter the dish with fresh thyme before serving.

Devilled venison kidneys

My father loved devilled meats. Devilled turkey drumsticks after Christmas was about the only dish he ever cooked and very good they were too. Make them as above, except add 2 tablespoons wine vinegar instead of the brandy. Then add a heaped tablespoon of strong mustard (smooth or wholegrain), two or three shakes of either Tabasco or Worcestershire sauce, and a pinch of either hot paprika, cayenne or finely ground black pepper. Then scoop in the cream and stir it until nicely mixed together.

Roast kidneys in their own fat

This is the sort of gutsy dish that eighteenth-century gourmets used to enjoy at fireside dinners while they roasted whole truffles in the ashes. It is difficult to be precise about the timing here, as it depends on both the size of the deer and their kidneys and also how thick a covering of fat they have. This varies according to the condition of the deer and can range from 5 cm (2 inches) down to none at all. If you prick the suet all over, it should render down to a lovely crisp skin. If not, then simply peel it off and enjoy the kidney inside. You can test its 'doneness' by piercing it with a skewer, but do remember that kidneys produce a lot of blood when skewered, right up to the moment when they are cooked all the way through, which, to my mind is overcooked.

I would serve these with spring greens briefly boiled in very salty water with grilled pine nuts scattered over them and mashed, or dauphinoise potato (p.178). Serve with mustard and a good bottle or two of claret.

VENISON HEART

I love venison heart. I love its really meaty taste and I love its texture, which is not unlike that of squid. Like squid, it's best cooked very fast for a firm juicy bite or else braised slowly and gently for a softer texture. Anything in between is very rubbery. Hart's hearts should surely feature somewhere in the ultimate romantic *diner à deux*. I have converted more than one person who thought they didn't like heart by simply frying slices of it in butter very quickly, leaving them to rest for a few moments, and serving them up plain and simple but lovely and rosy-pink, with just a squeeze of lemon on the top, like the liver recipe on p.200.

Hearts from the smaller species can be halved lengthways and grilled or roasted. Hearts from the large species need slicing into rings before frying. Trim off the fat and gristly parts from the top first. Some people like them stuffed and baked slowly – very traditional fare, though current meat inspections slash the heart, which makes this more difficult. Some Norwegians have just told me they steep venison hearts in a 10% brine for a few days and then hang them up to dry; it is delicious thinly sliced like bresaola, though I haven't had time to try it myself. I will, though.

Marinated venison heart with parmesan wafers

Serves 2

I ate nothing but venison heart one weekend when we were working at a game fair. My job was to dash back home and stock up with more venison burgers for the team to cook. I had prepared and marinated some venison hearts, and every time I galloped in I threw some slices into a frying pan. In the moments it took to load up the car, the slices were cooked and then savoured with very great relish. Fast food indeed – here it is. If you can't get hold of lovage, it is also good with juniper berries, rosemary or thyme, all powerful flavours.

1 large or 2 small hearts (about 450 g/1 lb)

100 ml (4 fl oz) olive oil

4 tablespoons red wine (or 2 of red wine vinegar)

Salt and pepper

Butter/oil for frying

2 tablespoons coarsely chopped lovage, (optional)

2 teaspoons juniper berries crushed, (optional)

1 tablespoon fresh rosemary or thyme(optional)

Parmesan wafers

100 g (3 oz) Parmesan or Grana Panada cheese

Trim the hearts of all fat and gristle. Slice the trimmed heart 1 cm ($^1/_2$ inch) thick (or in half, if very small) and place in a small dish. Mix together the oil, wine or vinegar, a good pinch of salt and some pepper, and the chosen herb. Pour this over the heart so that it is covered. Keep submerged for about 12 hours (though it will happily keep in the fridge for several days as long as the meat is covered).

When ready to cook, remove from the marinade, pat dry, and fry in a mixture of hot butter and oil for 1 minute per side, then draw the pan off the heat and allow the heart to continue cooking in the residual heat for a further 3–4 minutes, depending how rare you like it.

To make the Parmesan wafers, grate the cheese coarsely and make four loose rounds on a sheet of baking parchment. Place in a hot oven or under the grill till the cheese melts but before it starts burning, so keep an eye on it. Once cooled, remove carefully from the parchment and serve with the grilled heart.

Braised venison heart with gratin Savoyard

Serves 4

You can make a more substantial dish by preparing the gratin and heart in advance and serving this with thin slices of quickly sautéed venison liver – a great combination. Lovage is a very strong herb, so only a small amount is needed; alternatively, use fresh parsley, chervil or thyme.

Gratin Savoyard is made the same way as gratin dauphinois except that stock is used instead of milk or cream. It makes a great accompaniment to venison roasts, stews or steaks as it leaves you free to concentrate on the meat and sauce. Ideally, the cheese should be a mountain *tomme de Savoie*, but any good strong cheese will do.

600 g (1lb 4 oz) trimmed venison heart

4 shallots, finely chopped

Stock or hot water

Black pepper

Rowan or redcurrant jelly to serve (optional)

For the gratin Savoyard

500 g (1 lb+) waxy potatoes

50 g (2 oz) butter

2 cloves garlic, crushed

300 ml (^{1}/$_2$ pt) good venison stock

Ground nutmeg

Salt and pepper

50 g (2 oz) Tomme de Savoie or grated cheddar

A few leaves of fresh lovage, parsley or chervil

Cut the heart into small dice no more than 1 cm (^{1}/$_4$–^{1}/$_2$ in) square. Gently fry the diced shallots in butter till golden and remove to a small baking dish. Heat the pan up a bit more and very quickly brown the pieces of heart, then remove them to the baking dish. Add half a cupful of hot stock or water, a couple of turns of black pepper, and then cover the dish and bake in a low oven (Gas 3, 160ºC, 325ºF) for 2 hours, or until the pieces are tender. Check halfway through that it is not drying up; if it is, top up with water. When it is cooked, season with salt to taste.

While it cooks, prepare the gratin Savoyard. Line four ramekins with greased tin foil – they should be about 6–8 cm (2^1/$_2$–3 ins) diameter. Turn to p.178 for the preparation method, placing the layers in the ramekins instead of a large dish. They cook a little more quickly in the ramekins. When cooked, turn the potato rounds out of the ramekins, and invert them onto individual warm serving plates, arrange the heart and its rich gravy round about, scattering over it some chopped lovage, parsley or chervil.

HARTS' TONGUES

These are similar to lambs' tongues, i.e. a little fiddly to prepare but definitely a delicacy that repays the effort, so accumulate several to make it worthwhile. They need gentle simmering for several hours and then skinning. A red deer tongue will weigh approximately 200 g (7 oz), the other species proportionately less. I have never found it necessary to pickle them in saltpetre, which turns them deep red. I prefer the delicate, unadorned flavour even if the colour is greyer. When peeling off the skin, start with the thick upper part which should peel off easily. If it doesn't, they are not cooked. The thinner skin on the sides is sometimes more reluctant to peel off cleanly – have patience and if necessary use a small paring knife: this is quite normal.

Florentines of tongues, or any other meat

From *The Accomplisht Cook* by Robert May 1671

Pressed venison tongues

Serves 4–6

Find some round containers that neatly contain the tongues, either in pairs, yin-yang fashion, or in threes like the Isle of Man symbol. You also need a weight to press the tongues that fits inside the containers, otherwise it won't be possible to cut slices. If you are lucky enough to have a tongue press this is a simple procedure, if not, a heavy tin protected by clingfilm works fine.

800 g (1lb 14 oz) venison tongues

250 g (8 oz) carrots, peeled and chopped

250 g (8 oz) onion, peeled and chopped

1 teaspoon whole black peppercorns

1 teaspoon salt

Scrub the tongues if necessary. Place them in a pan with the carrots and onions and just cover with water. Bring to simmering point, and simmer or cook in a low oven for 2–3 hours or until tender. Leave them in the cooking liquid until they are cool enough to handle (the warmer they are at this stage, the better). Then peel off all the skin and place them in the container making sure they are a tight fit. If there are large gaps, add a small splash of the cooking liquid. Cover with the weight, if necessary putting something else heavy on top of it. Allow the tongues to cool completely under the weight.

To remove the pressed tongues, sit the container briefly in very hot water (or wrap hot tea towels round it) and then turn it upside down onto a plate. Sometimes it is necessary to run a knife round the edge to help it out. Serve with pickled capers, pickled beetroot, sauerkraut or something similarly tangy.

Harts' tongues in an onion and parsley sauce

Serves 4–6

This used to be a favourite of my elder daughter when she was a child. It is wonderful served with a mash made from equal quantities of carrots and celeriac. Hasselback potatoes (p.172) make a good texture contrast.

800 g (1 lb 12oz) venison tongues

250 g (8 oz) carrots, peeled and chopped

250 g (8 oz) onion, peeled and chopped

Stock or water to cover

150 ml (¼ pt) cream (optional but recommended)

Salt, pepper

2 heaped tablespoons chopped parsley

Scrub the tongues, place in a saucepan with the onions and carrots, and cover with stock or water. Bring to a simmer and cook for 2–3 hours or until the tongues are tender. Allow them to cool in the liquid until you can handle them, then peel off the skin. Keep them in a bowl or polythene bag with a few spoons of the cooking liquid to stop them drying out.

Rub the onion, carrot and cooking liquid through a sieve and return this liquid to the pan. Boil it fiercely to reduce it to a sauce consistency, and stir in the cream if used. Add salt and pepper to taste, and at the last minute add the parsley. Slice the tongues and place in a serving dish. Pour over the sauce and warm it all through thoroughly before serving dredged with some coarsely chopped parsley.

VENISON SWEETBREADS AND BRAINS

Sweetbreads is the culinary (and more attractive) term for the pancreas, a gland within the folds of the intestine near the diaphragm, and the thymus, a gland in the throat which is part of the immune system that is most important in immature animals and diminishes with age. The pancreas is present throughout the animal's life, and although excellent, is not quite so creamy and delicate as the thymus. Like all offal, they need to be very fresh, and removed for eating or freezing immediately after killing. Venison brain is similar, though even creamier in texture.

Venison sweetbreads or brains with pickled capers
Serves 2

This is simple and good. The amounts are for a starter. Since these are a springtime treat, choose something like a new season's salad herb (chervil is good) or those harbingers of summer, tiny baby broad beans with their bitter/sweet flavour.

200 g (7 oz) venison sweetbreads or brain

Salt

Seasoned flour

Butter and/or oil for frying

2 tablespoons capers or caper berries (optional)

1 lemon plus Malden salt (optional)

To prepare sweetbreads or brains, steep them in cold salted water (1 tablespoon salt per 600 ml / 1 pint) for 1–2 hours to remove any blood. Then simmer them very gently in plain water for only five or six minutes, strain off the liquid and allow them to cool, weighted under a plate. Remove any small gristly parts (there won't be many) with a sharp knife.

Sweetbreads can be cooked whole or sliced; brain is usually sliced. Dust the pieces lightly in the seasoned flour and fry them in butter (my preference) or oil until golden brown on both sides.

Serve them up very simply, with the pickled capers, either the intense small ones or the milder large caper berries, or with a squeeze of lemon juice and some Malden salt, or with a black butter sauce.

Alternative Sweetbreads (Fries)

This is a speciality reserved for those who shoot their own deer. Testicles are used for medicine by the Chinese but are also good to eat. Thirty-five years ago, when John was studying the deer on the Scottish island of Rum, he was asked to help in the annual castrating of the semi-wild young Highland cattle. We were just recently married. I stood outside the temporary compound, and as the 'bits' flew over the wooden paling, many ribald comments came my way as to what I should do with them, including how to cook them. I was told to peel them and boil them. In the privacy of my own kitchen I attempted this, but after what I perceived to be the fourth or fifth layer (there are really only two), I decided I was the butt of a joke and gave up.

Many years later in Latvia, along with eight other international cooks, I was roped into a cook-in for three-hundred. At the end of the afternoon, the host, Dainis Paeglitis, cooked up some stags' testicles and auctioned them off for charity. The second batch was shared by the cooks. They were delicious, rather like brains or sweetbreads.

Testicles need skinning first. Best way to do this is to plunge them into boiling water for a couple of minutes, then remove the outer skin. Slice them about 1 cm ($^1/_2$ inch) thick, roll them in flour seasoned with freshly ground pepper and sea salt, then fry them in butter so the outside is crisp and golden. Serve them up as for sweetbreads, above. If you want to be fancy, serve with steamed spinach, rocket or mizuna leaves. You need to squeeze a lemon over them afterwards, of course.

11. Pâté, pies and terrines

11. Pâté, pies and terrines

Smooth venison liver pâté
Makes 1 kg (2¹/₄ lbs)

Over the years, I must have hand-made nearly a ton of this pâté. I had one teenage customer who used to buy a small carton and warm it up in the microwave and eat it all in one go with a teaspoon as though it were a carton of ice cream. I still get requests for my pâté, so here is the recipe. Check that your food processor can manage this quantity before starting, and use wine vinegar that isn't too harsh. I repeat the warning about liver – don't be tempted to use it from a rutting stag or buck, and don't substitute margarine for the butter. Somebody once did both of these and it was foul.

500 g (1 lb+) venison liver

180 g (6 oz) butter, chopped

100 ml (4 fl oz) good red wine vinegar

2 eggs

2 teaspoons finely chopped garlic

1¹/₂ teaspoons salt

¹/₂ teaspoon finely ground black pepper

180 g (6 oz) very fine white breadcrumbs

1 small wineglass red wine

Cut the liver into 2 cm (1 inch) square cubes and put them into an ovenproof dish with the butter and wine vinegar. The liver should be just covered. Cover the dish and bake in a hot oven (Gas 7, 220ºC, 425ºF) for half an hour.

Crack the eggs into a food processor and add the garlic, salt and pepper. Tip in the hot, bubbling liver/butter mixture and immediately process it to a fine liquid. This cooks the eggs, so the liver must be bubbling hot. Then add the breadcrumbs and process again till smooth once more, and finally blend in the wine.

The consistency of this pâté is like firm butter. To make a softer, spreading pâté, use the process on the next page. Pack it into little pots. If wished, pour a layer of melted butter over the top and decorate with bay leaves, juniper berries, red and black peppercorns.Or melt some tart jelly, pour it over the pâté and decorate with slices of orange. You can freeze it for up to a month, though the next recipe rejuvenates it if it becomes crumbly.

Venison pâté with red wine, whisky, gin or brandy

In the mid-1980s, an elderly lady from Devizes would regularly write to me, courteously requesting that I send her one small pot of my 'delicious venison pâté' because she was to be entertaining 'an elderly gentleman' who was very partial to it. I always received a polite thank you letter explaining how much her elderly friend had enjoyed the treat. As the months, and finally years, wore on, I wondered about their relationship. And then the orders stopped. A few months later, I received a letter from the lady, hoping that her confession would not offend me. It transpired that the 'elderly gentleman' was in fact a Tibetan terrier who had saved her brother's life. After her brother's death, she decided that this 'elderly gentleman' deserved an occasional treat, and this he enjoyed until he finally rejoined his original master.

A batch of pâté as above (approx 1 kg /2¼ lbs)

Up to 150 ml (¼ pt) of red wine or whisky or gin or brandy

The cold pâté should be beaten, as blending or processing whips it up too much. I used to use an old Kenwood mixer on slow speed, which did a splendid job, slowly but powerfully mashing the pâté. Later, when making it in quantity for Christmas, I used the huge mixer in the butchery and stood over it emptying whole bottles of whisky into the churning pâté, to the amazement of our stockman who clearly thought it a tragic waste of whisky.

Crumble up the cold pâté and pound it until it turns into a paste. Add some wine, whisky, gin or brandy and continue adding and mixing until it is quite smooth; you may not need all the liquid. It should end up about the same consistency as mashed potato. It will firm up a little after it is put into dishes, but not much. It is very easy to spread onto warm toast.

Potted venison

This is Hannah Glasse's recipe from 1747. A quarter of it should be fat. You can use tin foil instead of brown paper, and a blender will grind it to a paste very quickly. Add the cloves sparingly as they are very strong – barely $^{1}/_{4}$ teaspoon to 500 g (1 lb+) of meat. For the rest, as she says, it is to taste, but start with half a teaspoon of salt, mace and nutmeg and adjust to taste.

> 'Take a piece of venison, Fat and Lean together, lay it in a Dish, and stick Pieces of Butter all over; tye a brown Paper over it, and bake it. When it comes out of the Oven, take it out of the Liquor hot, drain it, and lay it in a Dish. When cold, take off all the Skin, and beat it in a Marble Mortar, Fat and Lean together. Season it with Mace, Cloves, Nutmeg, black Pepper, and Salt to our Mind. When the Butter is cold, that it was baked in, take a little of it, and beat in with it to moisten it; then put it down close, and cover with clarified Butter. You must be sure to beat it, till it is all like a Paste.'
>
> *Hannah Glasse*

Venison and apricot terrine

Serves 6

Ingela Kassander is the marketing manager of Highland Game and this is her recipe. The Highland Game owner, Christian Nissen, arrived like a breath of fresh air into the Scottish venison industry in 1997 and together they have been responsible for enormous progress in the handling, presentation and energetic promotion of wild venison. They deserve all the accolades they get. Ingela's pretty terrine makes an impressive starter served with gherkins or spicy salad leaves drizzled with a walnut or hazelnut dressing, and is just the thing for a summer picnic.

75 g (3 oz) dried apricots, chopped

3 tablespoons brandy

500 g (1 lb+) minced venison

350 g (12 oz) minced belly of pork

1 teaspoon fresh ginger, grated

2 allspice berries, crushed

6 juniper berries, crushed

100 ml (4 fl oz) dry red wine or port

2 tablespoons olive oil

Salt and freshly ground black pepper

175 g (6 oz) thinly sliced pancetta or streaky bacon

1 egg, beaten

Mix the apricots with the brandy, cover and leave to soak for a couple of hours. Mix together the venison, pork, fresh ginger, allspice, juniper berries, salt and pepper with the wine or port and the olive oil. Cover and marinate overnight or as long as you can.

Preheat the oven to Gas 4, 180ºC, 350ºF. Line a terrine or loaf tin with the pancetta or streaky bacon, keeping 3–4 rashers for the top. Beat the egg into the marinated venison mixture, then use just under half to fill the base of the terrine, pushing a 1.25 cm (1/2 inch) ridge up all around the sides of the terrine. Spoon the apricots into the hollow created by the ridge, then cover with the rest of the venison mixture to encase the apricots completely. Smooth over and cover with the rest of the pancetta or bacon, folding over any stray strips.

Cover with tin foil, place in a bain marie and bake in the oven for 1 1/2 – 2 hours or until a skewer inserted into the middle comes out clean. Remove from the oven and place a weight on top, then chill. To serve, run a knife around the edge of the tin and turn the terrine out.

Raised venison pie
Serves 8–10

These make great presents, and every time we have a big party I do an enormous one as a centrepiece. You can also cook the mixture in a terrine without the pastry, or use the mixture to make individual raised pies which are gratifyingly filling. I use venison as the base and then pop in whatever I have in my freezer to add variety (though pure venison is satisfying too). 'Whatever' has ranged from game birds to squirrel to swans to hare to Highland beef. I also use a splash of the exotic spirits given by foreign visitors; some have lovely spices in them. The fatty meat (which should comprise about a third) can be pork belly, streaky bacon, mutton or lamb, beef, duck or whatever you think would add flavour. So feel free to adapt the recipe – add garlic or chilli, fresh ginger or herbs as you like. Half the fun is decorating the top of the pie.

1 kg (2¼ lbs) minced venison

350 g (12 oz) minced fatty meat

250 g (8 oz) venison steak (optional)

150 ml (¼ pt) red wine

3 tablespoons brandy or other spirit

2 tablespoon wine vinegar

2 teaspoons juniper berries, crushed

1 teaspoon each of salt, nutmeg and ginger

¼ teaspoon each of ground cloves and pepper

Mix all the pie filling ingredients thoroughly. They can be left overnight if wished but will be fine without. Grease your pie mould (or a cake tin with removable base). Make the hot water crust: put the flour into a large warmed bowl and make a well in the centre. Boil together the water, butter, lard, salt and nutmeg and tip it into the well in the flour. Stir well together, and as soon as you can handle it, knead it into a smooth slightly greasy paste. Use two-thirds to line the tin. Push it well into all the corners and keep it evenly thick all over. You don't want it too thick but if too thin it may split. Keep the remaining pastry warm.

Pack the filling in tightly, pressing it well down. Roll out the remaining pastry and cover the pie. Make a really good seal between the top and sides by folding and kneading them well together, then trim off any excess and crimp the edges with a fork. Brush with beaten egg and decorate as desired. Make two holes in the top to allow the steam to escape, and place some rolled up

For the hot water crust

700 g (1½ lb) plain flour

300 ml (½ pt) water

120 g (4 oz) butter

120 g (4 oz) lard

Pinch of salt

Pinch of nutmeg

Egg yolk/milk

paper into the holes to keep them open and prevent leakage onto the pastry. (These funnels are called 'Bristols' which, according to some sources, is rhyming slang for 'Bristol City'= titty. Others maintain it is a corruption of 'bristles' – the hog's hairs that surgeons left in a stitched wound to allow it to drain.)

Bake in a hot oven (Gas 6, 200ºC, 400ºF) for about 30 minutes, or until the top is golden brown. Then reduce the heat right down to Gas 3, 160ºC, 325ºF and continue to cook for a further 2-3 hours, depending on the thickness of the pie. Allow to cool completely (takes some hours), then pop it into a hot oven for a couple of minutes to heat the tin but not the pie. Carefully ease the tin off the pie with a knife. It keeps at least a week in the fridge if no-one discovers it's there.

A red deer pie with diagram of armature. From Conrad Hagger's *Neues Saltzburgisches Koch-Buch*, 1719.

Venison and pheasant marbled terrine

A beautiful terrine with a lovely marbled appearance when it is sliced. Pheasant and partridge make the best contrast to venison, but wild duck also works well. Cold terrines and pâtés need slightly heavier spicing than meats eaten hot.

350 g (12 oz) venison steak

350 g (12 oz) pheasant breasts

$^1/_2$ teaspoon ground ginger

$^1/_4$ teaspoon ground cloves

8 juniper berries, crushed

$^1/_4$ teaspoon black pepper

350 g (12 oz) minced pork belly

2 tablespoons brandy or whisky

Sprig of fresh thyme or coriander, chopped

2 cloves garlic, crushed

Salt

80 g (3 oz) fresh spinach leaves

8–10 stoneless prunes, sliced lengthways

200 g (7 oz) thinly cut mild bacon rashers

100 ml (4 fl oz) jellied game stock (optional)

To serve

vinaigrette and caper berries

Cut the venison and pheasant into strips. Sear them quickly in a very hot pan. Mix together the ginger, cloves, juniper and pepper, and scatter it over the meat so that it is well covered. In a bowl, mix together the pork belly, brandy or whisky, fresh herbs, garlic, and a pinch of salt. Line a terrine or loaf tin with the bacon, reserving some slices for the top. Make a thin layer of pork mixture on the base of the loaf tin. Wrap the venison and pheasant strips in the spinach leaves and lay them into the tin, filling all the gaps with more pork mixture and distributing the prunes evenly throughout the layers. Cover the top neatly with bacon rashers and wrap the whole dish in tin foil. Place the tin in a dish with water coming half way up it and bake in a moderate oven (Gas 4, 180ºC, 350ºF) for 2 hours. Then put a weight on the terrine and allow it to cool completely. If wished, melt the jellied game stock, season to taste, and pour over the terrine. It is easiest to slice when well chilled, but tastes best at room temperature. Serve with a drizzle of vinaigrette and some caper berries.

12. Cured and smoked venison

12. Cured and smoked venison

Bresaola, Bunderfleisch, Carpaccio, Coppa, Jamon, Jerky, Pemmican, Prosciutto, Salami – what mouthwatering prospects these names inspire. Curing and smoking meat is a big subject though, so regard this chapter as a useful starting-off point. Much depends on the quality of venison; its thickness, moisture content and more.

The original point of these processes was to preserve meat, but nowadays the different flavours and textures that they provide are more important than their keeping qualities since we have other ways of preserving meat. Smokes and cures used to be much stronger and saltier than we tend to like now, so the degree of cure has become a matter of personal taste - a balance of flavour, texture, and keeping quality.

Brining and dry salting draws moisture out of the meat, concentrating its flavour. So it is important to use venison in perfect condition – bruised or damaged meat will not cure or dry well, though it could be smoked and made into sausages.

Dry-cured venison

A dry-cure is a mixture of predominantly salt, but which includes sugar orhoney to soften the meat, and spices for flavour. The cure draws moistureout of the venison and replaces it with salt which preserves it. It canalso be air-dried after a short curing period. The secret, such as it is,is in knowing when the venison is cured. Too little and it is still uncured in the middle, though many people like it that way. If cured too long, it becomes tough and very salty. Curing times depend on the thickness and temperature of the meat, which will shrink by 25-50%. Small muscles cure quickly and need monitoring to ensure they don,t shrivel up. It is impossible to give exact timings - experiment and see what suits your taste. Always record the weight, thickness of meat and the curing time and temperature for future attempts. Muscles without tapering parts give best results; trim them of all outer muscle. Use coarse salt, not fine, but the sugar can be any type you like. Spices other than juniper are also good - try ginger, thyme, or toasted crushed coriander seeds. My cure is similar to gravadlax and has roughly the same texture.

2–3 chunky venison muscles, each approx. 1.5 kg (3 lbs)

1 kg (2¼ lbs) coarse sea salt

500 g (1 lb+) sugar

2 tablespoons finely ground black pepper

4 tablespoons juniper berries, crushed

Mix together the dry ingredients. Find a deep container that will accommodate the venison muscles. Cover the base with a little dry cure, then place the muscles on top and pack more cure round the edges, between and over the muscles so they are completely covered. While you do this, remember the feel of the fresh muscles. Weight them down, because once some of the water has been drawn out, they will float. Use something that will not corrode in the salt. For muscles of this size, leave for 8–10 days, turning the meat over twice. Lighter or thin muscles take less time.

When you turn them, press them to feel how firm they have become. Eventually you will be able to know when they are cured from the firmness. They should be firm but not rock-hard – for an indication, press your little finger onto the top of the muscle below your thumb. Remove the cured meat from the brine and pat dry. It freezes successfully at this stage and indeed it seems as though the curing process continues very slowly in the freezer. When wanted for use, slice as thinly as you can.

Venison salami

When making salami, saltpetre is not essential: what is essential is a dry atmosphere. Some people used to hang salamis high up in the chimney because there was a good draught of air, not to mention some cool smoke from time to time. Ideal temperature is 16–18°C (61–65°F) – see the drying box below.

6 kg (14 lbs) venison

2.5 kg (5 lbs) hard pork fat

3 tablespoons minced garlic

450 g (1 lb) salt

350 g (12 oz) brown sugar

3 tablespoons cracked black pepper

500 ml (16 fl oz) wine vinegar

1 teaspoon saltpetre (optional)

Pudding skins

Remove all sinews from the venison and either mince coarsely (along with the pork fat) or chop both finely into 1 cm (¹/₂ inch) dice. Thoroughly mix in all the other ingredients and pack the mixture as tightly as possible into the skins because it shrinks as it dries. Tie tightly and hang up to dry. A drying box as in the biltong recipe below can be used, or they can be hung high above an Aga-type stove. You may need to squeeze the skins tightly half-way through the drying to avoid air spaces.

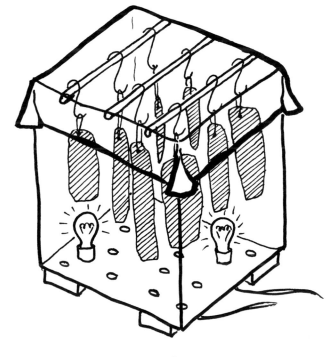

Drying box

BILTONG

Biltong is supposed to have been brought to South Africa by Dutch seamen, but could this extract from Sir Walter Scott's notes in *Waverley* perhaps point to the origins of biltong coming from Scotland after all?

'The Scottish Highlanders in former times had a concise mode of cooking their venison, or rather of dispensing with cooking it, which appears to have greatly surprised the French whom chance made acquainted with it. The Vidame of Charters, when a hostage in England, during the reign of Edward VI, was permitted to travel into Scotland, and penetrated as far as the remote Highlands (*au fond des Sauvages*).

'After a great hunting party, at which a most wonderful quantity of game was destroyed, he saw these Scottish Savages devour a part of their venison raw, without further preparation than compressing it between two batons of wood, so as to force out the blood, and render it extremely hard. This they reckoned a great delicacy: and when the Vidame partook of it, his compliance with their taste rendered him extremely popular.'

The Drying Box. My thanks to Andrew Conroy and others for endlessly discussing the merits and methods of biltong. The main difficulty in Britain is in drying the meat. Either use an electric fan, or build a drying box out of a tea chest (wooden box) about 45 x 45 x 60 cm (18 x 18 x 2 inches) high . Drill some holes 15 mm ($^1/_2$ inch) diameter in the base and the top. Wire up two 50-watt lightbulbs and place them in the bottom of the box. Hang the meat off rails set into the rim of the box, and seal all gaps to prevent flies. Yellow lightbulbs do not attract flies so much, and if you start to hang the meat in the evening, the surface will have dried off before flies get going the next day, though the spices should prove a deterrent. Depending on the thickness of the meat, it could take from 3 days to 1 week (or even longer) to dry sufficiently.

Biltong

Saltpetre is not easy to get hold of nowadays because it was used to make explosives, though some butchers seem to manage to get it. Its main function is to preserve the meat's bright colour so it is not essential. Sodium bicarbonate (bicarbonate of soda) inhibits mould so is useful in humid areas. Other spices, like chilli, can be added to taste but shouldn't overpower the meat. Choose muscles without too much sinew, either from the leg, loin or fillet.

5 kg (11 lbs) boneless venison

150 g (6 oz) coarse salt

150 g (6 oz) cracked black pepper

150 g (6 oz) crushed coriander seed

2 tablespoons brown sugar

1 head garlic cloves, crushed

1 teaspoon saltpetre (optional)

1 teaspoon sodium bicarbonate (optional)

125 ml (¼ pt) malt or wine vinegar

Cut each venison piece to a uniform thickness so it dries evenly. Remove all the sinews. Mix together all seasonings except the vinegar. Rub some of the seasoning into each piece of meat, then sprinkle a thin layer on the base of a plastic container and lay the strips of meat in it, sprinkling more seasoning and some drops of vinegar between each layer as you go. Put the container in a cool place for 12–18 hours. Then lift out the pieces of meat and let them finish dripping before hanging them up in a well-ventilated place until dried to taste. For my taste, the ideal biltong is dried but still nice and pliable. For a milder flavour, the spices can be quickly rinsed off in a dilute 10:1 solution of vinegar before drying.

Venison jerky – mild

Jerky is drier than biltong and made from thinner strips cut to the thickness of your finger. The word comes from *charqui*, a South American word for dried beef. The meat is normally cut with the grain rather than across it to give long strips that are really chewy. Novices and the dentally challenged can make slices across the grain but real men chew. There are hundreds of recipes ranging from the very mild to the extremely hot. I prefer mild jerky as it doesn't obliterate the venison. This recipe is from Harold Webster, probably America's greatest venison enthusiast. He enjoys hunting deer in the old-fashioned way, quietly and with bow-and-arrow, as he believes this is the best way to get unstressed venison.

1.8 kg (4 lb) venison

4.5 litres (8 pts) water

180 g (6 oz) salt

110 g (4 oz) sugar

2 tablespoons black pepper

10 bay leaves

1 teaspoon cloves

1 teaspoon dried sage

Remove all the sinew from the venison and cut it into slim strips the size of your finger. Boil some of the water and add all the pickle ingredients, stirring until the salt and sugar have dissolved in the water. Remove from the heat and pour into a plastic or ceramic container with the rest of the (cold) water. When it is quite cold, add the venison strips, stir them around, and keep them weighted down in the brine. Leave for 24 hours, stirring it occasionally. Then drain off the brine and trickle cold tap water through the meat container for an hour. Hang the venison in a cool oven (Gas ¹/₈, 50–55ºC, (120–140ºF) until the jerky is leather hard. You can also dry it in a smokehouse for extra smoky flavour or use the biltong-drying box on page 225.

Hot and spicy venison jerky

The full works. Apart from the common denominators of salt and pepper, jerky ingredients range from soy sauce, Worcestershire sauce, garlic powder, sugar, mesquite (liquid smoke), curry powder, pineapple juice, whisky, onion powder, oil, Tabasco sauce, cider vinegar, Hickory smoked salt, chilli sauce or teriyaki sauce. Take your pick. Everything is optional. Just steep the strips in it and dry. This is about right for 1–1 1/2 kg (2–3 lbs) venison.

2 teaspoons salt

2 teaspoons sugar

1 teaspoon black pepper

2 tablespoons vinegar

1 teaspoon garlic powder

2 teaspoons liquid smoke

3 drops Tabasco sauce

2 tablespoons soy sauce

2 onions, very thinly sliced

Mix all these marinade ingredients together. Cut the venison into strips as thick as your finger and submerge them in the marinade for 4–24 hours, turning occasionally. Thread the strips on meat skewers and allow to drain a little, then hang it in the oven and dry off the venison on its lowest setting, aiming for 60ºC (150ºF) for 6–8 hours, checking the strips are not touching each other. You may need to leave the oven door ajar to keep it as cool as that.

BRINE CURES FOR VENISON

Tjälknöl

In Sweden this is made with elk (moose) venison, the largest of the deer species. At one time people used to ride them. They gallop so fast on their great long legs that in the seventeenth century, riding elk was banned because criminals kept escaping from the police who only had horses. Tjäle is Swedish for hard frozen winter soil; Knöl means a round lump. My thanks to Cecilia Gliksten and Kersten Phillips for sharing their recipes.

Tjälknöl is often made at Christmas because it is ideal for serving a lot of people at a party. It would make a lovely starter for a wedding too. It's an odd way of curing the meat but it really does work, and the venison really does have to be frozen. A chunky joint is preferable to a long thin one here. You want to find a container for soaking the meat that will allow it to be covered with the liquid. If any of the meat is sticking out, you will need to keep turning it around in the brine. If you soak it in a thick polythene bag, the brine can be pulled round the meat.

2 kg (4¼ lbs) frozen boneless venison haunch

1 litre (1¾ pt) water

125 g (4¼ oz) coarse salt

2 tablespoons sugar

1 bay leaf

½ teaspoon crushed black pepper

15 juniper berries, crushed

Put the frozen joint into a narrow ovenproof dish and put it in a cold oven. Turn the oven on to a very low setting (Gas ⅛, 80°C, 175°F) and leave it in the oven for 12 hours. When you test it with a meat thermometer, the inside should still be pink at 65°C (150ºF).

Meanwhile boil up the water with the rest of the ingredients and allow them to cool completely. Put the hot joint into the cold liquid and leave it there for 5 hours. No longer, or it will be too salty. After 5 hours remove the meat from the brine and allow it to drain dry. Put it in a plastic bag in the fridge, or it can be frozen again for future use. It is served cold, very thinly sliced. See p.73 for serving suggestions.

Marinated venison carpaccio

Jane Grigson was my greatest food heroine, not only for her excellent recipes and scholarship in food history, but for her generosity of spirit. As a novice food writer twenty years ago, I found her enthusiasm and encouragement inspirational. During a correspondence, she sent this recipe to start me off on my quest for a good venison carpaccio. My thanks are due to her daughter Sophie for giving me permission to reproduce it here. It is really delicious, though I had to restrict it to home use because I could not reliably ensure that the tunnel left by removing the leg bone did not become sticky, and air-drying a large piece of meat in Scotland is not something that can be reliably accomplished either. Using a large single muscle overcomes the boning-out problem, of course, and a drying chamber would eliminate the vagaries of an unpredictable climate.

These are the amounts for a whole fallow haunch; use $^2/_3$ the amount for roe and $1^1/_2$ times for red deer. Ask your butcher to tunnel-bone the haunch or see p.269 to do this yourself.

4 kg (9 lb) boned whole haunch

2 litres (3$^1/_3$ pts) red wine

175 ml (6 fl oz) mellow sherry vinegar

400 g (14 oz) coarse sea salt

1 large onion, thinly sliced

1 large carrot, thinly sliced

1 large sharp apple, thinly sliced

1 chunk celeriac

Small bunch fresh thyme

1 tablespoon black peppercorns, cracked

1 tablespoon juniper berries, crushed

4 bay leaves

Bring all the ingredients for the brine to the boil and simmer for 20 minutes, stirring to dissolve the salt. Cool. Place the venison in a ceramic, stainless steel or plastic container and pour the brine over it so that it is completely covered. Cover with a lid or tin foil and leave for 10 days, turning the meat daily. Then drain off the brine and pat the meat dry, paying attention to the bone cavity. Wrap the meat in muslin. Hang in a cool airy place for about 10 days. After a week, you can press the meat to see if it has firmed up enough to slice thinly. When it is firm enough, unwrap it and rub it all over with olive oil, making sure the bone cavity is also oiled. Wrap the joint in greaseproof paper and keep in the fridge, slicing it as required. Serve with pieces of melon, black pepper and a dressing made from equal quantities of olive oil, orange juice and Madiera or sweet sherry.

Smoking venison

Smoking is one of the oldest methods of protecting meat from fly damage. Smoking meat for sale is a specialist subject, but it is good fun so here are some guidelines for home-smoking. The flavour of smoke attaches itself most readily to fat, so very lean venison will be milder in flavour unless brined and/or oiled beforehand. Equally, sausages that contain fat will absorb smoke more quickly. Venison can be cured and cold-smoked for eating raw (like smoked salmon) or it can be cold-smoked and cooked at a later stage, or it can be hot-smoked during which it is cooked and smoked at the same time.

At its most simple, joints of venison can be hot-smoked without brining, but care needs to be taken not to dry out the meat. Either make sure it remains pink, or else lard the meat. Use beef readings on a meat thermometer to determine the pinkness. Steaks do not perform very well as they are overcooked before the smoke has much time to take effect.

The more usual procedure is to brine meat before hot- or cold-smoking it. This helps the smoke to permeate. Plastic, ceramic or stainless steel containers are best for brining. Oak (or hickory), pine, fruit wood and alder are popular woods for smoking; in America, mesquite is also used, sometimes as a flavouring.

4 litres (6½ pts) water

2 litres (3¼ pts) Brown ale or stout

450 g (1 lb) salt

450 g (1 lb) brown sugar

2 teaspoons juniper berries, crushed

1 teaspoon cracked black pepper

1 teaspoon ground ginger

¼ teaspoon ground cloves

Boil all the ingredients together, cool and immerse the venison, turning it every day. A whole red deer haunch will need 7–10 days, a muscle block 1–3 days. Then remove from the liquid and dry for 2 days. Cold-smoke at a maximum temperature of 30ºC (85ºF) for 1–3 days. The venison will have a supple texture and can be thinly sliced or roasted afterwards. Some people like to dry it afterwards (up to 2 weeks), which intensifies the flavour and allows it to keep even longer. The conditions should be cool, dark and dry, and the meat should be screened against flies. After drying, this is best thinly sliced. For hot smoking joints, brine the meat as before, then smoke for 6–12 hours at 80ºC (175ºF). Use a meat thermometer to determine when the venison is cooked. When the centre reaches 65ºC (135ºF) it is done.

Raspberry tea smoked venison

Chef Paul Davidson showed me this very simple method of home-smoking venison – it was a popular starter in the hotel where he worked. He serves it with rosemary jelly. The meat should be about 6 cm (2½ inches) thick in order to remain moist and pink inside. The smoking pan needs to be heated on the stove-top as well as to go in the oven.

Starter for 8

500 g (1 lb+) venison loin or rolled haunch

Olive oil

Handful of thyme

4 raspberry tea bags

Equipment

Small dish to marinate venison

Cling film

Small frying pan

Flat bottomed ovenproof frying pan or tray

Aluminium foil

600 ml (1 pint) dry sawdust or fine wood shavings

Press the thyme onto the meat, place it in a tight-fitting dish or plastic bag, and completely cover it with olive oil. Leave to marinate in the fridge for 2-3 days.

Preheat the oven to Gas 8, 230ºC, 450ºF. Prepare the smoking pan by covering its base completely with a thin layer (less than 1 cm / ½ inch) of sawdust. Place the raspberry teabags on top. Then cut a sheet of foil and pierce it all over with a fork to make holes for the smoke to come through. Place the raspberry teabags on top. Then cut a sheet of foil over the sawdust and press it down so that it fits tightly, covering the sawdust completely.

Now heat a frying pan till very hot. Scrape the thyme off the venison and quickly brown it all over. There will be enough oil already on the venison to brown it. Place it on top of the pierced foil sheet, then cover the pan with a lid, or use more foil to make a tight-fitting lid. Place the pan over a high heat for 5 minutes, by which time there will be some smoke emerging from under the lid.

Now put the pan into the preheated oven for five minutes, then remove from the oven, take off the foil lid, and allow the meat to cool in the smoking pan. When it is quite cold, wrap it tightly in cling film and chill it in the fridge before slicing it very thinly. Serving with jelly and spicy herb salad.

13. *Venison sausages, stuffing and puddings*

How to make your own

13. Venison sausages, stuffing and puddings

How to make your own

Making sausages is really simple. After all, a sausage is only a mixture of meat and fat with some spicing stuffed into a casing. But unfortunately it's not quite as simple as handing over a list of ingredients, because everyone has a different reason for wanting to make sausages. Perhaps they are for home consumption, in which case you may want to use ingredients that would make them too expensive to sell. Or perhaps you want to make sausages suitable for someone with special dietary needs. Or perhaps you'd like to make really good sausage rolls for your children. Or maybe there is a whole carcase and lots of trimmings in the freezer to deal with. If you want to sell your venison sausages – and many small producers now do – then there are hygiene constraints that need to be addressed. This is not to say that commercial sausages need to be boring standard items, though – far from it. But everyone has different priorities.

The two most important pieces of advice I can offer are: firstly – go easy on the spices to begin with. Take a few teaspoonfuls of mixture and fry it up and then adjust the seasoning if necessary. In particular, take care in multiplying up a recipe for large-scale use, as spices don't always multiply up successfully. Secondly, write down every ingredient exactly at the time that you add it. If you wait till the end, you will have forgotten something, I promise you. There is nothing more frustrating than to have invented a brilliant sausage and then be unable to recreate it.

EQUIPMENT

You can make sausages at home without any special equipment at all. You can buy ready-minced venison and belly pork, you can hand mix your ingredients, and if you don't even want to stuff the filling into skins using a plastic funnel, you can roll them in flour and fry them without skins. Or make the best sausage rolls in the world.

MINCING (GRINDING) For small quantities or samples, the simplest is a metal hand mincer that can be clamped onto a work surface. It may not be able to cope with much sinew, so trim that off. Next size up is electric attachments that come with large domestic food mixers. These are robust and perfect for home sausage-making. If you make sausages to sell, you will want the type of small mincer a high street butcher would use. Industrial operations use a bowl cutter, which are inclined to turn the ingredients into slurry. I am sure we have all experienced sausages like that.

Most butchers use a fine mincing plate. Mince the meat once for a normal 'country' style sausage, twice for a 'smooth' one. The more you mince meat, the paler it becomes. Mince the fat at the same time. The meat pushes it through and stops it turning into a solid lump that clogs up the machine. A coarse plate is good for making salamis, pie mince and very large sausages. Make sure the mincer blades are kept razor sharp, as blunt blades squeeze moisture out of the meat.

MIXING This sounds obvious, but rather than adding each spice individually, mix all your spices and any other dry ingredients together and then scatter the mixture as thinly and widely as you can over the meat/fat so that the spices are distributed evenly. Hand-mixing is fine for making sausages at home. Wear plastic gloves for this. Indeed some butchers prefer to mix all their ingredients by hand before mincing as there is no risk of getting a clump of unmixed spices. Commercial producers may like to consider a mincer/mixer, which minces the meat straight into a mixer that works quite slowly, rather like a dough hook, and it doesn't turn the mixture into a paste.

FILLING At its most simple, all you need is a funnel with a wide tube long enough to take the sausage skins. You can poke the sausage meat down into it with a wooden spoon handle or your fingers. Food mixers with mincers usually have a sausage-filling attachment too, with different sizes of funnels to make anything from salamis to chipolatas. Next size up is a tabletop filler that clamps onto a surface and can take from 2.5–4 kg (6–10 lbs) mixture at a time. These are hand operated, which is helpful to the beginner since you can control the speed at which the mixture comes out. See p. 239. Knee-operated electric fillers are for the small-scale professional: it is part of every butcher's initiation to have to wield one of these. With inexperienced handling, sausage skins can flick like a hosepipe and the meat hurtle out of the skins with a loud bang to hit the opposite wall with quite some force.

PACKING AND FREEZING See page 272.

HEALTH AND HYGIENE Everything, including people, should be spotlessly clean. The more meat is chopped, minced and mixed with other things, the more surface there is to be contaminated. So keep everything as cold as possible and proceed as quickly as possible. Some people like to wear thin latex gloves when handling minced meat to stop it sticking to their hands.

MAKING SAUSAGES FOR SALE When you sell meat products considered 'medium or high risk', there is a raft of legislation which, in the current food climate, looks set to increase rather than decrease. Most requirements are based on common sense but unfortunately some are created to cope with manufacturers of the worst type, which places an unfair onus on those who actually want to do a good job instead of cheating their customers. Such regulations will cover your premises, which have to be registered or licensed, the storage and transport of your goods, how you monitor your ingredients and working practices and the labelling of your products. Every country has different regulations, so start by contacting your local Department of Environmental Health, Meat Hygiene Service or their equivalent. Usually they are very helpful to a beginner – it is their job, after all.

Commercial meat processing equipment is expensive, so it is worth investigating secondhand equipment which is quite easy to buy now that so many small butchers are closing. You can't go wrong buying food-grade tables and containers, but with secondhand machinery, consider the cost and availability of spare parts and a service engineer, also whether they might be made redundant by forthcoming legislation. If it is cheap enough there is less worry and you might be lucky – we once bought a haggis boiler at auction for £5, thinking it would tide us over till the following spring. It lasted for ten years.

This may sound daunting but it soon becomes routine and since your sausages will be so much better than your rivals who have to have theirs made up for them, it is easily worth it.

INGREDIENTS

This is where the fun starts – and the discussions and arguments about what a sausage should be. Every country has its local variations, all of which are the best in the world. Throughout most of Europe and certainly in America, sausages are made with meat, fat, spices and that's that. One hundred per cent meat. No breadcrumbs, no butcher's rusk, no filler and extenders, no oat or any other kind of meal. They regard British sausages as a crummy con trick. But using fine breadcrumbs is an honourable tradition that goes right back to the best of medieval cooking, and British people love their traditional sausages the way they are.

Making sausages at home gives great opportunity for experiment, and sometimes those small jars of unused exotic ingredients in the cupboard can, if thoughtfully used, come into their own with surprisingly successful results. The same goes for the bottles of strange spirits and liqueurs. When they work, I call them serendipity sausages. The key phrase is 'thoughtfully used'! You don't want to end up with a sticky mish-mash.

THE MEAT Any part of the deer can be used, but cut out thick gristle, as it will toughen. The heart adds great meatiness – trim off the fat on top first. Any meaty trimmings can be used as long as they are not outside edges that are sticky or blackened. That indicates a lot of bacteria. And, of course, you can substitute part of the venison with other choice meats (wood pigeon, rabbit or pheasant) and adjust the spicing accordingly.

THE FAT The norm used to be that about a third of sausage meat should be fat, though nowadays many sausages are made with far less. We make ours with about 14% and they eat well. If the deer is mature and in good condition, there could be a fair bit of fat on the trimmings. Venison fat is like suet so trim off excess and adjust when adding other fatty meat. However a lot of venison is so lean that you have to add fat from another species. My recipes assume there is little fat on the meat.

If you are concerned about fats, then choose fat from grass-fed animals. Their fat is far better for you than grain-fed animals. Mutton or hill lamb fat used to be recommended as being the most like venison. It is not easy to come by, but you may find a supplier at a farmer's market who is only too pleased to have a sale for their fatty trimmings. The same goes for beef, which is also good for sausages. Pork fat is the most traditional, partly because there used to be so much of it. However, I find that because

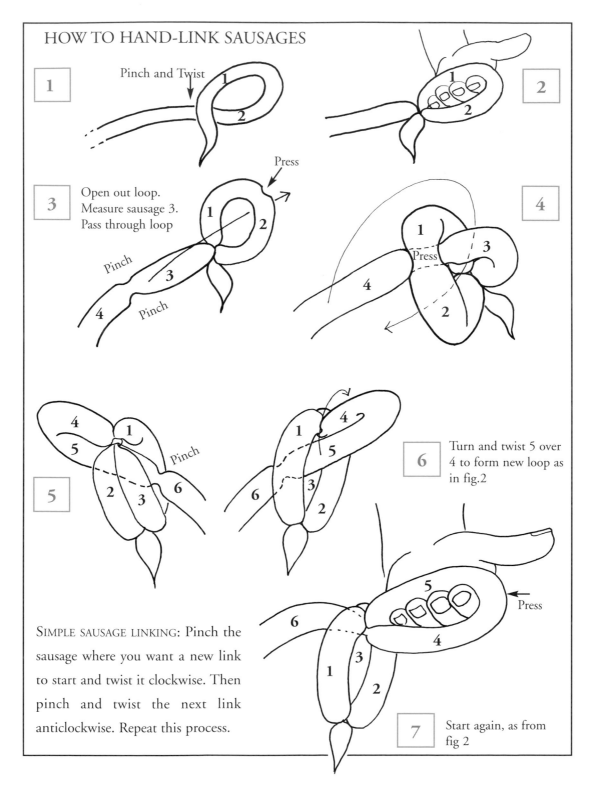

HOW TO HAND-LINK SAUSAGES

1 Pinch and Twist

2

3 Open out loop. Measure sausage 3. Pass through loop

Press

Pinch

Pinch

4 Press

5 Pinch

6 Turn and twist 5 over 4 to form new loop as in fig.2

SIMPLE SAUSAGE LINKING: Pinch the sausage where you want a new link to start and twist it clockwise. Then pinch and twist the next link anticlockwise. Repeat this process.

Press

7 Start again, as from fig 2

it is a soft fat, you need less of it to achieve the same lubricating effect. The downside is that pork is unsuitable for Jews and Muslims.

SKINS (CASINGS) There are two sorts of sausage skins: natural skins (casings) and collagen casings. Natural casings are more expensive as they are time-consuming to prepare. You buy them in tubs of brine, or dry-salted which need soaking overnight before use. Sausages made with natural skins will never be completely consistent in size, but that should only worry strict portion controllers. Beef casings (runners) are used for salamis and ox bungs for puddings like haggis. Pork casings are suitable for small salamis and plump sausages. Sheep casings are the finest, and make slim sausages and chipolata (cocktail) sausages. So far as I am concerned, natural casings are far and away the best and well worth the extra expense. I am surprised that more fuss is not made about them.

Collagen casings are man-made and the skins are thicker, more rubbery and sometimes have a tendency to burst in cooking. What I dislike most about them is the sweet flavourings they incorporate into the skins. These often smell delicious when they are cooking, but the taste and texture is invariably a disappointment. Still, they are cheap, robust to manufacture with, and just great for portion-controllers.

Whichever you use, feed them onto the filler tube leaving about 5 cm (2 inches) hanging over the end. Don't tie the end because an air bubble comes out first. Start turning the filler machine (or the motor) and hold the skins lightly onto the tube. Once the skin starts to fill, you will soon get the feel for how to control the speed and tightness of the skin coming off the end. If you encounter (or make) a hole in the skins just pinch above the hole and hold it closed while you start filling again so it doesn't pour out of the hole. The skill in filling sausage skins is in getting them full enough to be plump but not so full that you can't link them or so that they burst when cooking. Fill salami skins as tight as you can since the filling shrinks as it dries. But if you want to twist or link the sausages, the shorter your sausages are in proportion to their thickness, the slacker you need to leave the filling. Linking sausages is a satisfying activity rather like knitting (see diagram). Sausages – even industrial ones – are still always made about 10 cm (4 inches) long because that is the length they always came out when being hand-linked.

BINDERS Of course you don't have to use a binder in your sausages. However, an awful lot of people like the texture and flavour. Furthermore, if soaked in a flavourful liquid beforehand, you can cut down on the amount of fat needed. For home use, real breadcrumbs are good to use, either fresh or dried in the oven. However, for commercial use, remember that they contain yeast which affects keeping quality. That is why most commercial butchers use rusk, a refined wheat-based product that is capable of soaking up a great deal of water. It almost invariably comes ready-mixed with seasonings, colourings and preservatives, and so far as I am concerned, the sausage gourmet is not interested in these. I use toasted oatmeal for our sausages, which I think gives a lovely nutty flavour. Don't soak medium oatmeal beforehand or it turns into a solid mass. If you use large grains such as pinhead oatmeal or bulghar wheat, soak them in a delicious liquid for an hour to prevent them bursting the skins. Oatmeal has the advantage of being suitable for people with wheat intolerance, and many (but not all) coeliacs. A pure meat sausage gets rid of the problem completely.

SPICES AND HERBS These give sausages their character. Anyone passionate about spices may already be used to toasting and grinding fresh spices; it undoubtedly gives them vivacity. If your source is some spice jars that have been around for years, you may be surprised at how much stronger fresh spices are. Try to buy them from shops that sell lots as they are more likely to be fresh. When making up your own recipes into larger batches, be cautious about multiplying-up spices. A teaspoonful that works for 500 g (1 lb+) meat does not necessarily mean that 20 teaspoons will be right for a 10 kg (22 lb) batch. Err on the side of caution, and weigh everything scrupulously. Once you have it right, make up large batches of your spice mix and calculate the weight for a batch rather than weighing out individual spices which is more prone to error. The salt acts to distribute the spices.

Spices and herbs that complement venison fall into two categories: aromatic – juniper (good quality juniper never grinds to a fine powder; it will always remain in coarse bits), thyme, rosemary, lovage, sage, fennel or aniseed, turmeric, sweet paprika, cardamom, cloves and cinnamon; and hot spices – ginger, coriander, cumin, chilli, black pepper, cayenne pepper, hot paprika and mustard.

VEGETABLES AND FRUIT They add texture and succulence as well as flavour but intense flavours work best in sausages. Thus prunes are more effective than plums, dried ceps more effective than fresh. To add succulence, use onions, leeks, aubergines, mushrooms, tomatoes, spinach or peppers. For a more intense flavour, try redcurrants, prunes, dried fungi, dried tomatoes, olives, capers or garlic.

LIQUIDS Sometimes, a little liquid is needed to make the mixture soft enough for filling, especially when using breadcrumbs, oatmeal or the dreaded rusk. Exactly how much is needed depends on the meat. Defrosted meat is wetter. Also, watery ingredients (e.g. tomatoes, peppers) affect the consistency. Sometimes a simple sausage is just what's wanted, so water is fine for achieving the right texture. For variety, try adding wine, orange juice, diluted wine vinegar, strong ale (it may be necessary to boil it down to reduce it), whisky or brandy, or indeed those ends of bottles in the cupboard. If you use a beer kit instead of ale, you can use the diluted malted syrup without having to ferment it with unwanted yeast.

SPECIAL DIET SAUSAGES If you remove one of the main ingredients of a sausage, make sure that its texture, flavour or moistness is replaced. For low-salt sausages, just add a little more spice: mustard seed, perhaps, or cumin. For sausages with little or no fat you need to replace the slippery succulence that fat gives. You could soak your breadcrumbs or oatmeal in walnut oil for example, or add vegetables like onions, sweet peppers, aubergine, mushrooms, and to a lesser extent, tomatoes and spinach.

PRESERVATIVES, COLOURINGS AND FLAVOUR ENHANCERS Don't use them. If you develop a good sausage recipe they are completely unnecessary, and they can mask the look and the smell of meat that is going off. If your products are additive-free, your nose will tell you perfectly well whether your meat or product is fresh.

FRESH SAUSAGE RECIPES

Some of these are suitable for commercial use, others are more for the home cook. I have in most cases made them in approximately 1 kg, 2 kg or 4 kg ($2^1/_4$, $4^1/_2$ or 9 lb) batches so they can be more easily compared and multiplied up or down.

Venison sausages, a basic recipe

This one has less fat than the all meat ones. Reduce it further to 650 g (1½ lb) if you like. You can of course add other ingredients or leave some out. For example, you can use different binders or leave them out all together.

2.25 kg (6 lb) venison

1.25 kg (2½ lb) fat – pork, lamb, etc.

450 g (1 lb) breadcrumbs or medium oatmeal

50 g (2 oz) salt

15 g (½ oz) ground black pepper

15 g (½ oz) nutmeg

7 g (¼ oz) ground ginger

7 g (¼ oz) cloves

300 ml (½ pt) water or other liquid

Chop the venison and fat into 8 cm (3 inch) chunks, then mince them together using the fine plate (if using a small hand-operated mincer, cut the meat smaller, then use the coarse plate first and then the fine or it may be too hard to mince.) Mix the breadcrumbs or oatmeal together with the spices and scatter them into the meat. Mix thoroughly, adding the liquid until the right consistency is reached. Fill natural casings and link in the traditional way. Hang them up to dry-off before packing or cooking.

Variations on the basic recipe

Venison and tomato sausages

An excellent breakfast sausage that children like too. Make them as in the basic recipe above, adding in a 450 g (1 lb) tin of tomatoes and their juice, or 700–900 g (1$^1/_2$–2 lb) peeled fresh tomatoes. Reduce the liquid accordingly. Serve them with some basil leaves or a little pesto sauce. It seems almost impossible to buy fresh tomatoes in Britain that have any flavour so tinned tomatoes are best here, though buy good quality ones.

No-salt venison sausages with honey and mustard

Use the same basic recipe above, but remove the salt and replace it with 2 tablespoons wholegrain mustard and two tablespoons of honey. If the honey is stiff, warm it in a little of the water with the mustard so that it can be mixed in evenly.

Low-or no-fat sausages with onions and mushrooms

Use the basic recipe above and either reduce the fat to just 500 g (1 lb+) or eliminate it altogether. Then add in 500 g (1 lb+) peeled onions and 500 g (1 lb+) fresh mushrooms. If it is wild mushroom season, they will be even better. A tablespoon of dried mushroom powder intensifies the flavour, but is not essential. Three or four tablespoons fresh thyme or one of dried, go well with mushrooms. Add in 2 or 3 teaspoonfuls of chopped garlic too, if you like it – it's good for your heart, as are the onions and the oatmeal. So is a tot of spirit, so add in some brandy or whisky if the idea appeals.

   You could also use 1 kg (2$^1/_4$ lb) aubergine to keep the sausages moist. Cut them in half and bake in a microwave for 5 minutes till soft, then scrape off the cooked flesh. You might like to add a tablespoon of oregano to the aubergine. With healthy sausages like these you could end up living an awfully long time.

Venison and juniper sausages with pine nuts

These are the flavours of my garden in Périgord: pine nuts from the huge umbrella pines, juniper from the hedges and a touch of wine vinegar from the bottle that got left out in the sun. Juniper berries should be oily inside and therwfore don't grind very finely. Try adding some of the salt and crushing them together, sometimes that helps to break them down into smaller bits. Pine nuts are improved by sautéing them in a frying pan with a smear of oil until they are deep golden brown. Huge numbers of chestnuts also grow in Périgord, so you could use them instead of pine nuts. You could also make this mixture into burgers.

2.25 kg (6 lb) venison

1.25 kg (2¹/₂ lb) fat –
pork, lamb, etc.

450 g (1 lb) pine nuts or
chestnuts

15 g (¹/₂ oz) juniper
berries, crushed

50 g (2 oz) salt

30 g (1 oz) allspice

150 ml (¹/₄ pt) red wine
vinegar

Lightly spiced venison sausages

With its sweet peppers and cumin, and coarse cut meat, this recipe has a North African flavour so I have suggested lamb fat rather than pork, but either would do.

2.25 kg (6 lb) venison

1.75 g (4 lb) lamb fat

350 g (12 oz) sweet bell peppers

50 g (2 oz) salt

30 g (1 oz) ground cumin

30 g (1 oz) cracked black pepper

7 g (¼ oz) ground coriander seed

Chop the venison and fat into chunks of a size suitable for your mixer. Mince them together using the coarse plate. Chop and deseed the peppers and scatter them over the meat. Mix the breadcrumbs or oatmeal together with the spices and scatter them into the meat, mix everything thoroughly, then mince again through the coarse plate. If needed, add water until the right consistency is reached. Fill natural casings and link in the traditional way.

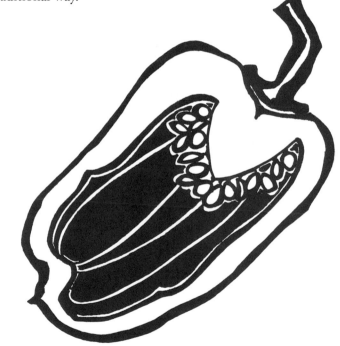

Hunter's venison sausage

This is Harold Webster's recipe. As well as being an expert cook and author, Harold is a keen hunter. This is an all-meat sausage so has a bit more fat. If it looks as though the sausages may be a little peppery, either cut out the cayenne and allspice or reduce the black pepper.

2 kg (4½ lb) cubed venison

2 kg (4½ lb) cubed fatty pork

2 **crushed** cloves garlic or ½ teaspoon powder

2 tablespoons salt

2 tablespoons coarse ground black pepper

½ teaspoon cayenne pepper (optional)

½ teaspoon ground allspice

¾ teaspoon ground mace

¼ teaspoon ground nutmeg

Approx 150 ml (¼ pt) hot water

Mix the venison, pork and crushed garlic together and mince with a fine blade. Stir all the spices together and mix them in to the meat well. Mince a second time. Add enough hot water to make a good sausage consistency, then fill pork casings with the mixture or make it into little patties.

Hot and spicy venison chorizo

You could devote a whole chapter to chorizo, a sausage that has leapt in popularity recently. There are as many variations as there are people who make them, and of course everyone's is the best, whether it is a hot Spanish one, a fiery Mexican one, a milder French one, *chouriço*, the Portuguese version or *chaurice*, the aromatic Franco-Spanish mélange created by the Creoles of Louisiana. The fieriness varies from less than one teaspoon of chilli powder per kg (2 lbs+) to 4 tablespoons per kg (2 lbs+). Not for me, that one. Here is a middling one; add or subtract as you will.

1.5 kg (3½ lb) venison

900 g (2 lb) fat belly pork

6 cloves garlic

2 small sweet bell or chilli peppers

1 tablespoon salt

2 teaspoons ground black pepper

1 tablespoon chilli powder

2 teaspoons cayenne pepper

1 teaspoon cumin

1 tablespoon smoked Spanish paprika

2 teaspoons dried thyme

120 ml (4 fl oz) wine vinegar

Cut the venison and pork belly into chunks. Chop the garlic and chilli or bell pepper into tiny pieces. Scatter over all the other ingredients and sprinkle the vinegar over them. Mince once for a coarse mixture, twice for a smoother one. It can be packed into sausage casings or simply formed into patties, or even just left as a sort of cooked seasoning that is added to spice up innumerable dishes.

Scotch whisky venison sausages

With venison, oatmeal, onions and whisky, these are good Scots fare. Until recently, you could have argued that garlic is not very Scottish, but an enterprising couple now grow really good garlic right up near the Moray Firth. The slight sweetness of the onion and sugar complements the whisky here. No doubt if you are Irish or American you will use whiskey or bourbon. Breathe deeply when you cook these. Slàinte!

2.25 kg (6 lb) venison

1.25 kg (2½ lb) beef or lamb fat

375 g (12 oz) onions

50 g (2 oz) garlic, minced

375 g (12 oz) medium oatmeal

50 g (2 oz) salt

50 g (2 oz) dark brown sugar

15 g (½ oz) ground black pepper

15 g (½ oz) nutmeg

300 ml (½ pint) Scotch whisky

Chop the onions, meat and fat into large cubes and mince once on the coarse plate. Mix together all the dry ingredients and stir them well into the meat. Mince again, and then mix in the whisky, adding some water if necessary for a good sausage meat consistency.

Variation

Venison sausages with brandy and prunes

Another good combination. Omit the sugar and oatmeal. Replace the onions with 375 g (12 oz) stoneless prunes and the whisky with brandy. If the prunes are very dry, soak them in water or wine for a few hours or overnight.

Venison stuffing

Any of the fresh sausagemeat recipes above can be used as a stuffing, and they go well with poultry and game birds. Take your pick. You can also make venison forcemeat balls, dust them with flour and roast them alongside a joint or game bird. We make a lot of stuffing for people to liven up their turkey.

Venison sausage rolls

Children love these. Use any of the sausagemeat recipes above, roll the mixture out on a floured board, and wrap in your preferred pastry. There is a recipe for short crust pastry on p.188 and flaky pastry on p.191. Equal quantities by weight of pastry to filling are about right for most tastes, though if you roll the pastry thinner it is better for you.

Venison salami

See p.224

Deer haggis

Some specialist suppliers make venison haggis and it now appears on restaurant menus as a little starter, teamed up with things like mashed celeriac and carrot cakes, a whisky-flavoured jus, or roasted neeps. Or they are rolled in puff pastry, deep fried in breadcrumbs, popped into vol-au-vent cases, and so on.

Haggis is part of that world-wide family of concoctions made from scraps of meat and offal packed into a pudding skin with some kind of meal and then boiled, baked or fried. 'Little bags of mystery' André Simon called them. Despite Robert Burns' eulogy to the sheep haggis, it is my contention that venison haggis is the original Scots haggis since deer were in Scotland long before the sheep. Recipes for 'haggies' made of various meats appear in early English cookery books, too, reflecting the origin of the word: hachis, to chop. Here is a recipe from a Highland Chief, which appears in F. Marian MacNeil's classic *The Scots Kitchen*. He will be referring to red deer offal. It is steamed (like a Christmas pudding) in a covered bowl, which makes it manageable by people without sausage-making equipment. It doesn't include the dreaded lungs either.

500 g (1 lb+) venison heart

500 g (1 lb+) venison liver

225 g (8 oz) venison suet, minced

225 g (8 oz) coarse or pinhead oatmeal

3 onions, finely chopped

Salt and black pepper

450 g (1 lb) suet crust (p.192)

Boil the heart and liver in water for half an hour. When cold mince the heart and liver very fine. To these add the suet, the coarse oatmeal, previously toasted in the oven or before the fire, the finely chopped onions, a tablespoon of salt, and a strong seasoning of black pepper. Mix all well together. Put into a pudding basin, cover with paste as for a venison steak pudding, and simmer for four hours. Serve in the basin, very hot.

14. Just Desserts

Six venison curiosities

14. Just desserts

Six venison curiosities

These recipes are curiosities, but all worth trying if you have the ingredients. They appeal to those who enjoy recreations and eccentricities. Some of these dishes formed part of a demonstration banquet for an international congress. I produced a nine-course banquet with deer ingredients in every course, including a vegetarian option, which involved reindeer cheese.

Nowadays the notion of including meat in a dessert dish is abnormal, but in the days when all the dishes were presented together on the table instead of being presented as separate courses, the boundaries between sweet and savoury were not very clear-cut – meat was often cooked with sugar. By the twentieth century, savoury dishes were entirely savoury and sweet dishes reserved for a dessert course. However, a more adventurous generation is now familiar with Middle and Far Eastern dishes, which combine these ingredients. And, of course, it was from the Middle East that these sweet/savoury flavours originally came to Britain. So we come full circle.

Hartshorn and hindberry jelly

Serves 4-6

Hindberry is an old country name for the raspberry: hinds certainly love them. And hartshorn jelly is a relic from the past. Many old cookery books include recipes for jellies that call for hartshorn as it was regarded as a tonic. It was also used to thicken a flummery (see next recipe). Hartshorn is deer antlers, and it was used in two ways: making jellies is the first. It was sold as dried shavings, almost certainly of velvet antler which is made of cartilage whereas hard antler is just dead, dry bone. Apart from the jelly produced by boiling up bones, hartshorn and isinglass (made from the swim-bladder of the sturgeon) used to be the only gelling agents available.

This jelly has a beautiful colour and texture. In the sixteenth and seventeenth centuries, jellies were a fashionable part of the banqueting course, and this one would have been much appreciated, served in tiny glasses and eaten while strolling about the grounds. If you don't have access to hartshorn, make it using bones with cartilage and sinew instead – this acquires the necessary firm texture. Unlike stock-making where you want lots of meat for colour and flavour, here you want bones scraped clean of meat as the jelly should be as colourless as possible.

500 g (1 lb+) hartshorn shavings, and/or

3 kg (6–7 lbs) knuckle bones with cartilage

300 ml (½ pt) white wine

500 g (1 lb+) hindberries (raspberries)

2 egg whites

Lemon juice

Sugar

Ground cinnamon, cloves

Cover the bones and hartshorn shavings with water and simmer for 4–6 hours, skimming. Strain carefully, cool and remove any fat. Add the wine and reduce to 600 ml (1 pint). Warm the raspberries, and sieve to release the juice. Add to the strained jelly, and then clarify it with egg whites (see consommé recipe on p.62 for method). Flavour it delicately with sugar, lemon juice and a tiny amount of the spices, then leave to set in a jelly mould. May also be served with reindeer milk ice cream or hartshorn biscuits (see below).

Hartshorn flummery

Serves 6-8

This is a Scots recipe from around 1700 quoted in Dorothy Hartley's *Food in England,* though a nearly identical version appears in Hannah Glasse's *The Art of Cookery* published in 1747. Mrs Glasse adds that it is best if left to stand for a day or two before turning it out. This flummery has cream beaten hard into it to make a delicate mousse. A dry or medium white wine is best for a little acidity and this obviously affects the amount of sugar used. The mousses are turned out and sent to table: 'Let the cups you pour it into be dipped in clear water. When you send to table you must turn it out and stick over the top with blanched almonds cut in slips. Eat it with cream or wine, whichever you like best.' But you can always just serve them in individual glasses. An electric beater will save you most of the lengthy beating that both reckon is essential to the success of the dish.

450 g (1 lb) hartshorn shavings

3.5 litres (6 pts) spring water

600 ml (1 pt) thick cream

300 ml ($^1/_2$ pt) white wine, chilled

4 tablespoons orange-flower water

Caster sugar to taste

Boil the hartshorn in the water very gently until it has reduced to 1.2 litres (2 pints), then strain it through a fine thick tea towel and allow to cool completely, by which time it should be a jelly. Bring the cream to boiling point, allow it to cool completely and then chill.

Once the cream is nicely chilled, warm up the jelly very gently till it is barely liquid. Remove from the heat and add the cream, white wine, orange-flower water and enough sugar to taste. Then 'beat it all one way for an hour and a half at least - for if you are not careful in thus beating it will never mix or look to please you.' Turn it into wetted moulds, chill and turn out when set once more.

Springerle (Hartshorn biscuits)

The second culinary use for antler was as a major source of ammonia. Powdered antler was burnt to produce ammonium carbonate or "spirits of hartshorn" – one of the main ingredients of smelling salts. 'Hartshorn salt' was used as an early raising agent in baking and it is still used in Germany and Scandinavia where brightly decorated hartshorn biscuits are a Christmas favourite. The biscuits smell of ammonia when cooking but this disappears afterwards. It gives a much lighter texture to thin biscuits than baking powder. Hartshorn salt or *Hjorthorns-salt* is relatively easy to buy in Scaninavian (http://swefoods.com) and German shops. Elsewhere, try the larger Chinese stores and ask for ammonium carbonate.

50 g (2 oz) butter

140 g (5 oz) sugar

½ teaspoon vanilla essence

1 egg

½ teaspoon hartshorn salt

2 tablespoons milk

Juice of ½ lemon

225 g (8 oz) flour

½ teaspoon aniseed, ground

Small pinch salt

Caster sugar to dust biscuits

Beat together the butter, sugar and vanilla essence, then beat in the egg. Dissolve the hartshorn salt in the milk and lemon juice (it will froth up) and add this to the butter and sugar. Stir in the flour, aniseed and salt. Using more flour if necessary, form a soft dough and roll it out on a floured board till 5 mm (¼ inch) thick. Cut it into biscuits and place onto baking sheets 2 cm (1 inch) apart to allow for spreading. Bake at Gas 5, 190ºC, 375ºF for 8–12 minutes. The biscuits should be pale, with the edges just starting to brown. Remove from the oven, and cool for 1–2 minutes, then dust with caster sugar or coloured sugar strands.

Reindeer milk ice cream

Serves 4

I once produced a nine course venison banquet that called for reindeer milk. It was provided by Mauri Neiminen who was researching reindeer milk in Finland and looking at ways of commercialising its products. Reindeer milk is extremely rich, nutritious and syrupy, with a fabulous flavour of milky fresh cobnuts. Reindeer are the only species routinely milked by the nomadic reindeer herders of northern Europe and Asia. In the 1970s, the red deer research team on the island of Rum and at the Glensaugh research station milked some red deer to analyse the milk: it was similarly rich and syrupy but the hinds were considerably less co-operative than reindeer. One couple above all who should be able to make reindeer milk ice cream is Alan and Tilly Smith who run the Reindeer Company near Aviemore. I was fascinated to see how biddable reindeer are. After a mere ten-minute struggle, a wild reindeer was harnessed next to his companion, and was calmly pulling a sled along the public road as though he had been doing it for years.

450 ml ($^3/_4$ pt) reindeer milk	Infuse the milk with the vanilla pod in a warm place for $^1/_2$ hour. Beat the egg yolks with 2 tablespoons sugar, then beat in the milk. Stir over a very low heat or in a bain marie till well thickened. Cool. Beat two egg whites stiffly and whip the cream. Fold these into the custard, adjust the sugar if necessary, then freeze.
Vanilla pod	
4 eggs	
2 tablespoons sugar plus sugar to taste	
200 ml (8 fl oz) double cream	

Real mincemeat tarts

It is not so long ago that most mincemeat contained real meat as well as suet, as one might suppose. The tradition goes back to medieval times and beyond, when chopped meat was frequently cooked with dried fruits, nuts, dates, citrus peel, spices and honey so that it was fairly sweet, like many Middle Eastern dishes still are today. To begin with, there was more meat than fruit, and the tarts were called chewets. As the years progressed, less and less meat was included, until by the twentieth century only the suet remained and dishes made with mincemeat now feature only in our dessert course.

If you make venison stock, you will have venison suet – there is usually a good layer to remove when the stock has cooled. This you can wash, chop and freeze for future use. It should be a smooth cream colour. The ideal mincemeat is not over-sweet; it should be moist but not cloying. Don't skimp on the brandy, as that is what preserves it. You will never want to use bought mincemeat again.

350 g (12 oz) minced venison

450 g (1 lb) raisins

675 g (1¹/₂ lb) currants

100 g (4 oz) candied peel

675 g (1¹/₂ lbs) venison or beef suet

900 g (2 lbs) apples

250 g (¹/₂ lb) moist sugar

250 g (¹/₂ lb) honey

100 g (4 oz) whole almonds

¹/₂ teaspoon ground nutmeg

¹/₂ teaspoon ground ginger

¹/₄ teaspoon ground cinnamon

Rind of 1 lemon

Juice of ¹/₂ lemon

¹/₄ – ¹/₂ pint brandy

Pastry to line tart cases

Chop the dried fruit, peel and suet, and grate the apple. Mix together all the other ingredients except the pastry and pack tightly into jars, pressing it down well to exclude all the air. Cover the jars tightly and leave to mature for at least two weeks; it will keep and improve for months. When ready to use, stir it well as some of the juices will have sunk to the bottom.

Line the tart cases with pastry, fill with mincemeat, cover with pastry lids, leaving a little hole for the steam to escape, and bake in a hot oven (Gas 6, 200ºC, 400ºF) till the pastry is cooked (about 15 minutes). Serve with clotted cream or reindeer milk ice cream.

Difhes of minced pies

From *The Accomplisht Cook,* Robert May 1671

Chocolate and hazlenut venison pudding
Serves 6

Unlikely though it sounds, grated kidney was used in several historic sweet dishes. Usually, pig's kidney is stipulated, but venison is infinitely better, and using sweet liver better still. They were cooked, grated and mixed into the other ingredients to give a rich, nutty flavour. Gervase Markham in *The English Housewife* (1615) has a recipe for Florentine, which is a spiced sweet pastry tart filled with grated kidney, sweet herbs, currants, sugar, cinnamon, fine breadcrumbs, eggs and cream. Jane Grigson adapts one of Carême's recipes for Pithivier that includes grated kidney. Some people can't manage without chocolate, so with those in mind, here is my venison version. It's good as a warm pudding with lots of cold cream, or else served cold and thinly sliced or cut into small cubes and covered with excellent chocolate sauce. It is extremely rich and remains sticky throughout. If you don't tell people what is in it, it is unlikely they will guess what lends that particular richness. Just watch out that vegetarians are not tempted to eat this scrumptious dessert, and only use really fresh liver from young or female animals.

125 g (4 oz) venison liver

Water

125 g (4 oz) butter

125 g (4 oz) sugar

3 eggs, separated into yolk and whites

6 tablespoons cocoa powder

125 g (4 oz) ground hazelnuts

Grated zest of 1 orange

1 tablespoon brandy

Chilled cream to serve (optional)

Simmer the venison liver in unsalted water for 10–15 minutes. Then drain and chop finely. When the liver has cooled a little, place the butter, sugar egg yolks and liver into a food processor and blend to a smooth paste. Add the cocoa powder, hazelnuts, grated orange zest and brandy and blend briefly till mixed. Whip the egg whites separately and fold them in. Butter either a deep cake tin 18 cm (7 inches) diameter or six individual soufflé dishes. Bake in a moderate oven (Gas 4, 180ºC, 350ºF) for 30 minutes. Serve hot or warm with cream as a pudding, or turn it out when cold and slice thinly. It is very rich indeed.

15. The nutritional value of venison

Human beings have been eating venison and other wild animals for over a million years. They have been eating the meat of domesticated animals for a few thousand years. Only in the last few hundred years was the diet of domesticated animals so radically changed as to alter the whole structure of their fat. And only in the last few decades have we realised the effect this has had on human obesity.

In terms of the time it takes for evolutionary adaptation, a few thousand years is almost negligible. A few hundred years counts for nothing. Therefore it is not in the least surprising to discover that the meat of wild, unimproved animals has the perfect structure for human beings. It is lean and full of iron, though when there is fat, it is rich in essential omega-3 fatty acids. It therefore has about the lowest GI (Glycæmic index) of any red meat. Because deer have not been 'improved' by domestication, the composition of venison remains what mankind has been adapted to eat for hundreds of thousands of years. Venison, in short, is what we are *designed* to eat. We were not designed to cope with domesticated animals lavishly fed on high-energy grain rations.

FAT AND OMEGA-3 Research has shown that ruminants (deer are ruminants, like cattle and sheep) fed on a diet of grasses and other 'unimproved' foods have a meat structure better suited to human beings than ruminants fed on a high-energy grain diet which produces the more harmful fats. So long as deer continue to feed on grasses and other low energy plants rather than domestic grains, this is likely to remain the case. We are learning more about the complex and fascinating story of fat: that while there are harmful fats that lead to obesity and diabetes, there are also essential fats that we need to grow, develop and maintain our bodies and brains. Most venison is naturally low in fat – if there is any it tends to be confined to the outside of the carcase and is therefore easily trimmed off by the butcher or cook, leaving very lean meat indeed. Young venison has less fat than skinless chicken. So although traditionally venison is regarded as winter food, its leanness actually makes it perfect for light, summer cooking. The Meat Research Institute at

Langford, Bristol pointed out that venison, like oily fish, is also a good source of essential omega-3 linoleic acids. As well as being necessary for growth and good brains, omega-3 helps to reduce potentially cancer-forming free radicals. This point was noted in 1997 by the World Cancer Research Fund, who recommend eating game meats in preference to domesticated meats for preventing cancer. Venison is also comparatively low in cholesterol – it has only about half that of chicken.

HIGH IN IRON AND PROTEIN Venison is much darker than beef or lamb. Its deep red colour indicates its high iron content, another valuable contribution to our modern diet which at the time of writing, now leaves over 90% of western women deficient in iron. The figures for venison given in the table below, (from McCance and Widdowson's *The Composition of Foods : Meat, Poultry and Game, 1995*) come from young farmed deer and it shows venison as an excellent source of iron and low fat protein. I compare venison with skinless chicken because, strangely, chicken is what dieticians and health advisors seem to recommend to people who shouldn't consume domestic animal fats, even though so much chicken is intensively produced with grain, feed additives, growth promoters and, in countries we increasingly import from, antibiotics. I have experienced scores of people who had been recommended to cut red meat out of their diet altogether; they became so bored with chicken that to discover that they could enjoy venison without breaking their diet was a joyous revelation.

COMPOSITION PER 100G			FAT g	PROTEIN g	ENERGY (Kcal)	IRON mg	CHOLESTEROL mg
VENISON, Haunch		Raw	1.6	22.2	103	3.3	50
		Roast	2.5	35.6	165	5.1	**
CHICKEN, Skinless		Raw	2.1	22.3	108	0.7	90
		Roast	7.5	27.3	177	0.7	105
BEEF, Topside		Raw	12.9	20.4	198	1.7	48
		Roast	11.4	29.9	222	2.3	68

** No reliable result available

GOOD FAT? Venison is promoted as low-fat meat. However, this should perhaps be qualified to say that *young* venison is low in fat, because at certain times of year mature deer, especially males, can lay down impressive amounts of fat in preparation both for the rut and a long cold winter. Top prize goes to reindeer which, having to contend with long Arctic winters of wind, snow and scant food, have been known to lay down some 10 cm (4 inches) of back fat in preparation. They are almost unable to run by the end of the summer. With good grazing, many other species when fully mature will also lay down thick deposits over the haunches and saddle and between the muscle – Chinese water deer are regularly as fat as mutton.

Until about 50 years ago, this fat was greatly appreciated, and now that we are beginning to understand more about the composition of 'good' as well as 'bad' fat, it

can perhaps be appreciated again. Actually, an awful lot of the stalkers that I have met have never stopped being hugely enthusiastic about venison fat. From medieval times until the 1970s, fat venison carcases were rated higher than lean ones. In 'Sir Gawain and the Green Knight', a fourteenth-century poem, the narrator relates with approval how, when the huntsmen tested the fat, 'Two fingers' width fully they found on the leanest.' Joachim Buchelaar's seventeenth-century still-life paintings in the National Gallery in London glory in some splendid carcases bulging with fat, which are clearly objects of desire. And Jane Austen, in *Pride and Prejudice* has her dinner guests saying, approvingly, that 'they had never seen so fat a haunch'. Armed with the knowledge that these characters are enjoying fat that has not been changed by feeding grain, we can perhaps appreciate their delight without feeling anxious on their behalf.

REFERENCES

Cordain, L. et al. *Fatty acid analysis of wild ruminant tissues; evolutionary implications for reducing diet-related chronic disease.* European Journal of Clinical Nutrition, 56, 2002.

Crawford, Michael, & Vergroesen, A J: *The Role of Fats in Human Nutrtion (2nd Edition)* Academic Press, London, 1989

World Cancer Research Fund and American Institute for Cancer Research: *Food, Nutrition and the Prevention of Cancer – a global perspective.* Washington, 1997

16. *Preparing and costing venison*

SKINNING AND HANGING VENISON

All the early accounts of hunting in the forests of England show that deer were skinned first, gutted afterwards, and then cut up on top of the skin in the woods. A fourteenth-century manuscript advises protecting the pieces in fern leaves before carrying it home. There is no mention of hanging it to mature. Later cookery books mention hanging skinned haunches, often patted with powdered ginger to keep the flies off (and make it taste good).

Nowadays, deer from farms and parks with facilities of their own, are also skinned first while the carcases are still warm, and gutted afterwards. Some game butchers have direct access to an estate so that they, too, can skin the warm carcase before gutting it. The advantages of doing it this way round are that the carcase is clean so it can be hung successfully for longer. Also, skinning while the carcase is still warm means that the surface dries out, making a protective layer on the outside. When properly hung, the dry surface of the carcase glows a deep, rich mahogany colour – a sign that all is going well with the venison. There is slightly more weight loss doing it this way round, but that initial evaporation concentrates the flavour and I consider it a price worth paying.

Wild (game) venison is usually gralloched (gutted) on the hill, or in the forest or park, immediately it has been killed. It is then cooled, transported and hung with the skin left on it until it is time to cut it up. The obvious advantage of this system is that the carcase is protected from contamination while being brought back to the game larder. The disadvantages are that eviscerating the carcase with the skin on leads to a certain amount of contamination from hair, and it is less easy, once it has cooled, to remove the skin without ripping off some of the muscle as well. More importantly, the skin retains moisture so the carcase inside never completely dries off. This makes the meat inside heavier, but also floppier and more difficult to butcher neatly. It can also encourage moulds that sometimes affect the smell and flavour of the meat (see p.27). So if at all possible, hang your venison without the skin in a dry fly-proof place with a good airflow. The ideal temperature is between minus 2 and 0ºC (28–32ºF).

BUYING AND BUTCHERING VENISON

It doesn't matter what species of deer you have; the muscles are all the same. In small species, it isn't worth boning out much. But since the current trend is for more meat to be boned, it helps to know where the bones lie and how to get at them. To make boneless roasting joints, either break down the joint into single muscle roasts, or roll and tie several together. Tying with string is preferable to elastic netting, which does not hold the meat so well and is awkward for the carver. A butcher's knot is the same as a packer's knot: a secured slip-knot. When rolling joints, use a skewer to hold the meat in place until you have tied the first few strings. Tie a string in the middle, then at neat intervals out towards the ends. Then trim the ends neatly. Some people like to pass a string twice round the length of the joint as well for good measure.

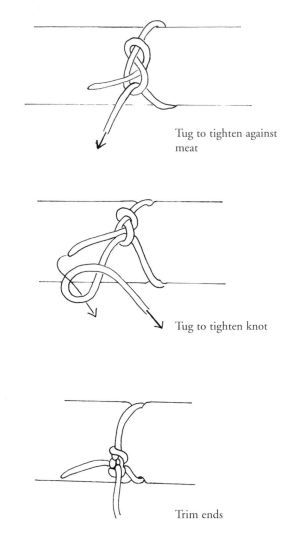

Tug to tighten against meat

Tug to tighten knot

Trim ends

HAUNCH

CHEF'S INFORMATION Unless otherwise specified, a whole haunch includes the rump and shank, as shown. When a whole haunch from the larger species is prepared for the carvery table, the flank and shank are removed, and the pelvic (aitch) bone is removed (see below). With small species, these can be left on, and the shank merely cut through so that the joint fits more easily into a roasting tin, just like a leg of lamb.

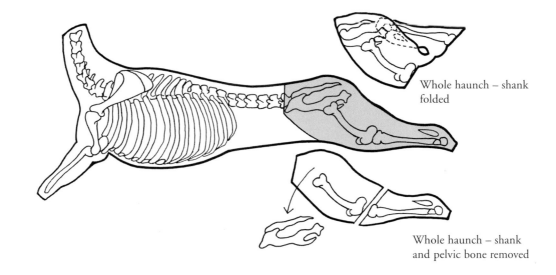

Whole haunch – shank folded

Whole haunch – shank and pelvic bone removed

Fig 1

Sever ligament between leg and pelvic bones

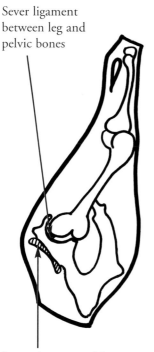

Start where sawn hip bone is exposed

Once a leg is boned, it can be divided into the four main muscles below, plus the shank. If further trimmed, each muscle divides into two. This is sometimes called an eight-muscle haunch or Denver cut. Haunches from small species like roe and Chinese water deer are so small as to make dividing them into separate muscles a fruitless exercise. If wanted for steaks, they are best treated like lamb, i.e. tunnelling out the leg bone and slicing into leg steaks. See diagram on page 269.

BONING A HAUNCH To break down a haunch into its separate muscles, turn it so the inside (closest to the other haunch) is uppermost and remove the pelvic (aitch) bone. Use the tip of the knife for this and always hold the blade facing away from your other hand. Start where the exposed hip bone has been sawn and follow round next to the bone until you reach the top of the leg bone (Fig 1). Inside the socket there is a ligament connecting the pelvic and leg bone: sever that and the socket becomes a useful place to grip the pelvic bone

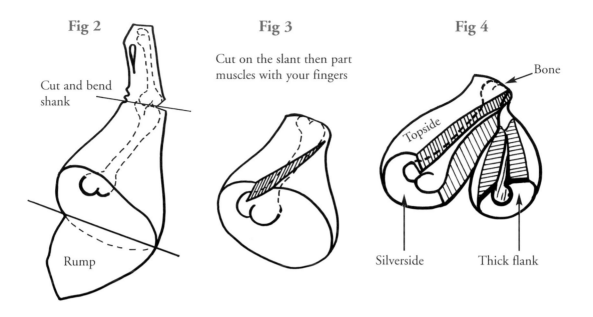

Fig 2

Cut and bend shank

Rump

Fig 3

Cut on the slant then part muscles with your fingers

Fig 4

Bone

Topside

Silverside

Thick flank

while you continue removing it. Next cut off the shank by cutting between the knuckle bones. Bend it backwards to sever the joint with the knife, and cut straight through the muscle (Fig 2). Now cut off the rump by slicing straight across under tip of the leg bone. (Fig 2) Then, using a natural seam that runs diagonally from the shank to the top of the leg, cut down between the muscles to the bone and start to part the thick flank from the silverside. (Fig 3). The knife should be tilted to follow the edge of the muscle. Bending the meat over the edge of your cutting block makes this job easier – you eventually see the thick silver sinew on the edge of the silverside. Remove the thick flank, cutting off the small bone at the knuckle end (Fig 4). Then remove the leg bone altogether, keeping the knife edge next to the bone, leaving just the topside and silverside. These can be parted most of the way with your fingers; you only need to cut the outer skin. These muscles can be sliced into steaks or rolled and tied. Each of these four muscles can also be divided into two smaller muscles. The smaller of the two silverside muscles is called the 'salmon cut' or 'haunch fillet'. There are more details of these cuts on p35-36.

TUNNEL BONING A HAUNCH Remove the pelvic (aitch) bone and shank as above. Then stand the haunch with the knuckle side uppermost and cut around the knuckle, making sure you also include the small bone that is attached to the thick flank. (If you manage to keep this attached to the leg bone, there is a little gap you can put your thumb in to

Fig 1

Fig 2

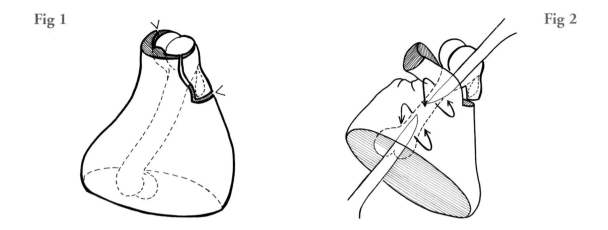

help grip the leg bone.) Then, keeping your boning knife close to the leg bone, free the bone from the muscle. Use your fingers if necessary, to feel where the bone is, but keep them away from the knife. Cut round the other end of the bone and pull it out. The haunch can either be sliced into leg (round) steaks or tied into a boneless joint. The cavity can be stuffed before tying.

SADDLE

CHEF'S INFORMATION A wholesale or catering saddle is cut between the 11th & 12th rib i.e. up to the neck, with the shoulder blade bones removed and rib bones cut back. A wholesale saddle may or may not include the rump (the boniest part of the haunch which contains part of the fillet). If it does not include the rump, ask whether the fillets (filet mignon) have been cut through at that point or whether they have been 'dropped' i.e. the haunch end of the fillet has been removed before cutting off the bone so that you get the whole fillet. Wholesale saddles include much forequarter meat as well as rump bones and substantial trimming may be required – anyone doing a costing should bear this in mind. Ask for a specification since it can alter the yield of prime quality meat dramatically – price alone is not always a reliable guide to

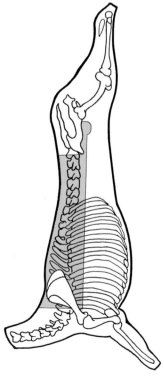

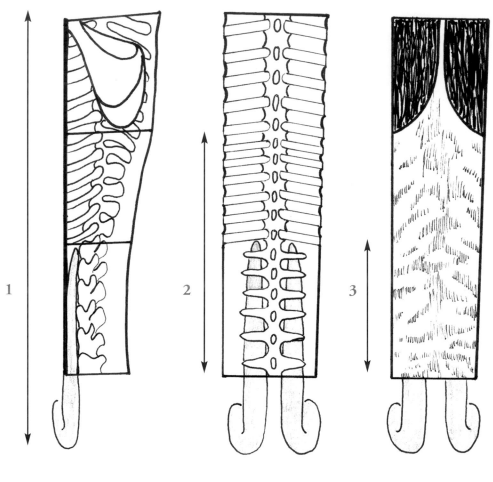

1. Wholesale (long) with dropped fillets

2. Catering (short) with dropped fillets

3. Table (best end) with dropped fillets

good value. To present a large saddle joint for the carvery table, it is usually cut off between the 6th and 7th ribs, i.e. where the shoulder bone cartilage starts. The very best saddle joint is between the rump and the rib bones, as this has the fillet underneath. On an old animal the skin and sinew can be very tough and this plus fat can weigh 15–20% of the striploin. There is considerable confusion over the names of the saddle cuts. See pages 32-34 to avoid costly mistakes.

BONING A SADDLE Cut off the forequarter from the saddle either between the 6th and 7th or 11th and 12th ribs as required. Next, drop the fillets (if wished) before you cut the saddle off the haunches, as this is easier while the carcase is hanging up. Make a cut through the muscle where the haunch parts from the saddle to mark where to start boning the fillets. Keep the knife close to the bones as you part the fillet from it. When it disappears into the haunch, remember the club-shape of the fillet and follow the muscle round next to the bone. When the fillets are dropped, cut off the saddle through the bone below the rump.

To bone out the saddle, first remove the fillets. Keep the knife close to the bones. Then remove the loin. Turn the saddle over and, keeping the knife close to the bone, run the knife down either side of the backbone. There is a row of small bones that impede the knife; work round these to avoid wasting meat. Pull off the outer skin and fat from the loin and, if desired, trim off the inner silver skin to leave a larder-trimmed (Denver) loin. The fillets can also have the silver skin and chain steak (side strap) removed to produce a larder-trimmed fillet.

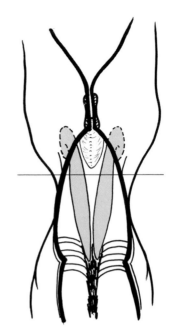

Dropping the fillets

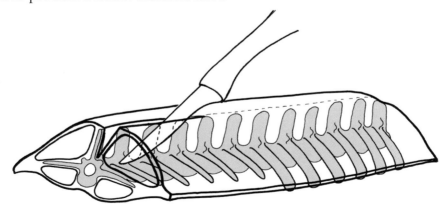

Boning saddle: removing the loin

Chops may be cut up to the 7th rib, i.e. before the shoulder blade cartilage starts. It is best to remove the chine (backbone), leaving just the rib bone. From the smaller species, cut them two or even three ribs thick for better cooking. Barnsley chops are cut straight across the backbone, i.e. a slice of saddle. French rack is also cut from this part and may even be cut longer if wished. Saw or clip the rib bones in a neat line parallel to the backbone. Then part the loin from the backbone and saw or clip the rib bones off the backbone. Remove all the outer skin and silver skin from the loin. Then cut away the fascia between the ribs, down to the loin. Finally, clean the bones completely of meat – a lengthy task so this can be expensive to buy. When two racks are sewn together to form a circle, with the loin on the outside and a gap in the centre to take stuffing, this is called a crown roast.

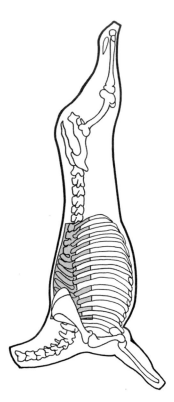

French rack

Chops

FOREQUARTER

Consists of the neck, shoulder, and breast. If the saddle has been cut off between the 11th and 12th ribs, there is correspondingly less forequarter meat. If the saddle is cut off between the 6th and 7th rib, the fore part of the loin can be boned out to make a neck fillet or neck steaks. If left on the bone, it can be cut into chops or French rack (see above). Shoulders can be boned and rolled, or presented as a bone-in joint. To bone a shoulder, tunnel out the blade bone in the same way as for the haunch (above). If you tie a couple of strings round a bone-in shoulder, it keeps it neater while cooking. The rest is usually diced for stewing, or minced.

YIELD – SOME FACTS AND FIGURES

Below are some actual average figures for head-shot red deer under 3 years – other species will have the same proportions. Use it as a rough guide – as always there are many variables: older carcases have more sinew and sometimes more fat; older males have proportionately more forequarter because of their thick neck muscles; animals in poor condition will have proportionately more bone and waste; in deer that are not head shot, bullet damage accounts for extra wastage. These percentages are of dressed (skinned) carcases. My thanks to Dick Elmhirst for contributing his valuable data.

Whole Carcase

	% OF CARCASE WEIGHT	% OF BONE IN CUT
Offal (heart, liver, kidney)	6%	0
Haunches, including rump	38%	20
Saddle, cut between 6th/7th rib	16%	14
Forequarter, neck, flank etc	40%	31
Saddle, cut to 12th rib	21%	19
Forequarter, neck etc	35%	26

Forequarter, cut between 11th/12th rib

Neck, bone-in	24%
Shoulder, bone-in	44%
Breast	32%

Breaks down into:

Boneless meat, untrimmed	70%
Bone	26%
Fat, waste	4%

Saddle, cut between 11th/12th rib and 6th/7th rib

	11th/12th rib	6th/7th rib
Loin, untrimmed	59%	63%
Fillets	10%	11%
Bone	19%	14%
Kidney	2%	2%
Trim, fat, waste	11%	10%

Haunches (leg), rump and shank on

Boneless untrimmed meat	80%
Bones and waste	20%

Breaks down into

Topside	21%
Silversides	22%
Rump	9%
Thick flank	17%
Shin meat	11%

PACKAGING AND STORING VENISON

VACUUM PACKING

A few people object to vacuum packing because of the small amount of moisture pulled out of the meat. Yet the same people seem perfectly happy to freeze it, which results in just the same amount of moisture loss. However, the benefits offered by vacuum packing and freezing far outweigh these very small amounts of moisture loss whose effect on the cooked dish is imperceptible.

As well as noting the 'use by' date on the labels, make sure the vacuum seal is always tight against the meat: this indicates the vacuum is intact. If the pack is slack, with air all round the meat, it means the pack has been punctured. If there are bubbles round the meat but the pack is otherwise tight and not leaking, the meat is comimg to the end of its shelf life. After about a week in its pack, vacuum packing sometimes give a curious smell to the meat, best described as 'bacony'. This is normal, and once the meat has been allowed to breathe in fresh air again, the smell disappears and the original bright colour and sweet smell is restored. So it is best to open vacuum packs half an hour or so before cooking. The longer the meat has been in the vacuum pack, the longer the smell takes to disappear. If it hasn't gone in an hour, the meat is coming up to its 'use-by' date. If it hasn't gone in two hours, it is past its 'use-by' date.

Freeze vacuum-packed meat as soon as possible. If the vacuum seal breaks in the freezer (the bag is no longer tight against the meat) rewrap it to prevent freezer burn. Vacuum-packed meat that is kept till near the end of its shelf life and then put in the freezer should have that fact written on it, and the meat allowed to breathe as above when defrosted.

HOME-FREEZING VENISON

Being lean, venison freezes well as long as it is well packed. It is the fat in meat that eventually goes rancid. I have eaten venison that was in a domestic freezer for three years and which was excellent. Where fat has been added (e.g. sausages) it is best used within six months. Proper packing with a thick wrapping and no air gaps is essential to prevent freezerburn. Freezer-burnt meat has a dried up surface which shows up as pale, starved-looking patches, or circles if the hole is a pinprick. In really bad cases, where only a thin film of cling-film was used, the whole surface could be affected. All freezer burn should be cut off before cooking, not because it will do you any harm but because it tastes horrible.

Protect all sharp bones, to prevent the wrapping from being punctured. Over-wrapping meat with clingfilm is good because it eliminates air, but do use several layers. Ideally, the wrapped meat should then be put in a sturdy plastic bag and submerged in cold water (leaving the opening out of the water, of course) to drive out as much air as possible before tying tightly. This is even more worthwhile if you wrap your meat in polythene bags only.

As well as being invaluable for extending fresh shelf life, vacuum-packed meat freezes well because a) the bags are thick and b) all the air has been removed. If you want to defrost frozen vacuum-packed meat in a hurry, fill a basin with cold or tepid water and immerse the whole sealed pack. Small items like steaks will be defrosted in about half an hour; a large joint may need a change of water and take an hour or two.

REFREEZING

Sometimes, understandable anxiety about refreezing meat can result in unnecessary waste. However, in some circumstances it is safe to refreeze defrosted venison – official guidelines warning that it should never, ever, be done are assuming a population of morons. So long as: 1) you are certain the venison was fresh when it was originally frozen; 2) it has not already been defrosted and refrozen before; 3) it is cooked immediately after the second defrosting, then the risk in refreezing is negligible. For example, if vacuum-packed frozen venison that would normally have a shelf life of 2 weeks is frozen after 2 days, and then is partly or wholly defrosted (e.g. in transit if you have bought some and are taking it home), that meat still has considerable shelf-life left so it is perfectly sensible to refreeze it quickly. I am clearly not talking about bits of meat that have been slung in the freezer because they are about to go off: they should never be refrozen. Apply common sense – and always write what has happened on the refrozen pack. Equally, I would not advise refreezing pork, wild boar, poultry or game birds under any circumstances because they are omnivores and more prone to bacteria, particularly poultry.

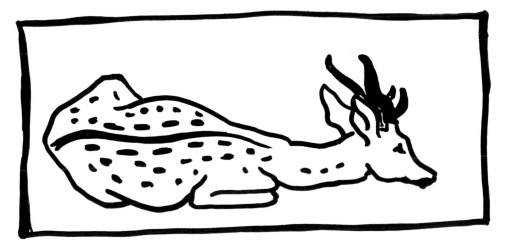

Rascal in repose

Sources of information

For further reading about deer, two good UK books about their natural history are *Deer* by Norma Chapman (1991 Whittet Books) and *The Natural History of Deer* by Rory Putman (1988 Christopher Helm Ltd.). *Fletcher's Game* by John Fletcher (Mercat Press 2003) is an account of his work with deer with insights into peoples' attitudes to them. *Heart and Blood* by Richard Nelson (1997, Knopf) also explores man's interaction with deer in North America and examines ways of controlling their population explosion. Both books are eminently readable.

For sausage making equipment in the UK
www.weschenfelder.co.uk (Tel: 01642 247524)
www.sausagemaking.org (Tel: 01204 433523).

For sausage making in USA, two informative websites are
http://home.pacbell.net
www.sausagemania.com.

The Venison Sausage Cookbook by Harold W. Webster (2002, Lyons Press) is spendidly practical.

To buy venison in the UK
Fletchers of Auchtermuchty (this is our business) offers a UK–wide mail order service and sells through farmers markets. www.seriouslygoodvenison.co.uk (telephone 0800 0836 476).

Many farmers markets and a few supermarkets now sell venison
Or contact the following societies, who all have an interest in deer:

British Association for Shooting and Conservation
www.basc.org.uk (Tel: 01244 573000)

British Deer Farmers' Association
www.bdfa.co.uk (Tel: 01629 827037)

British Deer Society
www.bds.org.uk (Tel: 01425 655434)

Deer Commission for Scotland
www.dcs.gov.uk (Tel: 01463 725000)

Deer Study & Resource Centre
www.deerstudy.com (Tel: 01782 657717)

Forestry Commission, in England
www.forestry.gov.uk/england (Tel: 01782 657717)

Forestry Commission, in Scotland
www.forestry.gov.uk/scotland (Tel: 0131 334 0303)

Game Conservancy Trust
www.gct.org.uk (Tel:01425 652381)

Outside the UK

Australian Deer Association
www.austdeer.com.au (Tel: +43 351 560 946)

Deer Industry Association of Australia
www.diaa.org (Tel: +43 3 5596 2323)

Federation of European Deer Farmers Associations
www.fedfa.org

New Zealand Deer Farmers Association
www.deernz.org   (Tel: +64 473 4500)

New Zealand Fallow Deer Society
www.nz-fallow.co.nz

North American Deer Farmers Association
www.nadefa.org (Tel: +1 651-345-5600)

North American Elk Breeders Association
www.naelk.org (Tel: +1 816 431 3605)

Index

A list of recipes appears at the start of each chapter on pages 45, 59, 83, 99, 129, 167, 197, 213, 221, 233, 251

red 13, 15, 16, 18

reindeer 15, 20, milk ice cream 256

roe 13, 15, 16, 22-3

rusa 16

sika 20-1

wapiti 15, 16, 18-19

white-tailed 15, 20-1

Deer Commission for Scotland 15, 276

Deer Industry Association of Australia 276

Deer Industry New Zealand 276

Deer Study & Resource Centre 276

demi glace 49

Denver leg 146, 265

desserts 252-8

dietary value of venison 259-264

Dods, Meg *Cook and Housewife's Manual* (1826) 50

dressed carcase 17, 19

dumplings 196

elk 15, 17-19, 94

Elmhirst, Jenny & Dick 187, 271

Errington, Humphrey 115

Escoffier 24

fallow deer 13, 15, 16, 20-1

farmed deer 16-17

farmers' markets 10

fat 28, 29, 40

content of venison 259-262

for cooking steaks 103

in burgers 95, 97-8

in sausages 239-40

kidneys roasted in their own fat 204

low fat sausages 243

fatty acids (omega-3) 259

Federation of European Deer Farmers Associations 276

fennel, bulb or Florence 44, 78, 81, 158-9, 173, 177

fennel seed 73

fifth quarter (offal) 197 – 212

fillet 31, 32, 33, 269-71, 272

haunch 36

first course dishes 59-82, 83, 197, 213, 233

flavour of venison 27, 30, 50-2

Fletcher, John 9, 212, *Fletcher's Game* (2003) 275

Forestry Commission 276

freezing venison 273-4

French rack 31, 34, 270

frikadellar 94

fruit 44, 168, 241

dried 241

figs 160, 201

grapes 126

plums 116, 126, 241

raspberries 44, 55, 144, 253

redcurrants 44, 118, 160

rowan berries, 44, 46-7, 118, 119

frying (steaks) 100-108

fungi 110-1, 146-7, 174